I0123933

Records

of the

Colony

of

New Plymouth

in

New England

ORIGINALLY PRINTED BY ORDER OF THE LEGISLATURE OF THE
COMMONWEALTH OF MASSACHUSETTS

Edited by

David Pulsifer

CLERK IN THE OFFICE OF THE SECRETARY OF THE COMMONWEALTH,
MEMBER OF THE NEW ENGLAND HISTORIC-GENEALOGICAL SOCIETY, FELLOW OF THE AMERICAN
STATISTICAL ASSOCIATION, CORRESPONDING MEMBER OF THE ESSEX INSTITUTE, AND OF THE
RHODE ISLAND, NEW YORK, CONNECTICUT AND WISCONSIN HISTORICAL SOCIETIES.

Acts of the Commissioners of the United Colonies of New England, 1643–1651

Volume IX

HERITAGE BOOKS
2016

HERITAGE BOOKS
AN IMPRINT OF HERITAGE BOOKS, INC.

Books, CDs, and more—Worldwide

For our listing of thousands of titles see our website
at
www.HeritageBooks.com

A Facsimile Reprint
Published 2016 by
HERITAGE BOOKS, INC.
Publishing Division
5810 Ruatan Street
Berwyn Heights, Md. 20740

Originally published
Boston:
From the Press of William White
Printer to the Commonwealth
1859

— Publisher's Notice —
In reprints such as this, it is often not possible to remove blemishes from
the original. We feel the contents of this book warrant its reissue despite
these blemishes and hope you will agree and read it with pleasure.

International Standard Book Numbers
Paperbound: 978-0-7884-1051-2
Clothbound: 978-0-7884-6401-0

COMMONWEALTH OF MASSACHUSETTS.

Secretary's Department.

BOSTON, APRIL 5, 1858.

By virtue of Chapter forty-one of the Resolves of the year one thousand eight hundred fifty-eight, I appoint DAVID PULSIFER, Esq., of Boston, to superintend the printing of the New Plymouth Records, and to proceed with the copying, as provided in previous resolves, in such manner and form as he may consider most appropriate for the undertaking.

Mr. Pulsifer has devoted many years to the careful exploration and transcription of ancient records, in the archives of the County Courts and of the Commonwealth. As a penman, and in all clerical qualifications, he has no superior. The studies and practice of his life have rendered him competent and reliable, as a decipherer of the handwriting of the earlier periods of our history, to a degree not equalled, perhaps, by any other person. He is accurate, vigilant, industrious, and indefatigable in this his chosen pursuit; and having a competent knowledge of colonial history, there is every reason to be assured that he will faithfully and successfully perform the service intrusted to him.

OLIVER WARNER,

Secretary of the Commonwealth.

INTRODUCTION.

THE subject of a combination of the Colonies was agitated in a meeting at Cambridge as early as June, 1638, but the confederation was not agreed upon until May, 1643. An account of the meeting in 1638 is given in the New Haven Colonial Records, edited by CHARLES J. HOADLY, Esq. It is found, in the answer of the New Haven General Court (held 29th of June, 1653) to the Massachusetts Declaration, as follows: —

" The confederation betwixt the colonies was no rash & sudden ingagem*, it had bine severall yeares vnder consideration. In anno 1638 there was a meeting at Cambridg aboute it, but some things being then propounded inconvenient for the lesser colonies, that conference ended w'hout fruit, and the foure jurisdictions, though knitt together in affections, stood in refferrence one to another loose and free from any express couenant or combination, till vpon a new invitation and propositions from the Massachusets, another meeting was appointed at Boston in May, 1643 ; so that magistrts, deputies and free-men, especially those of the Massachusets had aboute fiue yeares time to consider what they were aboute, the compass and consequences of such a consociation, and probably did improue it, and saw cause to renew the treaty so long suspended."

The following extracts from the Colonial Records of New Plymouth and Massachusetts show the action of the General Courts of those colonies in relation to the union of the four Col-

onies, previous to the signing of the Articles of Confederation by
the Commissioners.

On the twenty-seventh day of September, 1642, the General
Court of Massachusetts passed the following order: —

"The magistrates in & neare Boston w^{tu} the deputies of Boston, Charles-
towne, Cambridg, Watertowne, Roxberry, Dorchester, or the greater part of
them, are appointed to bee a comĩttē to treate wth any comission^{rs} from Plimoth, Coñectecot, or Newe Haven, about the union, & concerning avoyding
any danger of the Indians, & to have power to do hearin what they shall
find needfull for comõn safety & peace, so as they enter not into an offeucive
warr wthout order of this Courte./ "

At the General Court holden at Plymouth the vijth of March,
164$\frac{2}{3}$,

"Mr Edward Winslow & M^r Wiłłm Collyer are elected by the Court
to go to treate wth Massachusett Bay &c, about y^e combynaĉõn."

At the General Court of Massachusetts held May 10, 1643: —

"The Gov^{r}no^r, Mr Dudley, Mr Bradstreete, Mr Treasurer, Capt̄ Gibons,
& Mr Hauthorne are chosen to treat wth o^r freinds of Coñectecot, New Haven,
& Plimoth about a confederacy between us."

And at the same session the following order is recorded: —

"The Governo^r & Mr Dudley are appointed on the comĩttē to treate
wth o^r brethren & confederates of Coñectecot & Newehaven, & if either of the
former be hindered, Mr Bellingham is appointed in his steede."

Under date of June 6, 1643, the following order appears in
the Records of the General Court of Plymouth: —

"It is ordered and concluded by the Court, that Mr Edward Winslow
and M^r Wiłłm Collyer shall haue full comission & authoryty, in name of
the whole Court, to subscribe the articles of confederaĉõn (now read in
Court) wth the Massachusetts, Coñectacutt, and New Haven, and to subscribe
the same in name of the whole, and to affix thereto the comõn seale of the
goûment."

The Acts of the Commissioners of the United Colonies of

New England, now printed, being part of the New Plymouth Records, are contained in two folio manuscript volumes. It appears to have been the practice of the Commissioners at their meetings to put in writing their acts or conclusions, and to sign them; and it is probable that each colony was furnished by the Commissioners with the acts under their hands.

Gov. Winthrop says, "The names of the Commissioners and all their proceedings are at large set out in the books of their records, whereof every colony hath one." [Winthrop's Journal, II. 246.]

A folio volume of original minutes, from the year 1653 to 1662, much defaced, but recorded in the second volume, makes a part of the New Plymouth Records.

The original minutes of the meeting in September, 1646, and of the last day of the third month [May], 1653, and the greater part of the minutes of the meetings of Sept., 1648, and April, 1653, are all that are now known to be preserved belonging to the colony of Massachusetts. It is probable that the rest, together with the Book of the Acts of the Commissioners, referred to in this volume, were destroyed by the fire in 1747, of which an account is given by Secretary Willard, in a letter to Christopher Kilby and William Bollan, Esq., agents of the Province, in London, as follows : —

                                        " Boston, Decr. 21, 1747.
Gentlemen

      I am now to give you the sorrowful News of the grievous & surprizing Rebuke of Divine Providence on the Govern^{mt} of this Province in the Destruction of the Court House by Fire which happened in the Morning of the ninth Instant. It was generally concluded to have begun in the Floor under the chimneys of the Council Chamber & House of Represent^{ves} & was not discover'd till it was greatly increased ; All the Books of the General Court, Govern^r & Council & House of Represent^{ves} there in the House were wholly lost without saving one & all the Books of Commiss^{ns} and other Instrum^{ts} as well from the Crown as the Govern^{mt} of the Province with most of ye original Papers are likewise consumed."

In a letter received from J. HAMMOND TRUMBULL, Esq., Editor of the Colonial Records of Connecticut, dated Nov. 3, 1858, he says, "The Connecticut Manuscript is in excellent preservation." The Book of the Acts of the Commissioners belonging to New Haven Colony has not been preserved. That it was formerly kept is evident, not only from the statement of Gov. Winthrop, but by the following extract from the Records of the General Court held at New Haven the 27th of the third month, 1657 : —

"What conclusions of the comission[rs] are yet to be recorded shall be entred in one of y[e] new bookes that came last yeare from England."

The two volumes, first mentioned, are in the handwriting of different persons. The first volume appears to be in the handwriting of Nathaniel Souther, Nathaniel Morton, and other persons; the second volume appears to be wholly in the handwriting of Nathaniel Morton.

A few of the pages, left blank by those who recorded the Acts of the Commissioners, were subsequently used by John Cotton, Esq., of Plymouth, for indexes or tables of contents.

On the first and second pages of the first volume is recorded, "The agreement for the bounds betwixt Plymouth and Massachusetts," and on 279 and 280 the petition of Humphrey Johnson to the General Court of Plymouth, and answer thereto, which are printed in this volume. The pages of the manuscript are noted by a * in the margin. The following pages were left blank: 3, 4, 24, 42, 72, 174, 218, 219, 220, 261 to 277.

Some words omitted in recording, but found in the original minutes, are printed in brackets in the margin, as also some words from the originals, to correct mistakes in the record, are printed in the same manner. No blame, however, should be imputed to Secretary Morton or any one else on this account, as the minutes of the Commissioners appear to have been very hastily written.

The running title, and year and month in the margin, at the top of the printed page, are not in the original, but all other marginal entries, not in brackets, are found in the manuscript. In a few instances, words erased in the manuscript are printed with the erasures. The punctuation, with but a very little alteration, is retained.

The original Treaty between the Commissioners and the Narragansett sachems, or rather the part of the Treaty retained by the Commissioners, dated the 20th of the seventh month, 1645, engrossed on parchment, is preserved in the Archives of the Commonwealth. The marks of the Indian sachems as printed on page 48 were copied from it. The following, being part of the certificate or attestation of the witnesses, written on the back of the Treaty, was omitted in recording : —

" Signed ꝉ delifled in the p'sence of
> Richard Saltonstall
> Increase Nowell seč
> Simon Bradstreete.
> Willm Durand
> Benedict: Arnold
> Richard Callicott."

" Cutchamakin," " Abda," and " Pomunsh," who seem, by the record, to be parties to the Treaty, appear on the original as witnesses, Cutchamakin's name and marks being at the left of, and Abda and Pomunsh's under, the signature of Richard Callicott.

Reverting to the subject of the confederacy, it may be stated, that it lasted until the colonial governments were subverted in the reign of James II. New Haven had been, however, previous to that time, namely, in 1665, annexed to Connecticut, and, by the charter of William and Mary, Plymouth was united to Massachusetts.

In pursuance of letters from the right honorable the Lords Commissioners for Trade and the Plantations, dated the 20th of August and 19th of September, 1753, to the governors of several of his Majesty's Plantations in North America, a General Convention of Commissioners for their respective governments was held at the city of Albany, N. Y., in June following, for the purpose of having an interview with the Indians of the Five Nations, and making them presents on the part of the said governments, usual upon such occasions, in order to confirm and establish their ancient attachment to his Majesty and their constant friendship to his Majesty's subjects on this continent. After " brightening and strengthening the covenant chain " between the British Colonies and " the Six Nations," the Commissioners proceeded to the consideration of a plan for the union of the Colonies, prepared by Dr. Franklin, one of the Commissioners from Pennsylvania. By the plan, it was proposed that application be made for an Act of Parliament of Great Britain, by virtue of which, one general government might be formed in America, including the Colonies of Massachusetts Bay, New Hampshire, Connecticut, Rhode Island, New York, New Jersey, Pennsylvania, Maryland, Virginia, North Carolina, and South Carolina, to be administered by a President-General, to be appointed and supported by the crown; and a Grand Council of forty-eight members, to be chosen by the representatives of the people of the several Colonies met in their respective assemblies; which, though unanimously voted, was to be of no force until confirmed by the several assemblies.

Hutchinson says, " Not one of the assemblies from Georgia to New Hampshire, when the report was made by their delegates, inclined to part with so great a share of power as was to be given to this general government.

The plan met with no better fate in England. It was transmitted, with the other proceedings of the convention, to be laid before the king. The convention was at an end; and no notice was afterwards publicly taken of the plan."

That profound statesman, friend of the human race, and fearless defender of their rights, the Hon. John Quincy Adams, said, " The New England confederacy of 1643 was the model and prototype of the North American confederacy of 1774. In neither of the two cases was the measure authorized or sanctioned by the charters of the several colonies, parties to the compact. In both cases it was the great law of nature and of nature's God, — the law of self-preservation and self-defence, which invested the parties, as separate communities, with power to pledge their mutual faith for the common defence and general welfare of all. The New England colonists, conscious of this self-assumed sovereignty, expressly allege the *sad distractions* of their mother country, depriving them of her protection, and encouraging their enemies to combine for their destruction, as concurring with the other causes to impose upon them the duty of rallying all their energies for their own defence. The North American colonies, for the same assumption of sovereign power, appealed to their chartered rights as Britons, — and, finding that appeal fruitless and vain, to their natural rights as men, bestowed upon them by their Creator at their birth, and unextinguishable by human hands or human institutions. The compact of the New England colonies, without the sanction of their sovereign, was yet not against him. The union of the North American colonies turned the artillery of sovereignty against the sovereign himself, and demolished the throne of the oppressor with ordnance drawn from his own arsenals."

Sir Henry Vane, one of the early Governors of Massachusetts, said, " Antient Foundations, when once become destructive to those very ends for which they were first ordained, and prove hinderances, to the good and enjoyment of humane Societies, to the true Worship of God, and the Safety of the People, are for their sakes, and upon the same Reasons to be altered, for which they were first laid. In the way of God's Justice they may be shaken and removed, in order to accomplish the Counsels of his Will, upon such a State, Nation, or Kingdom, in order to his introducing a righteous Government, of his own framing."

" In Quarrels between Subjects and Soveraigns, about the Subjects Liberty and the Kings Prerogative, 'tis seldom seen, but the Error lies on the Soveraign's part, who is apt to be flattered into the presumptuous exercise of such an absolute Soveraignty and Legislative Dominion over them, as becomes no creature, and exceeds all the bounds of that contract he made with them, at his Inauguration."

James I. of England said, " I dare send the challenge (and will require no second) to maintaine as a defendant of honour, that my Brother-Princes and my Selfe, whom God hath aduanced vpon the Throne of Soueraigne Maiesty and supreame dignity, doe hold the Royall dignity of his Maiesty alone."

Sir Walter Ralegh said, " Such examples of the instability whereto all mortall affairs are subject, as they teach moderation, and admonish the transitory gods of Kingdoms not to authorize by wicked precedents, the evill that may fall on their own posterity : so do they necessarily make us understand, how happy that Country is, which hath obtained a king able to conceive and teach, That *God is the sorest and sharpest Schoolemaster that can be devised, for such Kings, as think this world ordained for them, without controlement to turn it upside-down at their pleasure.*"

" O eloquent, just, and mighty Death ! whom none could advise, thou hast persuaded ; what none have dared, thou hast done ; and whom all the world hath flattered, thou only hast cast out of the world and despised : thou hast drawn together all the far stretched greatness, all the pride, cruelty, and ambition of man, and covered it all over with these two narrow words, *Hic jacet.*"

To Hon. EPHRAIM M. WRIGHT and Hon. FRANCIS DE WITT, former Secretaries, and Hon. OLIVER WARNER, the present Secretary of the Commonwealth, a grateful acknowledgment is here recorded of obligation for many acts of personal kindness, as also for the cordial interest manifested in, and coöperation given to the work, from the commencement of my labors in the Secretary's Department, in June, 1853.

DAVID PULSIFER.

April, 1859.

Extract from the original minutes of the meeting of the Commissioners of the United Colonies of New England, held at New Haven, September, 1646.

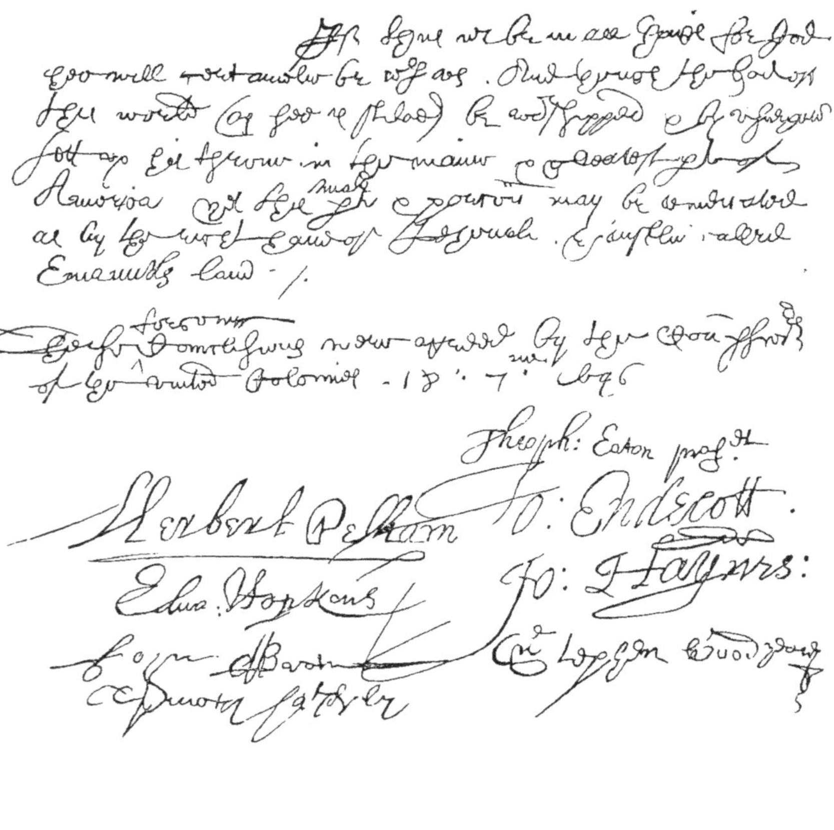

MARKS AND CONTRACTIONS.

A Dash ‾ (or straight line) over a letter indicates the omission of the letter following the one marked.

A Curved Line ˜ indicates the omission of one or more letters next to the one marked.

A Superior Letter indicates the omission of contiguous letters, either preceding or following it.

A Caret ◌̬ indicates an omission in the original record.

A Cross × indicates a lost or unintelligible word.

All doubtful words supplied by the editor are included between brackets, [ ].

Some redundancies in the original record are printed in Italics.

Some interlineations, that occur in the original record, are put between parallels, ‖ ‖.

Some words and paragraphs, which have been cancelled in the original record, are put between ‡ ‡.

Several characters have special significations, namely : —

@, — annum, anno.

ā, — an, am, — curiā, curiam.

ā, — mātrate, magistrate.

ƀ, — ber, — numƀ, number ; Roƀt, Robert.

c̆, — ci, ti, — acc̆on, action.

c̄ŏ, — tio, — jurisdicc̄ŏn, jurisdiction.

c̆, — cre, cer, — ac̆s, acres.

đ, — đđ, delivered.

ē, — Trēr, Treasurer.

ē, — committē, committee.

ğ, — ğũal, general ; Georğ, George.

ħ, — chr, charter.

ī, — begīg, beginīg, beginning.

ł, — łre, letter.

m̄, — mm, mn, — com̄ittee, committee.

ñi, — recom̄dac̄ŏn, recommendation.

m̄, — mer, — form̄ly, formerly.

m̆, — month.

ū, — nn, — Peñ, Penn ; año, anno.

ñ, — Dñi, Domini.

ñ, — ner, — mañ ñ, manner.

ŏ, — on, — mentiŏ, mention.

ŏ, — mŏ, month.

p̃, — par, por, — p̃t, part ; p̃tion, portion.

p, — per, par, pur, pear, — psuite, pursuite ; appd, appeared ; pson, person ; pte, parte.

ᵱ, — pro, — ᵱporc̄ŏn, proportion.

p̃, — pre, — p̃sent, present.

q, — qstion, question.

q̃, — esq̃, esquire.

r̆, — Apr̆, April.

s̃, — s̃, session ; s̃d, said.

s̆, — ser, — s̆vants, servants.

t̂, — ter, — neut̂, neuter.

t̄, — capt̄, captain.

û, — ner, — setˡal, seueral.

ũ, — abou, aboue, above.

v̆, — ver, — sev̆al, several.

w̃, — w̃n, when.

yᵉ, the ; yᵐ, them ; yⁿ, then ; yʳ, their ; yˢ, this ; yᵗ, that.

ᴣ, — us, — vilibᴣ, vilibus.

ℓ, — es, et, — statutℓ, statutes.

ℓc̆, &c̆, &cᵃ, — et cætera.

vizℓ, — videlicet, namely.

./ — full point.

Extract from the original minutes of the meeting of the Commissioners of the United Colonies of New England, held at New Haven, September, 1646.

If thus we be in all thing(s for God hee will certainelie be w'th vs. And though the God of this world (as hee i(s stiled) be wo'rshipped (by vsurpaĉõ sett vp hi(s throne in the maine (greatest pte of America yet thi(s ^small pte (porcõn may be vindicated a(s by the right hand of Jehouah . (iustlie called Emannuels land -/.

Theise ^forzoing Conclusions were agreed by the Comission'rs of the vnited Colonie(s . 18 : 7.ᵐᵒ 1646

Herbert Pelham
Edwa: Hopkins
John Browne
Tymothy hatherly

Theoph: Eaton pres.ᵗ
Jo: Endecott :
Jo: Haynes :
Stephen Goodyeare

CONTENTS OF VOLUME I.

Whereas there were two Comissions graunted by the two Jurisdicc̃õns the one of the Massachusets Goũment graunted vnto John Endicot gentlem̃ and Israell Staughton gent̃ The other of New Plymouth Goũment to Wilłm Bradford Esq̃ Governor and Edward Winslow gent̃ And both these for the setting out setling & determineing of the bounds and limmitts of the lands betweene the said Jurisdicc̃õns whereby not onely this pᵣnte age but the posterytie to come may liue quietly & peaceably in that behalf And forasmuch as the said Comissioners on both sides haue full power so to do as appeareth by the Records of both Jurisdicc̃õns. Wee therefore the said Comissioners aboue named doe hereby wᶜh one consent and agreement conclude determine and by these pᵣnts declare That all the Marshes at Conahasset that lye of the one side of the Riuer next to Hinghame shall belong to the Jurisdicc̃õn of the Mattachusets plantac̃õn. And all the Marsh yᵗ lyeth on the other side of the Riuer next to Scittuate shall belong to the Jurisdicc̃õn of New Plymouth excepting Threescore acres of Marsh at the mouth of the Riuer on Scittuate side next to the Sea which wee doe hereby agree conclude & determine shall belong to the Jurisdicc̃õn of the Massachusets And further we do hereby agree determine & conclude that the bounds of the limmitts betweene both the said Jurisdicc̃õns are as followeth vizᵗ From the mouth of the brooke that runeth into Conahassett Marshes (wᶜh we call by the name of Bound brooke) wᶜh a straight and direct line to the middle of a great pond that lyeth on the right hand of the vpper payth or com̃on way that leadeth betweene Weimouth and Plymouth close to the payth as we go along wᶜh was formerly named (and still we desire may be called) Accord Pond lying about fiue or six miles from Weimouth southerly, and from thence wᵗh a straight line to the Southernmost pt of Charles Riuer & three miles *southerly inward into the Countrey according as is exprest in the Patent graunted by his Maᵗⁱᵉ to the Company of the Massachusetts Plantac̃õn Prouided alwayes & neũthelesse concluded and determyned by mutuall agreement betweene the said Comissioners yᵗ if it fall out that the said line from Accord Pond to the Southermost part of Charles Riuer and three miles Southerly as is before expressed shall straiten or hinder any part of any Plantac̃õn begunn by the Goũment of New Plymouth or hereafter

*2

to be begun w^thin the space of tenn yeares after the date of these p^rnts That then notw^thstanding the said line it shalbe lawfull for the said Goûment of New Plymouth to assume on the Northerly side of the said line where it shall so intrench as aforesaid so much land as will make vp the quantytie of eight miles square to belong to euery such Plantacõn begun or to be begun as aforesaid wch wee agree determine and conclude to apertaine ꝗ belong to the said Goûment of New Plymouth And whereas the said line from the mouth of the said brook wch runneth into Conahassett salt Marshes (called by us bound brooke) and the pond called Accord Pond lyeth neere the lands belonging to the Towneships of Scittuate and Hinghame Wee doe therefore hereby determine and conclude that if any diuisions already made and recorded by either the said Townes do crosse the said line, that then it shall stand ꝗ bee of force according to the former intents ꝗ purposes of the said Townes graunting them (the Marshes formly agreed on excepted) And that no Towne in either Jurisdiccõn shall hereafter exceede, but containe themselues w^thin the said lines before expressed In witnesse whereof we the Comissioners of both the Jurisdiccõns do by these p^rnts Indented set our hands and seales the ninth day of the fourth month in the sixteenth yeare of our Soûaigne Lord King Charles And in the yeare of our Lord 1640

JO: ENDECOTT ☉   WILLIAM BRADFORD GOU^R. ☉
ISRAELL STOUGHTON, ☉   EDW: WINSLOW ☉

Articles of Confederation Betweene the

Plantations vnder the Goũment of the Massachusetts the Plantacõns vnder the Goũment of New Plymouth the Plantacõns vnder the Goũment of Connectacutt and the Goũment of New Haven wᵗʰ the Plantacõns in Combinacõn therewᵗʰ.

Whereas wee all came into these partſ of America wᵗʰ one and the same end ſ ayme namely to advaunce the Kingdome of oʳ Lord Jesus Christ and to enjoy the liberties of the Gospell in puritie wᵗʰ peace   And whereas in oʳ settleinge (by a wise pvidence of God) we are further dispersed vpon the Sea Coasts and Riuers then was at first intended, so that we cannot according to our desire wᵗʰ convenience comũnicate in one Goũment and Jurisdiccõn : And whereas we liue encompassed wᵗʰ people of seũall Nations and strang languages wᶜʰ hereafter may proue injurious to vs or our posteritie.   And forasmuch as the Natines haue forỹly committed sondry insolences and outrages vpon seũall Plantacõns of the English and haue of late combined themselues against vs   And seing by reason of those sad distraccõns in England wᶜʰ they haue heard of, and by wᵗʰ they know we are hindred, from that humble way of seeking advise, or reapeing those comfortable fruitſ of ptection wᶜʰ at other tymes we might well expecte. Wee therefore doe conceiue it our bounden dutye wᵗʰout delay to enter into a pᵗsent Consotiation amongst our selues, for mutuall help and strengh in all our future concernementſ : That as in Nation and Religion so in other respectſ we bee ſ continue *One according to the tenor and true meaneing of the ensuing Articles : Wherefore it is fully agreed and concluded by and betweene the pties or Jurisdiccõns aboue named and they joyntly and seũally doe by these pᵗntſ agree ſ conclude That they all bee and henceforth bee called by the name of THE VNITED COLONIES OF NEW ENGLAND.

2 The said Vnited Colonies for themselues ſ their posterities do joyntly and seũally hereby enter into *into* a firme ſ ppetuall league of ffriendship and amytie for offence and defence, mutuall advice and succour vpon all just

*6

II

(3)

occations both for p^{r}scrueing $\wp$ ppagateing the truth and liberties of the Gospell and for their owne mutuall safety and wellfare.

III

3 It is further agreed That the Plantaçõns wch at p^{r}sent are or hereafter shalbe setled w^{t}hin the limmetts of the Massachusets shalbe foreuer vnder the Massachusets $\wp$ shall haue peculier Jurisdicçõn among themselues in all cases as an entire Body and that Plyouth Connecktacutt $\wp$ New Hauen shall eich of them haue like peculier Jurisdicçõn and gouernment w^{t}hin their limmetts and in referrence to the Plantaçõns wch already are setled, or shall hereafter be erected or shall settle w^{t}hin their limmetts respectiuely Prouided that no other Jurisdicçõn shall hereafter be taken in as a distinct head or member of this Confederaçõn nor shall any other Plantaçõn or Jurisdicçõn in p^{r}sent being and not already in Combynaçõn or vnder the Jurisdicçõn of any of these Confederat$\wp$ be receiued by any of them nor shall any two of the Confederates joyne in one Jurisdicçõn w^{t}hout consent of the rest wch consent to be interpreted as is expressed in the sixt Article ensuinge.

IIII

4 It is by these Confederat$\wp$ agreed that y^e charge of all just warrs whether offensiue or defensiue vpon what pt or member of this Confederaçõn soe$\mathbf{u}$ they fall, shall both in men $\wp$uisions and all other disbursements be borne by all the p^{ts} of this Confederaçõn in differrent $\wp$porçõns according to

*7

their differrent abillitie in manner following, namely *that the Comissioners for eich Jurisdicçõn from tyme to tyme as ther shalbe occation bring a true account and number of all the males in euery Plantaçõn or any way belonging to or vnder their seuall Jurisdicçõns of what quallyty or condiçõn soe$\mathbf{u}$ they bee from sixteene yeares old to threescore being Inhabi$\mathbf{r}$s there. And that according to the differrent numbers wch from tyme to tyme shalbe found in eich Jurisdicçõn vpon a true and just account, the seruice of men and all charges of the warr be borne by the Poll : eich Jurisdicçõn or plantaçõn being left to their owne just course and custome of rating themselues and people according to their differrent estates w^{t}h due respects to their quallites $\wp$ exemptions among themselues though the Confederaçõn take no notice of any such p^{r}uiledg : And that according to their differrent charge of eich Jurisdicçõn and plantaçõn, the whole advantage of the warr (if it please God so to bless their endeavours) whether it be in lands goods or psons shalbe $\wp$portionably deuided among the said Confederat$\wp$.

V

5 It is further agreed That if any of these Jurisdicçõns or any plantaçõn vnder or in combynaçõn w^{t}h them be euuaded by any enemie whomsoeuer vpon notice $\wp$ request of any three majestrats of that Jurisdicçõn so invaded, the rest of the Confederrates wthout any further meeting or expostulaçõn shall forthwth send ayde to the Confederate in danger but in differrent

pporõons : namely the Massachusets an hundred men sufficiently armed ℇ puided for such a seruice ℇ jorney, and eich of the rest fourty fiue so armed and puided, or any lesse number, if lesse be required according to this pporõon. But if such Confederate in Danger may be supplyed by their next Confederats, not exceeding yᵉ number hereby agreed, they may craue help there, and seeke no further for the pʳsent : the charge to be borne as in this Article is exprest : And at the returne to bee victualled and supplyed wᵗʰ poder and shott for their journey (if there bee neede) by that Jurisdicõon which employed or sent for them : But none of the Jurisdicõons to exceed these numbers till by a meeting of yᵉ Commissioners for this Confederacõon a greater ayd appeare necessary. And this pporõon to continue till vpon know-*ledg of greater numbers in eich Jurisdicõon which shalbe brought to the next meeting some other proporõon be ordered. But in any such case of sending men for pʳsent ayd whether before or after such order or alterraõon, it is agreed that at the meeting of the Comissioners for this Conferacõon, yᵉ cause of such warr or invasion be duly considered : And if it appeare that the fault lay in the parties so invaded that then that Jurisdicõon or plantaõon make just satisfacõon, both to the Invaders whom they have injured, and beare all the charges of the warr themselues wᵗhout requireing any allowance from the rest of the Confederatℇ towards the same And further that if any Jurisdicõon see any danger of any Invasion approaching, and there be tyme for a meeting, that in such case three majestrates of that Jurisdicõon may suṁon a meeting at such convenyent place as themselues shall think meete, to consider ℇ puide against the threatned danger Prouided when they are mett they may remooue to what place they please Onely whilst any of these foure Confederatℇ haue but three majestrats in their Jurisdicõon, their request or suṁons from any two of them shalbe accounted of equall force wᵗʰ the three menõoned in both the clauses of this Article, till there be an encrease of majestratℇ there.

6 It is also agreed that for the mannageing ℇ concluding of all affaires pper ℇ concerneing the whole Confederaõon two Comissioners shalbe chosen by and out of eich of these foure Jurisdicõons namely two for the Mattachusets two for Plymouth two for Connectacutt and two for New Hauen being all in Church fellowship wᵗʰ vs wᶜʰ shall bring full power from their seůall geñall Courts respectiuely to heare examine weigh ℇ determine all affaires of our warr or peace leagues ayds charges and numbers of men for warr diuision of spoyles and whatsoeů is gotten by conquest recciueing of more Confederats *for* plantaõons into combinaõon wᵗʰ any of the confederates and all thinges of like nature wᶜʰ are the pper concoṁitants or

*8

VI

consequents of such a Confederaçõn for amytie offence ℓ defence not inter-
*9   medleing wᵗh the goůment of any of the *Jurisdicçõns wᶜh by the third
Article is pʳserued entirely to themselues. But if these eight Comissioners
when they meete shall not all agree, yet it is concluded that any six of the
eight agreeing shall haue power to settle and determine the businesse in
question : But if six do not agree that then such ꝑposiçõns wᵗh their reasons
so farr as they haue beene debated be sent and referred to the foure gefiall
Courts vizᵗ the Mattachusetts Plymouth Conccttacutt and New Haven :
And if at all the said Gefiall Courts the businesse so referred be concluded,
then to bee ꝑsecuted by the Confederates and all their members   It is further agreed that these eight Comissioners shall meete once euery yeare
besides extrordinary meetings (according to the fift Article) to consider treate
ℓ conclude of all affaires belonging to this Confederaçõn wᶜh meeting shall
euer be the first Thursday in Septembʳ. And that the next meeting after the
date of these pʳnts wᶜh shalbe accounted the second meeting shalbe at Bostone in the Massachusetts the third at Hartford the fourth at New Haven the
fift at Plymouth, the sixt and seauenth at Bostone   And then Hartford New
Hauen and Plymouth and so in course successiuely, if in the meane tyme
some middle place be not found out and agreed on wᶜh may be coṁodious
for all the Jurisdicçõns.

VII   7 It is further agreed that at eich meeting of these eight Comissioners
whether ordinary or extraordinary, they orr six of them agreeing as before,
may chose their President out of themselues whose office and worke shalbe to
take care and direct for order ℓ a comely carrying on of all ꝑceedings in the
pʳsent meeting : but he shalbe invested wᵗh no such power or respect, as by
wᶜh he shall hinder the ꝑpounding or ꝑgresse of any businesse or any way
cast the scales otherwise then in the pʳcedent Article is agreed.

VIII   8 It is also agreed that the Comissioners for this Confederaçõn hereafter
at their meetings whether ordinary or extraordinary as they may haue Comis-
*10   sion or opertunitie do endeavoure *to frame and establish agreements and orders
in gefiall cases of a ciuill nature, wherein all the Plantaçõns are interressed for
pʳserueing peace among themselues, ℓ pʳventing as much as may bee all occations of warr or differrenceℓ wᵗh others, as about the free and speedy passage
of justice in euery Jurisdicçõn, to all the Confederats equally as to their owne,
receiueing those that remooue from one plantaçõn to another wᵗhout due
certefycatℓ, how all the Jurisdicçõns may carry it towards the Indians, that
they neither grow insolent nor be injured wᵗhout due satisfacçõn, lest warr
break in vpon the Confederates through such miscarryages. It is also
agreed that if any servant runn away from his master into any other of these

confederated Jurisdiccōns That in such case vpon the Certyficate of one Majestrate in the Jurisdiccōn out of wch the said servant fled or vpon other due proofe: the said servant shalbe delifled either to his Master or any other that pursues and brings such Certificate or proofe. And that vpon the escape of any prisoner whatsoefl or fugitiue for any criminall cause, whether breake-ing prison or getting from the officer or otherwise escapeing vpon the certifi-cate of two Majestrats of the Jurisdiccōn out of wch the escape is made, that he was a prisoner or such an offender at the tyme of the escape, The Ma:^{trates} or some of them of that Jurisdiccōn where for the p^rsent the said prisoner or fugitiue abideth shall forthwth graunt such a warrant as the case will beare for the app^rhending of any such pson, and the deliuery of him into the hands of the officer, or other pson who pursues him And if there be help required for the safe returneing of any such offendor, then it shalbe graunted to him that craues they same he payinge the charges thereof.

9 And for y^t the justest warrs may be of dangerous consequence espe-cially to the smaler plantacōns in these vnited Colonies, It is agreed that neither the Massachusetts Plymouth *Connectacutt nor New Hauen, nor any of ye members of any of them, shall at any tyme hereafter begin vndertake, or engage themselues or this Confederacōn or any part thereof in any warr whatsoefl (sudden exegents wth the necessary conscquents thereof excepted) wch are also to be moderated as much as the case will pmitt) wthout the con-sent and agreement of the forenamed eight Comissioners or at least six of them, as in the sixt Article is puided: And that no charge be required of any of the Confederat{ in case of a defensiue warr till the said Comissioners haue mett and approued the justice of the warr, and haue agreed vpon the sufli of money to be levyed, wch sufli is then to be payd by the seflall Confederates in pporcōn according to the fourth Article.

10 That in extraordinary occations when meettings are sufloned by three Ma:^{trats} of any Jurisdiccōn, or two as in the fift Article If any of the Comissioners come not due warneing being giuen or sent It is agred that foure of the Comissio^{rs} shall haue power to direct a warr wch cannot be delayed and to send for due pporcōns of men out of eich Jurisdiccōn, as well as six might doe if all mett: but not lesse then six shall determine the justice of the warr or allow the demaund{ or bills of charges, or cause any levies to be made for the same

11 It is further agreed that if any of the Confederates shall hereafter break any of these p^rsent Articles, or be any other wayes injurious to any one of thother Jurisdiccōns: such breach of agreement, or injurie shalbe duly

IX

*11

X

XI

considered ℓ ordered by yᵉ Comissioᵣˢ for thother Jurisdiccōns, that both peace
ℓ this pᵣsent confederacōn may be entirely pᵣseruied w'hout violacōn.

12 Lastly this ppetual Confederacōn and the seũall Articles and agreements thereof being read and seriously considered both by the geñall Court for
the Massachusetts and by the Comissioners for Plymouth Conectacutt ℓ New

Hauen were fully allowed ℓ confirmed *by three of the forenamed Confederates namely the Massachusetts Conectacutt ℓ New Hauen Onely the
Comissioners for Plymouth haueing no Comission to conclude, desired respite
till they might advise w'h their Generall Court, wherevpon it was agreed and
concluded by the said Court of the Massachusetts and the Comissioners for the
other two Confederates That if Plymouth Consent, then the whole treaty as
it stands in these pᵣnte Articles is and shall continue firme ℓ stable w'hout
alteracōn : But if Plymouth come not in : yet the other three Confederates
doe by these pᵣnts confirme the whole Confederacōn and all the Articles
thereof : onely in September next when the second meeting of the Comissioners is to be at Bostone, new consideracōn may be taken of the sixt Article
wᶜh concernes number of Commissioners for meeting ℓ concluding the affaires
of this Confederacōn to the satisfaccōn of the Court of the Massachusetts,
and the Comissioners for thother two Confederats, but the rest to stand
vnquestioned.

In testymony whereof the Geñall Court of the Massachusetts by their
Secretary and the Comissionᵣs for Conectacutt ℓ New Hauen haue subscribed
these pᵣnte Articles this xixᵗh of the third month commonly called May
Anno Dñi 1643.

At a meeting of the Comissioners for the Confedacōn held at Boston
the seauenth of Septembᵣ, It appeareing that the Geñall Court of New Plyñ
ℓ the seũall Towneships thereof haue read considered ℓ approoued these Articles
of confederacōn, as appeareth by Comission from their Geñall Court beareing
date the xxixᵗh of August 1643 to Mᵣ Edward Winslow ℓ Mᵣ Wilᵗm Collyer
to ratifye and confirme the same on their behalf wee therefore the Comissioners
for the Mattachusetts Conecktacutt ℓ New Hauen doe also for oᵣ seũall Goũt-
ments subscribe vnto them.

JOHN WINTHROP Goũ Massachusᵗs.
THO DUDLEY   THEOPH: EATON
GEO: FENWICK   EDWA: HOPKINS
                                            THOMAS GREGSON.

*At a meeting of the

Commissioners for the vnited Colonies of New England holden at Bostone the seaventh of Septemb[r]

1643

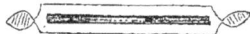

THE Articles of Confederacõn agreed at Bostone the xix[th] of May last being now read Mr Edward Winslow ₹ Mr William Collyer Comissioners for the Jurisdiccõn of New Plymouth deliuered in an Order of their Geñall Court Dated the xxix[th] of August 1643 by wch it appeares that the said Articles of the xix[th] of May weere read approued and confirmed by the said Geñall Court ₹ by all their Towneships and they the s[d] M[r] Winslow ₹ M[r] Collyer were both authorized to ratifie them by their subscriptions and chosen ₹ sent as Commissioners for that Jurisdiccõn w[th] full power to treate and conclud in all matters concerncing warr and peace according to y[e] tenor and true meaneing of the said Articles of Confederacõn for this p[r]sent meetinge

An order made by the geñall Court of the Massachusetts was now also p[r]sented ₹ read, dated the xx[th] of May 1643. By w[ch] it appeares That John Winthrop and Thomas Dudley Esqrs were chosen Comissioners for the Jurisdiccõn of the Mattachusets, and invested w[th] the like full power for this meeting.

An order made by the Geñall Court for Conneetacutt was p[r]sented and read dated at Hartford the fift of July last : By w[ch] it appeares that Georg Fenwick Esq̃ ₹ M[r] Edward Hopkins were chosen Comissioners for that Jurisdiccõn* and invested w[th] the like full power for this meeting

An order made by the Geñall Court for the Jurisdiccõn of New Hauen was p[r]sented ₹ read dated the vj[th] of July 1643 by w[ch] it appeares that M[r] Theophilus Eaton and M[r] Thom̃ Gregson were chosen and sent as Comissioners for that Jurisdiccõn w[th] the like full power for this meeting.

John Winthrop Esq̃ was chosen President for this meeting according to the vij[th] Article in the Confederacõn.

Vpon a motion made by the Comissioners for New Hauen Jurisdiccõn

It was graunted and ordered That the Towne of Milford may be receiued into Combinačõn and as a member of the Jursdicčõn of New Hauen, if New Hauen and Milford agree vpon the termes ℮ condičõns among themselues The like liberty was also granted in regard of the Towne of South-hampton

The Comissioners were informed that Vncus Sagamore of the Munhegen Indians haueing in warr taken Miantinomy Sagamore of the Narrohiggunsets prisoner, had brought him to be kept at Hartford till he might receiue aduice from the English how to pceed against him for sondry treacherous attempts against his life besides this last suddaine Invasion w'hout denounceing warr, and when Vncus was unpvided to w'hstand the great force Miantinomo brought against him : Wherevpon the Commissioners did seriously consider Miantinimos course and carriage, And though they knew and well remembred his ambitious designes to make himself vniũsall Sagomore or Gouernor of all these p̃ts, and his plotts to remooue whatsoeũ stood in his way, And though they haue had many concurrant ℮ pregnant testymonyes from the Indians in seũall p̃ts of the Countrey, of his treacherous plotts by guifts *to engage all the Indians at once to cutt of the whole body of the English in these parts w'h were further confirmed by the Indians Geñall p'paračõns, messages, ℮ soudry insolencies and outrages by them comitted against the English and such Indians as were subjects or frend℮ to the English, so that all the English Plantačõns were to their great charge and damnage forced to arme to keepe stronge watches day and night and some of them to trauell w'h Convoyes from one plantation to another yet leaueing these consideračõns w'h discouer the pride treachery cruelty and malicious disposičõn of the man, and to the English might haue beene sufficient puocačõns to a warr agͭst him: The Comissioners weighed the cause ℮ passages as they were clearely represented ℮ sufficiently euedenced betwixt Vncus ℮ Myantynomo and it appeared that a Tripartite agreement was made and concluded at Hartford betwixt Vncus and Myantinomo w'h some referrence to the English ; in w'h one of the Articles were, That though either of these Indian Sagamores should receiue injuries from the other, yet they should not make warr one of them against the other till they had first complayned, and that the English had heard their greevances, ℮ had declared ℮ determyned what was just ℮ right betwixt them : And that if either of them should attempt against the other w'hout consulting w'h the English, the English might then assist against the Invader: Notw'hstandinge Myantinomo and his Confederats haue sondry wayes manefested their enmity ℮ treacherously plotted and practised against the life of Vncus But especially of late since they were p'pareing ℮ ripening their plotts against

*15

the English *first a Pequin Indian one ˄ Vncus his subjects shott Vncus wth an arrow through the arme but aymeing at his life añ presently fled to the Nanohiggansets or their Confederats ꝑclaymeing in the Indian plantačõns that he had killed Vncus: but when it was knowne Vncus was not dead though wounded, the Traytor was taught to say that Vncus had cutt through his owne arme wth a flint, and had hyred the Pecott to say hee had shott and killed him. Myantinomo being sent for by the Goūnor of the Massachusetts vpon another occation brought the Pecott wth him: but when this disguise would not serue, and that ye English out of his owne mouth found him guilty ⁅ would haue sent him to Vncus his Sagamore to bee ꝑceeded against, Myantinomo desired he might not be taken out of his hands, ꝑmiseing he would send himself to Vncus to be examined ⁅ punished, but contrary to his ꝑmise, and fearcing as it appeares his owne treachery might be discoūed, he w^thin a day or two cutt of the Peacotts head that he might tell no tales. After this some attempts were made to poison Vncus, ⁅ as is reported to take away his life by sorcery. That being discoūed some of Sequassons company an Indian Sagomore allyed to, ⁅ an intimate confederate wth Myantinomo, shott at Vncus as hee was going downe Conectacutt Riuer wth a arrow or two: Vncus according to the foresaid agreement complayneing to the English they sought to make peace betwixt Vncus ⁅ Sequassen: but Sequassen refused, ⁅ expressing his dependance vpon Myantinomo p^rferred warr before peace they fought and Vncus had the victory. Lastly Myantinomo w^thout any ꝑuocačõn from Vncus (vnlesse the disappoyntment of former plotts ꝑvoaked) and suddainly w^thout denounceing warr came vpon Vncus wth nine hundred or a thousand men when Vncus had not half so many to defend himself: Vncus had before the battell told Myantinomo he had many wayes sought his life offered by single combat betweene themselues to end the quarrell and spare blood: But *Myantenomo p^rsumeing vpon his number of men, would haue nothing but a battell, and since Myantenomo was taken prisoner the Indians affirme that the Mohawkes haue beene sent vnto, and are come w^thin a dayes journey of the English plantačõns, but stayed by Miantenomo till hee may attaine his liberty, and then they will carry on their designes whether against ye English or Vncus or both is yet doubtfull.

These thinges being duely weighed ⁅ considered the Comissioners apparently see that Vncus cannot be safe while Myantenomo liues but that either be secret treachery or open force his life wilbe still in danger. Wherefore they thinke he may justly put such a false ⁅ blood-thirsty enemie to death, but in his owne Jurisdicčõn, not in the English plantačõns, And adviseing that in the manner of his death all ñicy and moderačõn be shewed, contrary to the practise of the Indians who exercise tortures ℓ cruelty. And Vncus haueing hitherto shewed himself a frend to the English, and in this craueing their advice, if the Nanohiggansetts Indians or others shall vnjustly assault Vncus for this execucõn, vpon notice and request the English pmise to assist and ptect him, as farr as they may ag:ˢᵗ such vyolence.

The Comissioners do think it fitt to aduise euery geñall Court that they would see that euery man may keepe by him a good gunn ℓ sword one pound of pouder wᵗʰ foure poundℓ of shott wᵗʰ match or flints sutable, to be ready vpon all occasions, and to be carefully viewed foure tymes a yeare at least, And that ouer and aboue this euery generall Court do see that they keep a stock of pouder shott ℓ match euer by them. And it is conceiued by the Comissioners that one hundred poundℓ of pouder and foure hundred pounds of shott wᵗʰ match sutable at the least be ꝑuided for euery hundred men

*18

throrow all the vnited Colonies *of New England, and that the Comissioners at each meeting report how the seſall Jurisdiccõns are furnished.

It is thought fitt and ordered That there be one and the same measure throughout all yᵉ Plantacons wᵗʰin these vnited Colonies, wᶜʰ is agreed to be Winchester measure viz·ᵗ eight gallons to yᵉ bushell.

It is judged meete by the Comissioners yᵗ there be trayneings at least six tymes euery yeare in each plantacõn wᵗʰin this Confederacõn.

The ꝑporcõns of men to be sent for by any of the Jurisdiccõns in case of any pᵣsent danger, vutill the Comissioners may meete according to the fourth Article in the Confederacõn: is for the Massachusets one hundred and fifty men Plymouth thirty Connectacutt thirty and New Hauen twenty fiue And according to this ꝑporcõn are all numbers to be ordered in case of any warr that may fall out vntill the next meeting of the Comissioners in Septembᵣ 1644

Whereas complaints haue beene made against Samuell Gorton ℓ his Company, and some of them weighty ℓ of great consequence, And whereas the said Gorton and the rest haue beene formerly sent for, and now lately by the generall Court of the Massachusets wᵗʰ a safe conduct both for the comeing and returne, that they might giue answere and satisfaccõn, wherein they haue donn wrong. If yet they shall stubbornely refuse The Comissioners for the vnited Colonies think fitt that the Majestrats in the Massachusets ꝑceed against them according to what they shall fynd just: aud the rest of the Jurisdiccõns will approue and concurr in what shalbe so warrantably donn, as if their Comissioners had beene pᵣsent at the Conclusions Prouided that this conclusion do not prejudice the Goūment of Plymouth in any Right they can justly clayme vnto any tract or tracts of land besides that

possessed by the English ℓ Indians who haue submitted themselues to the Goūment of the Massachusetts.

1643.

September.
*19

*In regard of the diũsitie of expressions wch are ℂ may be used in t̄ l e Comissions comeing from the seũall Jurisdic̃õns wch may occation disputs, It is thought fitt and ordered that this ensuing forme bee hereafter used by all the Confederates.

At a gc̃fi.ll Court holden at   for the Jurisdic̃õn of   the   day of

A. and B. were chosen Comissioners for this Jurisdic̃õn for a full and compleat yeare as any occation or exigents may require aud pticulerly for the next yearely meeting at   the first Thursday in September And were invested wth full power and authoryty to treate of ℂ conclude of all thinges according to the tenure ℂ true meaneing of the Articles of Confedac̃õn for the vnited Colonies of New England concluded at Boston the xix^th of May 1643.

The forme of ye Commission to be used.

Vpon informac̃õn and complaynt made by Mr Eaton and Mr Gregson to the Comissioners of sondry injuries and outrages they haue receiued both from the Dutch and Sweads both at Delaware Bay and elswhere the pticulers wth their proofes being duly considered. It was agreed and ordered That a ł̃re be written to the Sweadish Goũnor expressing the pticulers and requireing satisfaction wch ł̃re is to be vnderwritten by John Winthrop Esq̃ as Goũn^r of the Massachusetts and President of the Comissioners for the vnited Colonies of New England. And whereas the Dutch Goũnor wrote to the Goũnor and gc̃fi.ll Court of the Massachusetts complayneing against Hartford as by his ł̃re dated the xx^th of July last appeares vnto wch Mr Winthrop in pt answered the second of August referring to the Gc̃fiall Court for the Massachusetts and to this meeting of the Comission^rs for a further ℂ full answere, It was thought fitt that in that answere the wrongs donn both to Hartford and New Hauen be expressed requireing answere to the pticulers: and ꝑfessing that *as wee will not wrong others, so we may not desert our Confederates in any just cause.

*20

These foregoing conclusions were subscribed by the Comission^rs for the seũall Jurisdic̃õns the xvj^th of Septemb^r 1643.

JOHN WINTHROP Pres^d
THO: DUDLEY
GEOR: FENWICK
THEOPH: EATON
EDW: WINSLOW
W^M COLLIER
EDWA: HOPKINS
THO: GREGSON.

At a meeting of the

Comissioners for the vnited Colonies at Boston the
vijth Septemb^r 1643

IT was agreed that the Gou̅ment of the Massachusets in the behalf of the vnited Colonies of New England giue Conoonacus and the Nanohiggunsets to vnderstand that from tyme to tyme we haue taken notice of the violac̃on of that league betweene ye Massachusets and themselues, (notwthstanding the manefestacons of loue & integryty towards them by the English) wch they haue discouered as by other wayes, so lately by their concurrance wth Myantenomo their Sachim in his mischeevous plotts to roote out the Body of the English Nation purchaseing the ayde of all the Indians by by gnifts threats and other allurements to their p^ty (except a few vizt Vncus and his men, whom they haue not spared to invade notwthstanding A tripartie Couenant to the contrary, betweene the Gou̅ment of Conectacutt Myantenomo & Vncus Sagamore of the Mohegan vnder their hand& & markes : But vnderstanding how peacable Conoonacus & Mascus the late father of Myantenomo gouerned that great people, we rather ascribe these late tumults outbreakings & malitious plots to the rash and ambitious spirit of Myantenomo then any affected way of their owne. And therefore once more notwthstanding all those former vnworthy passages so well knowne vnto us, as a people inclineing to peace & desireing their good we do in our owne names and in the behalf, & wth the consent of the vnited Colonies tender them peace & such loueing correspondency as hath form̃ly beene euer obserued on our p^ts vizt the seu̅all Gou̅ments of the Massachusets Plymouth Conectacutt & New Hauen wth all such as are

in Combynac̃on & confederac̃on wth them both *English and Indians as Vncus Sagamore of the Mohegins & his people Woosamequine and his people Sacanocoe & his people Pumham & his people, whose peace and lawfull liberties we may not suffer to be vyolated. And if the Nanohiggansetts be desireous of peace as formerly we shalbe as carefull to p^rserue their peace & liberties from vyolac̃on : but shall expect more faythfull obseruance then we haue form̃ly found from Myantenomo in the tyme of his Gou̅ment requireing answere wth as much expedic̃on as the waight of the case requireth. And whereas Vncus was aduised to take away the life of Myantenomo whose lawfull Captiue he was,   They may well vnderstand that this is without violaçõn of any Couenant betweene them ç vs for Vncus being in confedaçõn wᵗh us, and one that hath dilligently obserued his Couenants before mençõned for ought we know, ç requireing advice from us vpon serious consideraçõn of the pʳmisss,. vizᵗ his treacherous ç murtherous Disposiçõn against Vncus çẽ and how great A Disturber hee hath beene of the Cõmon peace of the whole Countrey we could not in respect of the justice of the case safety of the Countrey and faythfullnes of our frend do otherwise then approue of the lawfullnes of his death, which agreeing so well wᵗh the Indians owne manners and concuring wᵗh the practise of other Nations wᵗh whom we are quainted, we pswade oʳselues how euer his death may be greeuous at pʳsent, yet the peacable fruits of it will yeild not onely matter of safety to the Indians but pñtt to all that inhabite this continent.

That assoone as the Comissioners for Conectacutt and New Hauen shall returne into those parts that then Vncas be sent for to Hartford wᵗh some considerable number of his best ç trustyest men, and that then he being made acquainted *acquainted* wᵗh the advice of the Comissioners *Myantenomo be deliûed vnto him that so execuçõn may be donn according to justice ç prudence Vncus carrying him into the next pt of his owne goûment and there put him to death Prouided that some discreet ç faythfull psons of yᵉ English accompany them and see the execuçõn for our more full satisfacçõn, and that the English meddle not wᵗh the head or body at all : And this being donn that notice be giuen to all yᵉ Confederates by łres That so the Massachusets goûment may thereupon send to Nanohiggunsett, ç Plymouth may take due course wᵗh Woosamequin as after is aduised.

*23

That Hartford furnish Vncus wᵗh a competent strengh of English to defend him against any pʳsent fury or assault of the Nanohiggunsets or any other.

That in case Vncas shall refuse to execut justice vpon Myantenomo. That then Myantenomo be sent by Sea to the Massachusets, there to be kept in safe durance till the Comissioners may consider further how to dispose of him.

That Plymouth labour by all due meanes to restore Woosamequin to his full liberties in respect of any encroachments by the Nanohiggansets or any other Natiues that so the pprieties of the Indians may be pʳserued to themselues, and that no one Sagomore encroach vpon the rest as of late : And that Woosamequin be reduced to these former termes ç agreements betweene Plymouth and him.

JO : WINTHROP Presid   EDW : WINSLOW

THO : DUDLEY   Wᴹ COLLIER

GEO : FENWICK   EDWA : HOPKINS

THEOPH EATON   THO : GREGSON.

At A meetinge of the Comissioners for

the vnited Colonies in New England at Hartford the fift of Septemb.ʳ 1644

1644.

September.

THE articles of Confederacõn being read an order of the gefiall Court of the Massachusets dated May the xxixᵗh 1644 was prsented and read whereby it appeared Mr Symon Brodstrecte and Mr Wiltm Hawthorne were chosen Comissioners for one full and compleat yeare being invested wᵗh full power (authoryty according to the tenor of the said Articles and an order made therevppon at A meeting at Boston the vijᵗh of Septemb.ʳ 1643.

Mr Edward Winslowe and Mr John Browne were in like manner chosen Comissioners for the Colony of New Plymouth as appeared by an order of their gefiall Court dated the fift of June 1644.

Mr Edward Hopkins and Georg Fenwicke Esqᵖ were chosen Comissioners for the Colony of Conectacutt as appeared by an order of their gefiall Court dated yᵉ last of July 1644.

Mr Theophilus Eaton and Mr Thomas Gregson were likewise chosen Comissioners for the Colony of New Hauen as appeared by an order of their gefiall Court dated the xxvijᵗh of Octobʳ: 1643.

Mr Edward Hopkins was chosen President for this meeting.

The Comissionrs for the Massachusetts mooued that a due order might be attended in the subscriptions of the Acts and determinacõns of this and any future meetings of the Comissioners for the vnited Colonies, and expressed not onely their owne appᵗhensions but the judgment of their gefiall Court, That by the Articles of Confederacõn the first place did of Right belong to the Massachusetts, as being first named and so thother Colonies in like order, wᶜh being taken into consideracõn, and the Articles of Confederacõn

read, It appeared euidently to the Comissioners *that no such pruiledg had beene euer ppounded graunted or practised by the Comissioners for the Jurisdicõns in either of their forᵐ meetings, and yet the first subscription was made in the prsence of the gefiall Court of the Massachusetts. And to prvent future inconuenienc vpon this occation they thought fitt to declare that this Commission is free and may not receiue any thing (not expresly agreed in the Articles as imposed by any gefiall Court, yet out of their respects to

(16)

the Goûment of the Massachusetts they did willingly graunt that their Comissioners should first subscribe after the President in this and all future meetings. And the Comissioners for the other Colonies in such order as they are named in the Articles vizt Plymouth Conectacutt and New Hauen.

The Comissioners being put in mynd of the differrences betwixt the Narrohiggansets and Vncus and the former engagements of the English to Vncus and his expectaĉon of succors from them in regard of some Assaults p^rtended to be made vpon him by the Narrohiggansetts, as also of a Charge layd vpon Vncus by the Narrohiggansets of takeing a ransome or at least a part thereof for the life of their late Sachime, whō afterward{ notw^thstanding he put to death. It was conceiued requisite before a full consideraĉon could be taken of the said differrenc{ or any determinaĉon therevpon, that two Messengers should be sent to both the said Sachims wth the following Instructions.

> Instrucĉons for Thomas Stanton { Nathaniell Willett sent by the Comissioners for the vnited Colonies of New England to Pessicus Canoonacus { other the Sachims of the Narrohiggansett Indians and Vncus Sagamore of the Mohegan Indians.

You shall informe the aboue menĉoned Sagamores respectiuely That the Comissioners for all the English Colonies namely the Massachusetts New Plymouth Conectacutt and New Hauen who haue full power { authorytie from all the said Jurisdicĉons to consider and conclude both of peace and warr, and by all just meanes to guide for the safety { welfare of the Countrey are now mett together at Hartford. I

*That the said Comissioners haue heard that the Narrohiggansett Sagamores and their company do charge Vncus { the Mohegan Indians that an agreement was made for the Ransome of the late Narrohigganset Sachim And that Vncus hath receiued part of the said ransome wch Vncus denyeth to haue receiued vpon any such consideraĉon, and therefore hath hitherto refused to returne the same. 2
*27

That diuers Acts of hostillity haue lately passed betwixt the Narrohiggansets and the Mohegan Indians wch are like to breake forth into an open warr to the disturbance of the publike peace vnlesse some seasonable course be taken to p^rvent it. 3

That they Comissiou^rs haue therefore sent you both to the Narrohigganset and Mohegan Sagamores to let them know that if they please either to come themselues, or to send any considerable men of theirs to ppound their seuerall greevances whether concerneing the foremenĉoned ransome or any other matter, and to bring due proofe of their complaints: 4

1644.

September.

They Comission's w'hout any ptiall respect to either pty will consider their differrenc̃, and giue answerable advice to them both to settle peace and A neighbourly correspondence w'h due satisfac̃öñ for injuries betwixt them.

5

That the Comission's hereby do p̃mise ꝑ assure them, that they or their messengers shall haue free liberty to come and returne, and to treate and p̃secute their affaires in peace w'hout molestac̃öñ or any just greeranc̃ from the English. And in the name of the Comiss's you shall require of both pties that during this treaty no acts of hostillyty passe either against any of their seꝗall plantac̃öns, or of their people in their occations or Sagamores or Messengers in their tranells.

6

If either of the pties put in excuses and seeme vnwilling to come, you may remember them of the treaty made and concluded at Hartford betwixt the Narrohigganset Indians, and the Mohegans, by w'h they engaged themselues, that vpon any differrenc̃ or offences before they entred vpon warr, they would first acquaint the English w'h their greevances and receiue advice and direction from them.

7

*28

But if notw'hstanding they refuse to come or send *you shall from the Comission's demaund from the refuseing pty what their purpose and resoluc̃öñ is whether for peace or warr betwixt themselues, and on what termes they stand w'h the English Cononies, whether they purpose to hold and continue all former treaties ꝗ agreements made either w'h the English of the Massachusetts or the English at Hartford, or whether they account them all as broken and voyd that they Comission's may accordingly order their occations.

8

You shall endeavour pticulerly ꝗ clearely to acquaint ꝗ open euery one of the former Articles both of the Narrohigganset and Mohegan Indians, and you shall take their answere in writing to eich pticular, And when you haue so donn reade their answere in the seꝗall pts of it to them that they may vnderstand how yᵘ vnderstand their answere, ꝗ that we may know they owne it, and that there is no mistake

HARTFORD Septembᵣ: 6ᵗh: 1644

Youghco the Sachim of Munhausett vpon long Island presenting himself to, the Comission's desired that in regard he was a Tributary to the English, and had hitherto obserued the Articles of agreement, he might receiue from them A certyficate whereby his relac̃öñ to the English might appeare and he p̃serued asmuch as might be from vnjust greevances and vexac̃öns (though the Colonies be no way engaged to protect him) yet herevpon the following certificate was giuen him

To all whom it may concerne, whereas Longe Iland wth the smaler Iland� adjacent, are graunted by the Kings Matie of Greate Brittaine to the Lord Starling, and by him passed ouer to some of the English in these vnited Colonies And whereas the Indians in the Easterne pt� of long Iland are become tributaries to the English and haue engaged their land� to them: And whereas Youghcoe Wiantause Moughmaitow and Weenagaminin do p�esse themselues frends both to the English and the Dutch and that they haue not beene injurious to either of them in their psons cattle or goods, nor by wampam or any other meanes haue sought to �cure the Mohawkes or any other Indians to annoy or hurt either of the Nations, and pmise still to continue in a peaceable and *and* inoffensiue course toward� them both and that if it may appeare that any of their men in any secrett way haue beene actors in any thinge against either English or Dutch, vpon due notice and proofe they will deliuer all such to deserued punishment, or �vide due satisfac̃ōn for all injuries � offences donn. It is our desires that the said Sagamores and their companies may enjoy full peace w'hout disturbance from ye English or any in frendship wth them, whilest they carry themselues in wayes of peace w'hout engageing themselues in the quarrells of others or doing wrong to any.

Septembr: 9th 1644.

*Whereas the Comission^rs for the Massachusetts by vertue of A joynt Conquest layd clayme to some part of ye lands lately belonging to the Pecoats, desireing that a diuision might either now be ordered, or some course � tyme appoyn'ted in w'h it might be setled: Mr Fenwick for himself and some Noble psonages, by patent interessed in the lands in question, desired that nothing might be concluded against their Right � Title in their absence, and p�esseth y^t Pecoat Harbor and the land� adjoyncing were of great conc̃ernement to those interressed in Conectacutt Riuer, and that they had a speciall ayme and respect to yt when first they consulted about planting in these pt�. The rest of the Comissioners considering the demaund and answere thought fit that due and convenyent respect be giuen to those noble � worthy psons absent to pleade their owne interrest, and that all patents of equall Authoryty receiue the same construc̃ōn, both in refferrence to pprietie in land� � jurisdic̃ōn: And Mr Fenwick was desired to acquaint those in England interressed, that the question might be yssued w'h convenyent speed. And vpon this occasion Mr Fenwick desired a meete �por̃ōn of the Tribute receiued from the Indians as a fruite of the Conquest attayned by A com̃on charge wherein the Gentlemen interressed in Say-Brooke-fort bare a considerable part.

Whereas the most considerable psons in these Colonies came into these

1644.

September.

ptℓ of America that they might enjoy Christ in his ordinancℓ w^{t}hout disturbance, and whereas among many other precious mercies the ordinances haue
beene and are dispenced among us w^{t}h much puritie and power. The Comis-
sion^{r}s tooke it into their serious considera$\widetilde{co}$n how some due mayntenance
according to God might be $\wp$uided and setled both for the p^{r}sent ℓ future for
the encouragement of the ministers who labour therein and concluded to
$\wp$pound ℓ co$\widetilde{m}$end it to eich ge$\widetilde{n}$all Court. That those that are taught in the

Mr Browne de-
sired further
considera$\widetilde{co}$n
about the 2 last
clauses of this
conclusion

word in the se$\widetilde{u}$all planta$\widetilde{co}$ns be called together, that euery man volun-
taryly set downe what he is willing to allow to that end ℓ use And if any
man refuse to pay a meete $\wp$por$\widetilde{co}$n, that then hee be rated by authoryty in
some just ℓ equall way, And if after this any man w^{t}hhold or delay due
payment, the ciuill power to be exercised as in other just debts.

*30

*This ensuing $\wp$posi$\widetilde{co}$n of A ge$\widetilde{n}$all Contribu$\widetilde{co}$n for the mayntenance of
poore Schollers at the Colledg at Cambridge being p^{r}sented to the Comission^{r}s
by Mr Shepard pastor to the Church at Cambridg was read and fully approoued
by them ℓ agreed to be comended to the se$\widetilde{u}$all ge$\widetilde{n}$all Courts as a matter
worthy of due considera$\widetilde{co}$n and entertainement for advance of learneing and
w^{c}h we hope wilbe chearfully embraced.

To the Honored Commission^{r}s.

Those whom God hath called to attend the welfare of Religious Co$\widetilde{m}$on
weales haue beene prompt to extend their care for the good of publike
Schooles by meanes of w^{c}h the Co$\widetilde{m}$on wealth may be furnished w^{t}h knowing
and vnderstanding men in all callings the Churches w^{t}h an able ministery in
all places and w^{t}hout w^{c}h it is easy to see how both these estates may decline
and degenerate into grosse ignorance, ℓ consequently into great and vni$\hat{u}$sall
$\wp$phanesse. May it please y^u therefore among other thinges of Co$\widetilde{m}$on Concernement and publike benefitt to take into yor considera$\widetilde{co}$n some way of comfortable mayntenance for that Schoole of the Prophets that now is: For
although hitherto God hath carryed on that worke by a speciall hand and
that not w^{t}hout some euedent fruit and successe yet it is found by too sad
experience, that for want of some externall supplys many are discouraged
from sending their children (though pregnant and fitt to take the best impression) therevnto, others y^t are sent their $\wp$ents enforced to take them away too
soone or to their owne houses too oft as not able to minister any comfortable
and seasonable mayntenance to them therein. And those who are continued
not w^{t}hout much pressure ge$\widetilde{n}$ally to the feeble abillities of their $\wp$ents or
other priuate frends who beare the burthen therein aloane, If therefore it
were commended by you at least to the freedome of euery famyly (w^{c}h is able

and willing to giue) throughout the plantaçõns to giue yearely but the fourth part of a bushell of Corne, or somethinge equivolent therevnto. And for this end if euery minister were desired to stirr up the hearts of the people once in the fittest season in the yeare to be freely enlarged therein and one or two faythfull and fitt men appoynted in each towne to receiue and seasonably to send in what shalbe thus giuen by them : It is conceiued that as no man would feele any greevance hereby, so it would be a blessed meanes of comfortable puision for the dyett of diuers such studients as may stand in neede of some support, ꝑ be thought meete and worthy to be continued a fitt season therein. And because it may seeme an vnmeete thing for this one to suck ᵒ draw away all that norishment wᶜʰ the like Schooles may neede in after tymes in other *Colonies, your wisdomes therefore may set downe what limmitaçõns you please, or choose any other way you shall think more meete for this desired pʳsent supply, yoʳ religious care hereof as it cannot but be pleaseing to him whose you are and whom now you serue, so the fruit hereof may hereafter aboundantly testyfye that your labour herein hath not beene in vayne.

The Goûment of Massachusetts may receiue Martins vineyard into their Jurisdicçõn if they see cause

The Jurisdicçõn of Coneetacutt hath the same liberty for Southhampton vpon Long Iland.

Whereas a Question hath beene formerly ꝑpounded betwixt the Massachusetts and Mʳ Fenwick about the ruñiug of the Massachusetts line in referrence to Woranoake where Mʳ Hokins ꝑ Mʳ Whitcing haue purchased landꝭ from the Indians, ꝑ haue built and are possessed of a trading there wᵗʰ the Indians. And whereas the pʳsent Comissionʳs for the Massachusetts ꝑduced an order of Court made at Massachusetts wherein Mʳ Fenwick ꝑmised to cleare the title to Woronoak as not wᵗʰin yᵉ Massachusetts line at or before this meeting or els to submitt yt to the Massachusetts Goûment, The Comissionʳs fynd that Mʳ Fenwick hath not yet cleared his title by Patent to Woronoak, ꝑ therefore see not for the pʳsent but that the trading house and landꝭ at Woroack doth fall vnder all just orders made at the Massachusetts wᵗʰ other trading houses and land wᵗʰin that Jurisdicçõn, till the title be further cleared But the ꝑprietie of the land to be left to the Purchasors they makeing their title appeave, ꝑuided it exceede not a thousand acrees.

It is ordered that no ꝑson wᵗʰin any of the vnited Colonies shall directly or indirectly sell to any Indians either pouder shott bulletts guñs swords daggers arrow heads or any amunition vnder the penalty of twenty for one nor shall any Smyth or other ꝑson whatsoeuer mend any gunn or other fore-

September.
This last clause
is also con-
firmed.

*32

menc̃oned weapon belonging to any Indian vnder the aforesaid penalty And it is comended vnto the serious consideracõn of the seũall Jurisdiccõns whether it be not expedient ℇ necessary to prohibit the selling of the aforesaid ammunition, either to the French or Dutch or to any other that do comonly trade the same wᵗh Indians.

Whereas there was a petition pʳsented to the Comissionʳs for a pporcõn of pouder and other guifts giuen to New England in gefiall It is thought fitt that what appeares *to be so giuen shalbe deuided according to a just pporcõn reserueing the pticuler guifts giuen to each Jurisdiccõn as ᵱper to themselues.

The Comissionʳs fynding that in that intercourse of occations wᶜh they may haue wᵗh their neighbours whether Dutch French Sweeds or others ayd may be demaunded or liberty ℇ pmission for voluntaries to strenghen and assist one pᵗy wᶜh may bee lyable to misconstruccõn and hassard the peace of the Colonies It is therefore ordered that no Jurisdiccõn wᵗhin this Confederacõn shall pmitt any voluntaries to goe forth in a warlike way against any people whatsoeũ, wᵗhout order ℇ direccõn of the Comissionʳs of the seũall Jurisdiccõns.

Whereas the Trade wᵗh the Indians in these pts is or may be of great Concernement, but wᵗhall subject to many questions and differrenc℮ as whether eich Jurisdiccõn shalbe limmited and restrayned to their owne knowne and allowed bound℮, whether in each Jurisdiccõn each pticuler pson shall haue liberty at his discretion to mannage a pticuler trade according to his optunitie, or whether the trade shalbe rented out to some either at certaine yearely rate, or such pporcõn by the hundred or skinn, or whether as the Colonies are now vnited so a gefiall stock be raised for, ℇ throughout them all, into wᶜh each man shall haue liberty to put in as he is able ℇ willing The Comissionʳs conceiued this latter more pfitable ℇ honorable and accordingly agreed to com̃end it to their gefiall Courts in their seũall Jurisdiccõns wᵗh these following consid eracõns.

I   It is conceiued that a stock of fiue or six thousand pound℮ may begin such a Trade, but Tenn thousand or more may comfortably, and to good advantage be ymployed in yt

2   That in each Plantacõn euery man may either put in his pporcõn vnder his owne Name (puided he put not in lesse then xxᵗ, or diuers may put in vnder the name of some one whom they gefially trust and are satisfyed in, And in such case he whose name is used, to be called an vndertaker or feoffee, and all the rest adventuʳs.

3   That in each Jurisdiccõn two or three be chosen by the vndertakers to

mannage this joynt stock, by puideing Comiodities for trade, setling tradeing houses hireing factors or servant{ to trade w'h the Indians, receiueing the Beauer or other ꝓceed of the trade from them w'haccount{ from tyme to tyme and what els may be necessary and ordered as ꝑp to their plac{ { these to be called Committees.

*That if the seũall Geñ: Courts approue this course of trading by a joynt stock euery man may have tyme w'hin three mouths after to vnder write what hee will furnish for the trade, and six months after to pay it in. Prouided that whateuer any man vnder writes no more shalbe accounted or expected then what he payeth in w'hin the aforesaid six months

4

*33

For the payment of euery mans ꝑporċõn, either money English comiodities fitt for Trade wampom Beauer English Corne or cattell fitt for the Butcher or markett shalbe accepted: so that by the Comittees they bee duly { indifferently rated, that they may equall to the payment of others that no man be wronged.

5

That this way of tradeing w'h due p'uiledges be established by each Geñall Court for tenn yeares { that all Interlopers both our owne and others be restrayned asmuch as may be.

6

That the accounts of this joynt stock be made by the aforesaid Comittees euery yeare and tendred to the view of the Comissio'rs in each Jurisdicċõn before this yearely meeting in Septemb'r And that after the first yeare so much of the gayne and ꝑfitts (if it please God to prosper the trade) be deuided as the Comission'rs for the Colonies w'h the aforeśd Committees shall thinke meete.

7

The aforesaid Comittees to haue such allowance and consideraċõn for their care and paynes in mannageing this joynt stock as the vndertakers shall thinke meete.

8

Whereas it is conceiued there wilbe a geñall Court in each Jurisdicċõn this next ensuing month or the begiñing of Novemb'r. where these ꝑposiċõns may be seriously considered, the Comission'rs ꝑmise mutually to certefy each other what entertainement they fynd that accordingly each Jurisdicċõn, { trader may order theire owne occations.

9

Some of the Inhabitants of Roade Iland haueing intimated a willingnes to be receiued into and vnder the Goũment of one of the Colonies. The Comission'rs considering that by an vtter refusall, they may by the discords and diuisions among themselues, be exposed to some greate inconvenyenc{, { hopeing many of them may be reduced to a better frame by goũment, thought fitt that if ye major pt { such as haue most interrest in the Iland will absolutely { w'hout reservaċõn submitt either the Massachusetts ˌ Plymouth may receiue them.

1644.

September.

*34

Confirmed.

*It is agreed by way of explanacōn of the fourth Article that in each meeting of the Comission's in Septemb', they alwayes bring w'h them the true number of all their males from sixteene to sixty yeares of age   That till the next yeares meeting in any occation of ayde the number of men to be sent from each Jurisdiccōn shall continue as was ordered in Septemb' 1643 but all charges past w'ch fall vpon the Colonies by the Articles shalbe payd according to y' number of males last yeare brought in and all future charges for this yeare according ^ the number to be brought in in September 1645.

There being a question ppounded of what esteeme and force a verdict or sentence of any one Court w'hin the Colonies ought to be of in the Court of another Jurisdiccōn the Comission's well weighing the same, thought fitt to commend it to the sevĩall gefĩall Courts, that euery such verdict or sentence may haue a due respect in any other Court through the Colonies where occation may be to make use of it and that it be accounted good euidence for the plaintiffe vntill either better euidence or some other just cause appeare to alter or make the same voyde, and that in such case the yssuing of the cause in question be respited for some convenient tyme, that the Court may be aduised w'h, where the verdict or sentence first passed.

The Comissioners for the Massachusetts informeing what ayde had formerly beene afforded to Mons' de la Toure at his owne charg by some Merchants or other volunteers out of the Bay w'hout publike order or allowance that Mons De Aulney hath since giuen out Comissions to take any vessells belonging to the said Bay : that Mons' de la Toure is or lately was in the Bay desireing further ayde aganst Mons' De Aulney that the Ma:trates in the Massachusetts haue not onely refused to graunt any further Assistance, but by a publike declaracōn haue strictly forbidden all theires (saue in their owne defence) either as volunteers or any other way to do any hostile Act against Mons' De Aulney or any of his till further consideracōn ῍ order.   And y' the Counsell for the Massachusetts haue written to Mons' De Aulney that the former ayde was carryed by priuate men, hyred by Mons' De la Toure at his owne charg and had no Comission, countenance nor any allowance from the gefĩall Court or Goûment there setled, that if it appeare any injurie haue beene donn by any of them in that Course, they will as they may, puide for a due repaire and for that purpose are ready and do desire that in a faire treaty consideracōn may be taken of all former passages and greevances

*35

betwixt the English now vnited *in these Colonies and himself and his Company, y' due satisfaccōn may be giuen and receiued and peace and a neighbourly correspondenč p'serued ῍ continued betwixt them   And in the meane tyme that their Merchants may pceed in their lawfull trades w'hout dis-

turbance, but what answere or successe they may receiue or fynd is yet
doubtfull, wherefore they desired advice from the Comission⟨r⟩s how to ꝑceede
further in these treaties or affaires w⟨th⟩ Mons⟨r⟩ De Aulney.

The Comission⟨r⟩s seriously considering the p⟨r⟩misss did fully approoue the
late offer of a faire and neighburly treaty to consider of greevanc⟨e⟩ mutually
that just repairacõns may bee accordingly made and if occation require
themselues shalbe ready to second and confirme that foremenconed offer that
justice may be furthered and peace w⟨th⟩ the sweet fruits of it continued but if
notw⟨th⟩standing those just ꝑposicõns made by y⟨e⟩ Massachusets Mons⟨r⟩ De
Aulney shall refuse to treat, or neglect to call back his foresd Comissions,
if he shall ꝑfesse a Resolucõn for warr or ꝑceede in Courses of actuall
hostilitie assaulting or seizeing any of the vessells belonging to any of the
Colonies either at Sea or in any harbour, before any attempt or further just
ꝑvocation haue beene offerred by any of the English, then it shalbe lawfull
for the gefiall Court of the Massachusetts to graunt a lymmitted Comission
to any of theires to repaire themselues and by seizeiug any vessells of his
to recoft their losses. And further if it bee apparent to the said gefiall
Court that Mons⟨r⟩ De Aulney be so resolued vpon warr that peace and
neighbourly correspondency cannot bee had vpon any equall termes. Then
it may be lawfull for the said Court in the name and for the use of the said
vnited Colonies to treate w⟨th⟩ Mons⟨r⟩ De la Towre ⟨e⟩ if he be willing to
purchase all his right and title to the land⟨e⟩ forte and app⟨r⟩tenices at S⟨t⟩ Johns
Riuer, or if hee will not part w⟨th⟩ it, they may then take the best ⟨e⟩ speedyest
course they can according to rules of justice ⟨e⟩ prudence at his charge to
secure Mons⟨r⟩ De la Towres fort there, that yt fall not into the hands of such
an implacable enimie. But in such case the Comission⟨r⟩s for the vnited
Colonies are to be sufiioned assoone as the season will ꝑmitt to afford their
further advice and direcõn in a businesse of so great importance and concernement.

Whereas a peticõn was delifled to the Comission⟨r⟩s desireing the mending
· of some places in the way from the Bay to Concetacutt It was agreed that it
be left to M⟨r⟩ Hopkins President, to take care for the ꝑuideing some man or
men to fynd ⟨e⟩ lay out the best way to the Bay, ⟨e⟩ tho charge to be borne by
the whole.

qr

*A motion being made by the Comission⟨r⟩s of Plymouth that satisfaccõn
might be required of Mons⟨r⟩ De Aulney for the injurie donn to them at
Matthebiquatus in Penobscott The Comission⟨r⟩s thought meete to deferr the
same till they see what Answere the said Mons⟨r⟩ De Aulney will returne to a

*36

Łre sent him by the Ma:^trates of the Massachusets wherein that pticuler is
menĉõned, and that therevpon it be taken into further consideraĉõn.

Whereas by a wise Prouidence of God two of the Jurisdicĉõns in the
westerne part⸹ viz⸹ Concetacutt and New Hauen haue beene lately exercised
by sondry Insolencies and outrages from the Indians. As first an English man
rúñing from his Master out of yᵉ Massachusets was murthered in the woods
in or neere the limmitts of Concetacutt Jurisdicĉõn and about six weeks after
vpon discouery by an Indian the Indian Sagamor⸹ in those pts promised to
deliuer the murtherrer to the English bound, and haueing accordingly brought
him wᵗhin the sight of Vncowa by their joynt consent as it is informed he was
there vnbound ⸹ left to shift for himself, wherevpon tenn English men forthwᵗh
comeing to the place, being sent by Mʳ Ludlow at the Indians desire to
receiue the Murtherrer, whoe seeing him escaped, layed hold of viij^t or ix
Indians there pʳsent amongst whom there was a Sagamore or two, and kept
them in hold two dayes, till foure Sagamores engaged themselues wᵗhin one
month to deliû the prisoner And about a week after this agreement, an
Indian came pʳsumptuously, ⸹ wᵗh guile in the day tyme, and murtherously
assaulted an English weoman in her house at Stamford, ⸹ by three wound⸹
supposed mortall left her for dead after hee had robbed the house, by wᶜh
passages the English were pvoaked, ⸹ called to a due consideraĉõn of their
owne safetie, and the Indians generally in those ptes arose in an hostile manner, refused to come to the English to cary on treaties of peace departed
from their wigwrams left their Corne vnweeded ⸹ shewed themselues tumul-
tuously aboute some of the English Plantaĉõns, and shott of peec⸹ wᵗhin
heareing of the Towne, and some Indians came to English ⸹ toald them the
Indians would fall vpon them soe that most of the English thought it vnsafe
to trauell in those pts by land and some of the Plantaĉõns were put vpon
strong watch and ward night and day, and could not attend their priuate
occations and yet distrusted their owne strengh *for their defence, wherevpon
Hartford and New Hauen were sent vnto for ayde, and saw cause both to
send, both into the weaker part⸹ of their owne Jurisdicĉõns thus in danger
And New Hauen for convenyency of Scittuaĉõn sent ayd to Vncowah though
belonging to Concetacutt, of all wᶜh passages they pʳsently acquainted the
Comission's in the Bay and had allowance and approbaĉõn from yᵉ geñall
Court there wᵗh direcĉõn neither to hasten a warr nor to beare such insolencies
too long, wᶜh courses though chargable to themselues, yet through Gods
blessing they hope the fruite is and wilbe sweete and wholesome to all the
Colonies, the Murtherrers are since deliuered to justice, the publike peace
pʳserued for the pʳsent ⸹ pbably may be better secured for the future The

*37

Comission^rs for Conectacutt ℮ New Hauen for their Jurisdicc̃ons who haue expended these charges in the aforesaid cause ℈pounded how they should be borne whether by the Colonies or the aforesaid Jurisdicc̃ons wch being considered ℮ the Articles for Confederac̃on read, the greater part of Comission^rs conceiued that till warr be begunn vpon some one of the Colonies by an Actuall Assault, no charg shalbe expected from the rest of the Jurisdicc̃ons. And the Comission^rs doe joyntly agree that in any such Assault or warr begunn vpon any one of them no charge is to be borne by the rest till all the grounds and occations of the warr be considered, and the Jurisdicc̃on invaded cleared by the Comission^rs according to the Articles, but being cleared then from the begining of the warr the charge to fall vpon the Colonies according to their ℈porc̃on, wherein the French busines (if there be cause) shalbe taken into considerac̃on, and the order now entred in this meeting of the Comission^rs shalbe of no force to guide the matter of charge in any warr wch may follow any further then the Articles thus expounded require.

Vpon certaine differrenc℮ betweene the Massachusetts and Mr Whiting wth others concerneing an agreement beareing date the xiiij^th of the fourth month 1641 concerning two patent℮ vpon the Riuer of Pascataque The Comission^rs for the Massachusetts pleaded that their geñall Court intended not to graunt any land℮ to the foresaid gentlemen but onely to receiue from them *what then was conceiued to be theires vpon a supposic̃on that the Patent℮ of the said gentlemen were auntienter then that of the Massachusetts and desired that some course might be thought vpon and setled, whereby the Townes on the said Riuer might enjoy such liberties as other Townes in the Bay doe according to a clause in the said Agreement, or otherwayes they shalbe forced to surrender wch being duly considered, it appeared to the rest of the Comission^rs y^t in the agreement menc̃oned the Court of the Massachusetts do graunt or consent to the reseruac̃on therein expressed ℮ ℈mise to assist them by all legall courses in the mayntenance of those reseruac̃ons, And that in makeing the said agreement there was a debate ℮ agitac̃on both aboute the Massachusetts line and date of the two Patents but they were by the said Court layd aside that the said Agreement might ℈cede and be concluded, And the Comission^rs conceiue that that clause wherein there is mention of liberties referrs onely to Jurisdicc̃on, and cannot infring or weaken the Gentlemens ℈prictie in ye land℮ reserued by the said agreement: yet they thinke it reasonable and just, that the Gentlemen afford some such further accomodac̃on in land to the Inhabitant℮, as by wch they may comfortably subsist and enjoy ordinances among them though no such thing be expressed or ℈uided for in the agreement before menc̃oned.

*38

Vpon the reading of A lre from the Goũnor of yᵉ Massachusetts to the Comissionᵣs dated the second of the vijᵗh month 1644 and vpon a serious consideracõn among themselues how the spreading course of Error might be stayed, and the Truths wherein the Churches of New England walke set vpon their owne firme ℓ cleare foundacõns The Comissionᵣs ppounded to and receiued from the Elders now pᵣsent at Hartford as followeth :

Quest.

Whether the Elders may not be intreated seriously to consider of some confession of doctrine and discipline wᵗh solid ground℄ to be approoued by the Churches, ℓ published by consent (till further light) for the confirmeing yᵉ weake among our selues, ℓ stoping the mouths of adũsaries abroad.

Ans :

Wee who are here pᵣsent in all thankfullnes acknowledg yoᵣ Christian and Religious care to further the good of our Churches and posterytie, and do readyly entertaine the motion: and shall use our best dilligence ℓ indeavour to acquaint the rest of our breethren wᵗh yt, and shall study to answere yoᵣ desires ℓ expectacõn assoone as God shall giue a fitt season.

*39

*Whereas there hath beene some differrence betweene the Massachusetts and New Plymouth concerneing A plantacõn now called Seacunck, to wᵗh Jurisdiccõn it should belong and appertaine, wᶜh was now referred by both pties to the Comissionᵣs and an abstract or coppy of a clause of Plymouth Patent expressing ℓ limmiting their bounds shewed vnto them : By wᶜh it appeareth that A Countrey or place called Poccanokick (als̃) Sewamsett is graunted vnto them. The Comissionᵣs not conceiuing that the clause (als) Sewamset as there expressed should streaten their limmits and improueing an opportunitie of the Narrohigganset Deputies now pᵣsent do find Seccunck clearely wᵗhin the limmits so graunted to new Plymouth, And therefore adjudg that vnlesse better euedence be brought at or before the Comissionᵣs meeting the next yeare in Septembᵣ) Seacunck doth and should fall into the Jurisdiccõn of New Plymouth.

Thomas Stanton vpon his returne informed that hee had fully acquainted the Narrohigganset Sagomores wᵗh the contents of his instruccõns that they consulting amonge themselues and wᵗh Einemo one of the Nayantick Sachems had sent a Sagamore wᵗh other considerable psons as their Deputies wᵗh direccõn and full power to charge Vncus and to treate wᵗh the English pmiseing to ratify ℓ confirme what the said Deputies shall agree ℓ conclude, wherevpon the Comissionᵣs gaue a full heareing bothe to the Narrohigganset Deputies and to Vncus Sagamore of the Mohegans concerneing a pᵣtended ransome for Myantinomo And as the yssue found, that thoug seũall discourses had passed from Vncus and his men that for such quantities of Wampom and such pcells of other goods to a great value, there might have beene some pbabillitie of sparcing his life, yet no such peells were brought : But Vncus denyeth and the Narrohigganset Deputies did not alleadg, much lesse proue that any ransome was agreed, nor so much as any treaty begunn to redeeme their imprisoned Sachim. And for that Wampoms and goods sent as they were but smale peells and scarce considerable for such a purpose, ꝑ part of them disposed by Myantinomo himself to Vncus his Coũsellors and Captaines for some favoure either past *or hoped for, ꝑ part were giuen and sent to Vncus ꝑ to his Squa for prserueing his life so long and vseing him curteously during his imprisonment. Wherefore the Comissionᵣs declared to the Narrohigganset Deputies as followeth.

1 6 4 4 .
September.

*40

That they did not fynd any proofe of any ransome agreed.

1

It appeared not that any Wampom had beene pay'd as A ransome or part of a ransome for Myantinomos life.

2

That if they had in any measure proued their charg agn:ˢᵗ Vncus. The Comissioners would haue required him to haue made answerable satisfacc̃on.

3

That if hereafter they can make satisfying proofe the English will consider the same ꝑ pceede accordingly.

4

The Comissionᵣs did require that neither themselues nor the Nyanticks make any warr or injurious assault vpon Vncus or any of his company vntill they make proofe of yᵉ ransome charged. And that due satisfacc̃on be denyed vnlesse he first assault them.

5

That if they assault Vncus the English are engaged to assist him.

6

Herevpon the Narrohigganset Sachim aduiseing wᵗʰ the other Deputies engaged himself in the behalf of the Narrohiggansets ꝑ Nayanticks That no hostile Acts should be comitted vpon Vucus or any of his, vntill after the next planting of Corne. And that after that, before they begin any warr they will giue thirty dayes warneing to the Goũnor of the Massachusetts or Coneetacutt.

The Comissioners approoueing of this offer, and takeing their engagement vnder their hand ꝑ required Vncus as hee expected the continuance of the fauoure of the English to obserue the same termes of peace wᵗʰ the Narrohiggansets and theires

These foregoing conclusions were subscribed by the Comissionᵣs for the seũall Jurisdicc̃ons this xixᵗʰ Septembᵣ 1644.

EDWA : HOPKINS Presidⁿᵗ.
SYMON BRADSTREETE
WILẸM HATHORNE
EDW: WINSLOW
JOHN BROWNE
GEOR : FENWICK
THEOPH· EATON
THO : GREGSON.

*Weetowishe one of the Narrohigganset Sachims Pummumsh (als) Pufiumshe and Pawpianet two of the Narrohigganset Captaines being sent w'h two of the Narrohigganset Indians as Deputies from the Narrohigganset and Nayantick Sachims to make proofe of the ransome they p'tended was giuen for their late Sachims life As also to make knowne some other greevance they had against Vncus Sachim of the Mohiggins did in conclusion pmise and engage themselues (according to the power committed to them) That there should be no warr beguñ by any of the Narrohigganset or Nayantick Indians w'h the Mohegan Sachim or his men till after the next planting tyme: And that after that, before they begin warr, or use any hostillity towards them, they will giue thirty dayes warneing thereof to the Goũment of the Massachusetts or Concetacutt.

Hartford the xviij'h of Septemb':

1644

The marke of WEETOWISHE

The marke of PAWPIAMET

The marke of CHIMOUGH

The marke of PUMUMSHE

The w'hin named Narrohiggansets Deputies did futher pmise That if contrary to this agreement any of the Nayantick Pecoatts should make any assault vpon Vncus or any of his, they would deliuer them vp to the English to be punished according to their demeritts. And that they would not use any meanes to pcure the Mawhakes to come against Vncus during this truce.

*Boston Massachusets the

28th of the fift Month 1645
July

At a meetinge extraordinary

of the Comissioners for the Vnited Colonies called by speciall Order of the gefiall Court of the Massachusetts John Winthrope Herbert Pellame Esqrs Mr Thomas Prence Mr John Browne gent George Phenwick & Edward Hopkins Esqrs Theophilus Eaton and Mr Steeven Goodyer

The sefiall
Comissions
Mattachusets

An Order of the gefiall Court of the Massachusetts dated the xiiijth of the third month 1645 was shewed whereby John Winthrope and Herbert Pellame Esqrs were chosen Comissionrs according the tenure of the Articles for this prnte yeare vntill new be chosen.

Plym

An Order of the gefiall Court of Plymouth dated the fourth of the fourth month 1645 was likewise pduced whereby Mr Thom Prence and Mr John Browne were chosen Comissionrs according to the tenure of the Articles for this prnte yeare.

Conectacut

A like Order of the gefiall Court at Hartford for the Jurisdiccõn of Conecetacute was pduced whereby George Fenwick & Edward Hopkins Esqrs were chosen Comissionrs according to the tenure of the Articles &c for this prnte yeare wch order was dated the ixth of the fift month 1645.

New Hauen

A like Order of the gefiall Court at New Hauen dated the xxxth of the eight month 1644 was shewed forth whereby Mr Theophilus Eaton and Mr Steeven Goodyer were chosen Comissioners according to the tenure of the Articles &c for a yeare then following.

John Winthrope was chosen President for this meeting of the Comissioners

(31)

1 6 4 5.

July.

The occasion of the meeting

The Comissioners desired to know the special occation of this meeting, the Comissioners of the Massachusetts answered That it was concerneing the french businesse wch not being fully p^rpared this day and the warrs betwixt Pissicus and Vncus being beguñ and requireing speedy course &c It was agreed to take that first into consideracõn according to the p^rsent state of Affaires, It was thought fitt to send messengers forthw^th to both the pties to pcure the Narrohiggansetts and Mohiggen Sachems to come or send to Boston and Instruccõns were drawne accordingly as followeth.

Instruccõns for Serjeant John Davies Benedict Arnold and Francis Smyth sent by the Comission^rs for the vnited Colonies of New England to Pissecus Canonnacus and other the Sachems of the Narrohiggansetts and Neantick Indians And to vncus Sagamore of the Mohegans.

I

*44

Instruccons for the messeng^n to the Sachims

*You shall informe thaboue mencõned Sagamores respectiuely that the Comissioners for all the English Colonies namely the Massachusetts New Plymouth Coneetacutt and new Hauen whoe haue full power and Authoryty from all the said Jurisdiccons to consider and conclude both of peace and warr and by all just meanes to puide for the safety and welfare of ye Countrey are now mett together att Bostone.

2

That the Comission^rs take knowledg both of some vnderhand Assaults on eich pte made one against the other contrary to the true meaneing of the late truce betwixt them at Hartford and of seũall hostile Invasions made by the Narrohiggansets vpon and against Vncus and the Mohegan Indians to the disturbance and breach of the peace wch the English haue sought to settle.

3

That therefore the Comission^rs haue sent you both to the Narrohiggansets and Mohegan Sagamores to let them know That if it please them to come themselues or to send any considerable men of theirs fully instructed to declare and proue vppon what occations and grounds this warr is thus broken out, and fully authorised to treate and conclude as occation shall require, the Comission^rs w^thout any ptiall respect to either pty will consider the same and take ye best Course they cann to restore and confirme peace betwixt them for their mutuall safety and advantage.

4

The Comission^rs do hereby pmise and assure them that they or their Messengers shall haue free liberty to come and returne to treate psecute and conclude their affaires in peace w^thout molestacõn or any just greevance from the English. And in the name of the Comission^rs you shall require of both pties, y^t during this treaty no acts of hostilitie passe either against any of their seũall Plantacõns or any of their people in their occasions or any of their Sagamores or messengers in their travells too & froo.

If either of the pties put in excuses & seeme vnwilling to come or send to surcease or suspend the warr begunn you shall remember them of their former treaty made & concluded at Hartford fiue yeares since w'h M'r Heaynes and other majestrat& there by w'ch they are both engaged to acquaint the English w'h their greevances and receiue advice and direccõns from them.

1645.

July.

5

But if notw'hstanding they refuse to come or send y'u shall acquaint them that the English are engaged to assist against these hostile Invasions, and that they haue sent some of their men to defend Vncus. You shall therefore from the Comission's demaund of the refuseing pty what their purpose is eich to other, and on what termes they stand w'h the English Colonies whether the former Treaties *for peace stand and remayne in force, or whether they will assault the English now w'h the Mohegans that y'e Colonies may prride accordingly.

6

*45

You shall endeavour pticulerly and clearely to open euery one of the former Articles to the Sagamores both of the Narrohiggausetts and Mohiggan Indians that y'e may fully vnderstand the same, and you shall take their answere' in writing to eich pticuler and when you haue so donne reade their answere in the seũall pts to eich of them, that y'e may owne the Returne they make, and that wee may know there is noe mistake.

7

Our said Messengers being returned Benedict Arnold our Interpretor informed vs upon his Oath of the answere hee receiued and what vsage he found from the two Sachims of Narrohigganset& and Naantick as appeares in the declaracõn hereafter inserted. They brought us also a letter from M'r Roger Williams wherein hee assures us the warr would p'scntly breake forth and that the Narrohigganset Sachims had lately concluded a Neutrallyty w'h Prouidence and the Townes vpon Aquidnett Iland. Wherevpon the Comissioners considering the great pvocations offerred and the necessyty we should be put vnto of makeing warr vpon the Narrohiggañ &õ and being also carefull in A matter of so greate waight and geñall concernement to see the way cleared and to giue satisfaccõn to all the Colonies did think fitt to aduise w'h such of the Majestrats & Elders of the Massachusetts as were then at hand, and also w'h some of the Cheefe Millitary Comãnders there who being assembled it was then agreed. First that our engagement bound us to ayde and defend the Mohegan Sachim 2'ly That this ayde could not be intended onely to defend him and his in his fort or habitacõn, but (according to the Coñon acceptacõn of such Couenants or engagements considered w'h the ground& or occasion thereof) so to ayde him as hee might be p'serued in his liberty and estate. 3'ly That this ayde must be speedy least he might bee swallowed vp in the meane tyme & so come too late

The messeng'rs returne

Aduice about the warr

Conclusion of the warr

1 6 4 5.

July.

The number
of men
Boston 190
Plym' 40
Conect' 40
New haū 30

*46

40 men sent to
ayde Vncus
from the Mas-
sachusⁱˢ

The Major
sent to

The men
brought in

Humfrey Ath-
erton Leiften-
ant ₵ Daueis
Serjeant.

4ˡʸ The justice of this warr being cleared to our selues and the rest then prˢent it was thought meete that the case should be breifly stated and the reasons ₵ grounds of the warr declared and published wᵗʰ declaraĉōn hereafter inserted

5ˡʸ That a day of humiliaĉōn should be appoynted, wᶜʰ was after agreed to be the fift day of the weeke following

6ˡʸ It was then also agreed by the Comissionrs that the whole number to be raised in all the Colonies should bee three hundred. whereof from the Massachusett₵ one hundred and nynety Plymouth fourty Conctacutt fourty and New Hauen thirty.

*According to the Counsell and determinaĉōn aforesaid the Comissrs considering the prˢent danger of Vncus the Mohegan Sachim (his forte haueing beene diuers tymes assaulted by A great Army of the Narrohiggansets ₵ĉ) agreed to haue fourty Souldiers sent wᵗʰ all expedition for his defence, and because a considerable number of men had form̄ly beene sent to him from Conectacutt and New hauen, and that the Narrohiggansets ₵ĉ might know that the rest of the Colonies were resolued to joyne in this warr and not to sit still and deferr the tyme by Messages It was agreed that those fourty men should bee sent from the Massachusets, and because the businesse would admitt no delay (notice being giuen to the Com̄ission₵s that yᵉ Ayde sent him from Conectacutt and New Hauen were returned hoame) so as there was not tyme to stay the conueineinge either of the geñall Court or of the standing Counsell It was ordered by the Comissionrs that those fourty men might and ought to be raised ₵ĉ by the prˢent Authoryty Wherevpon they acquainted the Goū ˄ herewᵗʰ who gaue assent and advice therevnto and wᵗʰall sent out summons for the geñall Court to be assembled aboute fiue or six dayes after vpon this the Comissionrs for the Massachusets one of them being President sent first to the Majors of the Regiments of Suffolk and Middlesex for their assistance in raiseing the said fourty men: But fearcing that would not succeed so speedyly as was required they sent warrants wᵗʰall to the Constables of six of the nearest Townes intemateing the vrgent and pressing occation ₵ requireing them to impresse so many men and some horses to be ready at Bostone wᵗʰin two dayes ₵ĉ The Majors endeavoured to rayse the voluntcers, but they returned us answere they could haue men, but they expected to be ympressed So the Constables brought in our full number and we sent them forth wᵗʰin three dayes armed and victualled vnder the Com̄aund of Lieftennant Humphrey Atherton and Serjeant John Davies wᵗʰ foure horses and two of Cutchamakins Indians for their guides and gaue Lieftennant Atherton A Comission and Instrucĉōns by which himself and Serjeant Davies vnder him were to con-

duct the said fourty men to Mohegan and to stay there vntill Captaine Mason
should come to them, as in the said Commission and Instruccons more fully
appeares : And it was further ordered that the forces to be sent from Concetacutt & Newhauen should joyne w'h Leiftennant Atherton at Monhegan and
should be there by the xxviij'h of this month at furthest & Leiftennant Atherton not to attempt vpon the Towne otherwise then in Vncas his defence before they came and then Captaine Mason to haue cheife comaund of all those
companys vntill they should meete w'h the rest of our forces in the Narrohiggansets or *Nyanticks Countrey and the rest of the forces from the Massachusetts and Plymouth being to joyne together at Seacunck now called Rehoboth and so to proceede And comission to the same purpose in forme of a
letter was sent to Captaine Mason by Leiftennant Atherton as followeth.

1 6 4 5.

July.

To attempt the
towne in Vn-
cas defence.

*47

Capt Mason his
Comission

Loueing frend Captaine Mason we are assured you haue full notice before
this how thinges stand betwixt the Colonies & the Narrohiggansets and their Confederates All the Companies hitherto sent haue beene limmitted to defend Vncas w'hout invadeing his enemies Now we see our selues called to a warr in the
full compas and extent of it fourty men vnder the direccõn of Leiftennant
Atherton are sent from the Massachusetts thirty wilbe sent from New hauen
wee desire and hope Leiftennant Silly may haue the ouersight of them And
fourty are to be sent from Connetacutt the charge of the whole company is
intrusted to your care we so now ayme ⌐   ⌐ at the ptextion of the
Monhegans that wee would haue no optunitie neglected to weaken the Narrohiggansets and their confederats in their number of men their corne canowes
wigwams wampam and goods. Wee looke vpon the Nyanticks as the cheif
Incendiaries and causes of the warr and should be glad they might first feele
the smart of it. The Massachusetts & Plymouth will send another Army
to invade the Narrohiggansets or to deuide themselues as the seruice
may require, and as oppertunity serueth : You shall from tyme to tyme haue
notice of their pceedings, we rest assured of yor experience and prudence in
these affaires and neede the lesse to aduise for the safety of yor men, prserva-
cõn of all puisions whether for dyett or seruice, and pticulerly that Vncas Fort
be secured when any strengh is sent forth against the Enemie lest hee and
wee recciue more dammage by some Indian stratageme then the enemie.
What booty you take or prisoners whether men weomen or children you may
send them to Seabrook fort to be kept and improoued for the advantage of
the Colonies in seũall pporcõns answering their charge &c.

These dispatches being made and Leiftennent Atherton beinge vpon his

1645.

July.

march the gefiall Court assembled where the Goũnor declared vnto them the occasion of calling this Court, and the Comission^{rs} being all p^rsent, the President seconded him and tould them that the Comissõrs had drawne vp a Declaraçõn of the justice and necessyty of this warr wch was openly read to them, wch being done the Deputies desired to haue it wth the seũall Treaties & Agreements made wth the Narrohiggansets &c, that ye might consider of the cause and so pceede: The same day they sent three or foure of themselues to the Majestrats wth a Bill to this effect: vizt. That in regard the fourty Souldiers were gone forth w^thout Comission from the gefiall Court, That a Comission might be sent after them, The Comissioners being p^rsent wth the Ma:^{trates} when this Bill came to them they *declared to the Majestrats how they had pceeded and vppon what grounds Wherevpon the Ma^{trates} returned the Bill w^thout consenting to yt, the Deputies not satisfyed wth this, desired a conferrence in wch the case was debated The Deputies aleadged that seing the Court was now assembled before the fourty men were gone out of the Jurisdicçõn they ought to haue Comission from this Court, otherwise if any blood should be shed, the Actors might be called to an account for it: It was answered that however it did pperly belong to the Authoritie of the seũall Jurisdicçõns (after the warr was agreed vpon by the Comission^{rs} & the number of men) to guide the men and meanes to carry on the warr yet in this present case the pceeding of the Comissioners & ye Comission giuen was as sufficient as if it had beene done by ye gefiall Court.

*48

I   First it was a case of such p^rsent & vrgent necessyty as could not stay the calling of the Court or Counsell

2   2ly In the Articles of Confederaçõn power is giuen to the Comission^{rs} to consult order and determyne all affayres of warr &c and the word <u>determine</u> comprehend& all acts of authority belonging therevnto.

3   3^{ly} The Comissioners are the sole judges of the necessyty of the expedition

4   The gefiall Court haue made their owne Comission^{rs} their sole Counsell for these affaires

5   These Counsells could not haue had their due effect except they had power to pceede in this ease as they haue donn wch were to make the Comission^{rs} power and the mayne end of the Confederaçõn to be frustrate & that meerely for obserueing A Ceremony.

6   6^{ly} The Comission^{rs} haueing sole power to mannage ye warr for number of men for tyme place &c They onely know their owne Counsells & determinaçõns, and therefore none can graunt Comission to act according to these but themselues

7ly To send a new Comission after them or any confirmačõn of that wᶜh

they haue would cast blame vpon the Comission⁢s and weaken their power as if they had ꝑceeded vnwarrantably

After much agitačõn ⅋ long tyme spent herein it was at last agreed That the Court would allow the ꝑceedings of the Comission⁢s in this case for the matter thereof but they would reserue the manner of ꝑceedinge as to their owne Comission⁢s to further consideračõn and so go on to expedite the pʳsent busines ꝑpounded to them by the Commissioners. And first they agreed that it did belong to the Comission⁢s onely to appoynt one to haue comaund in cheife of all the forces to be sent from the seûall Colonies and therefore desired them to consider of a man fitt for so weighty a service : The Comission⁢s willing *to shew all respects to the Massachusetts agreed to make choyce of one out of that Colony, and accordingly diuers able and sufficient men being ꝑpounded at last they made choyce of Major Gibbons and acquainted the gefiall Court therewᵗh that if they had any just exception against him it might be considered : The gefiall Court not objecting any thing the Comission⁢s sent for Major Gibbens who accepted the charge and had comission and instrucčõn as followeth.

The Comission⁢s of the vnited Colonies of new England being to appoynt A Comaunder in Cheife ouer all such millitary Forces as are to be sent forth ⅋ ymployed not onely in ayde of the Mohegan Sachem but also against yᵉ Narrohiggansets Nyanticks and other their Confederats, who in making warr vpon Vncas the Mohegan Sachem contrary to former treaties and agreements are now become aswell our enemies as his, in regard of our engagement. The said Comission⁢s haueing sufficient knowledg of yᵉ pyety courage skill and discretion of You Major Edward Gibbons do hereby comitt vnto you the charge comaund conduct and gouerment of all the said Millitary forces wᵗh all such Armes ⅋ Amunition ꝑvision and other appurteñences wᵗh all Officers therevnto appoynted, to be ordered mannaged and disposed of vpon all occasions by Yoʳ self and yoʳ Counsell of warr according to the course of millitary Discipline and according to such Instrucčõns as You may receiue from the said Comission⁢s from the tyme of Your setting forth in your March vntill your returne or sufficient discharge sent you from the same authoryty You haue power also hereby (wᵗh aduice of yoʳ Counsell of warr to use and execute Marshiall Discipline vpon all offendders and delinquents as occasion shalbe by fynes corporall punishments and capitall punishments also if neede shall require. And all ꝑsons whatsoeũ ymployed vnder you in this service are hereby required to yeild due obedyence and subjection to all Your lawfull

1645.

July.

Comaunds according to the quallity & power wherew'h you are hereby invested. You haue also power to Comaund all such Barkes and other Vessells w'h are to be set forth in the said service w'h all Seamen Souldiers and Amunition and puisions in them: And the said Comission'rs doe hereby constitute and appoynt Captaine Miles Standish Captaine John Mason Captaine John Leverct Leiftennant Robte Silley (or such others as shall haue cheefe Comaund of the Forces comeing from New Hauen) Leiftennant Humfrey Atherton, and the rest of the Leiftennants vnder Yo'r Comaund to be Yo'r Counsell of warr whereof Yo'rself to be President and to haue a casting voyce : And you and yo'r said Counsell or the greater number thereof shall haue power from tyme to tyme as

*50

a Counsell of ˄ *to mannage all affaires concerning the same and to joyne to you any other descreete and able officer or officers to be of your said Counsell as you see meete. You haue also power hereby vpon any necessary occasion to make new officers and to giue them titles sutable to their places. Giuen vnder the hands of the said Comission'rs at Boston in the Massachusetts the 19'th of the 6 month 1645.

> Instructions for Serjeant Major Edward Gibbons Comaunder in cheife of our millitary forces and for such as are joyned to him as a Counsell of warr.

Whereas You Serjeant Major Edward Gibbons are appoynted Commaunder in cheefe of all such forces as are or shalbe sent forth of the seuall Colonies as by Yo'r Comission bearcing the date of these p'nts doth more fully appeare And whereas there is joyned to you by the same authoritie as a Counsell of warr diuers of yo'r cheife Officers psons of approoued worth and fidellyty as in the said Comission they are more fully expressed And whereas the scope and cause of this expedition is not onely to ayde the Mohegans but to offend and invade the Narrohiggausets Nyanticks and other their Confederates who vpon makeing warr vpon Vncas the Mohegan Sachem contrary to their engagements are become as well our enemies as his Yet it being the earnest desires of the Comission'rs if it may be attayned w'h justice honour and safety

Peace first desired

to pcure peace rather then to psecute warr It is first comended to yo'r good discreetions to take any fitt occasion (or if w'h safety you may w'hout any considerable delay or danger to your pceeding) to use meanes to draw on such a peace w'h you haue hereby power to treate of and conclude, wherein you

Charges payd

are to take due consideracōn of the charges the Colonies haue expended in the warr w'h you may estimate by the number of men sent forth at seuall

& Vncas charges

tymes by their continuance abroad w'h wages and puisions aptaincing, And of the damnage w'h Vncas hath sustained since the warrs began wherein it were meete (if it may be donn w'h convenyency) hee were consulted w'h that both the Colonies and hee may receiue just satisfaccōn and repayre, w°h if the Narrogansets cannot p'sently make A considerable pt may be payd in hand, and the rest by a yearely tribute. But w'hall according to our engagements you are to puide for Vncas his future safety y' his plantacōns be not invaded, that his men and Squawes may attend their planting fishing and other occasions w'hout feare or injurie And that Vssamequine Pomham, Sokakonoco, Cutchama-kin & other Indians frends or subjects to the English be not molested w°h will disturbe the peace and drawe on further charge and Inconvenience: But a peace well framed will hardly be secured vnlesse either some of y° cheife Sachims deliuer their Sonnes as Hostages or that some considerable pt of the Countrey be yeilded to the English for plantacōns wherein there may be forts built by the *English and mayntayned (at least in pt) by a tribute from the Narrohiggansets to secure the Agreement. And it might pbably conduce to the settleing or p̄serueing of peace, if A trade were setled betwixt the Colo-nies and them, by w°h they might be supplied w'h necessaries, but pecces & poder kept back w°h other traders furnish them w'h. Yf You cannot conclude a peace w'h them vpon the termes aboue mencōned, to p'uent greater Incon-veniences, you may abate somewhat of our charges, and of the Damnage Vn-cas hath sustayned, but much care must be taken to secure both our and his future peace which if it may be donn by raiseing fortes & keepeing Garrisons in the Narrohiggansets and Nyantick Countreys at their charge, thōgh we re-quire Hostages as aboue, they may bee restored when the Fortifycacōns are finished & their payments made, And the Articles for future peace are to be agreed & confirmed by the Comission'rs of the vnited Colonies at their next meeting, otherwise to be of no force

    But if peace may not be obtayned in such way as before expressed, you are then w'h all prudent seleritie to p̄secute w'h force of Armes the said Narrohiggansets & Nyanticks and all such as shall assiste them vntill you may (through the Lords assistance) haue subdued them or brought them to Reason And if the necessitie of the service shall require a further supply of men or p̄uisions (be it one hundred more or lesse) vppon your letters of aduice to the Goūnors of the seūall Colonies, sup-ply shalbe speedyly sent vnto you according to the ppor̄cōn agreed. You are to make fayre warrs w'hout exerciseing cruelty and not to put to death such as you shall take captiue if you can bestowe them w'hout daunger of your owne. You are to use yo'r best endeavours to gayne the Enemies Canowes or vtterly to destroy them, and herein you may make good use of the Indians our con-

Margin notes:
Vncas future safety to be prouided for

& Vssamequin Pomham Sokakonocco Cutchamakin &c.

Hostages or considerable plac& for a forte.

*51

A trade setled w'h them

Hostages & forts for secu-rity of the peace

p̄secut. warr.

Supply of men & prouisions

Cannowes

1645.

August.
English strag-
lers

A tickett for
any taken up.

*52

federates as you may doe vpon other occasions, haueing due regard to the honor of God, whoe is both our sword and sheild, and to the distance wch is to be obserued betwixt Christians and Barbarians, as well in warrs as in other negotiaĉõns, if you fynd any English Straglers traders or others whom you shall suspect to giue intelligence or to furnish wth Armes or Amunition, or to giue any other ayd to the Enemie, you may secure them or send them to Bostone, All other of our Countrey men carrying themselues peaceably (̨ inoffensiuely shalbe at peace wth you. And if you haue occasion to make use of any their boats or vessells, cattell, puisions or other goods you shalbe very tender of indamnageing them, And you shall giue them a tickett whereby they may receiue due satisfacĉõn from the Colonies or some of them. *When you shall meete wth the forces wch come from the Confederates of Plymouth Coneetacutt and New Hauen or any of them Yo^r self and yor Counsell may order and dispose of them into such bodyes, and vnder such of the Comaundors as you shall fynd to be most convenyent and most agreeable to the seruice, haueing care to giue no just occation of offence or discontent to any of the Comaunders or Offieers of any of the Colonies.

Wee doubt not but Your self and your Counsell knowing well how p^rcious the liues and healths of our men are among all our Colonies, and how greate charg this warr is like to bring vpon us wilbe very carefull in p^rserueing and husbanding both to the best advantage, so as we shall not neede to giue you any Instrucĉõns or Direcĉõns about the same, but shall rest satisfyed in the confydence wee haue of your wisdomes and faythfullnes, to be ymproued through the Lords assistance (̨ blessing vpon you in this service for his owne glory and his peoples safety and p̨speritie in this wildernes.

Yf the Enemie fly so as you cannot come to fight wth them it may be expedient that you build one or more fortyficaĉõns in the most convenient places of the Narrohiggansets or Nyantike Countreys into wch you may by the help of the Indians our frends gather and p^rserue the Enemies Corne and other goods for the advantage of the service.

Lastly (yet aboue all the rest) we comend to yor Christian care the vpholding of the worship of God in yor Army and to keepe such watch ouer the confusaĉõn of all those vnder yor charge, as all pphanenes ympieties, abuse of the sacred name of God luxury and other disorder may be avoyded or duly punished, that the Lord may be pleased to go forth before you, and prosper all yor pceedings and returne you to us in peace wch we shall dayly pray for.

BOSTON the 19th of the 6th month 1645.

The Comissioners considering that of necessyty they must ymploy seuall vessells to carry puisions by Sea for the Army and to attend such occasions as the service may require, agreed that the men ymployed in such vessells should be an ouer number aboue the three hundred, and to be payd by the Colonies in their due apporcons, And in like occasions the other Colonies haue and will send an ouer number as occasion shall require w'th the genall Court approoued.

The President informed the Comissioners that since Myantenomy his Death the Narrohigganset Sachems by messengers sent him a p'sent expressing their desire to keepe peace w'th the English ; but desireing to make warr with Vncas for their Sachems Death, Mr. Winthrope then Gou̅nor would not receiue it vpon any such termes, The messengers desired they might leaue it, till they had further aduised w'th their *Sachems, and the p'sente not accepted nor disposed off remaynes in Spetie, to be ordered as the state of thinges now required. Wherevpon the Comission's thought fitt to returne it by expresse messengers conceiueing thereby the Indians would see the resolucōn of all the Colonies for warr : and accordingly Captaine Harding M' Welborne & Benedict Arnold had Instruccōns giuen them as followeth.

Instruccōns for Captaine Harding M' Welborne and Benedict Arnold sent by the Comission's of the Vnited Colonies to Piscus Canownaeus Janemo and other Sagamores of the Narrohiggansets and Nyantick Indians

You shall informe the Sachems aboue menconed that the Comm'rs for all the English Colonies assembled & yet continuing at Boston haue formerly by treaties and more lately by messengers vsed their best endeauors to p'serue the peace of Countrey in genall ; And pticularly to p'vent or stay the warr betwixt them and the Mohegans but hitherto their Messengers discouraged and abused haue returned w'thout successe The Narrohigga & Nyantick Indians haue begu̅ & psecuted warr vpon Vncas, haue wounded and slayne diuers of his men, seized many of his Canowes, taken some prisoners, spoyled much of his Corne, and haue not onely refused a faire treaty wherein all differrenc & greeuances might haue beene heard and wayed and due satisfaccōn orderred according to justice but haue reproached the English threatened to kill them, if they but stirr out of doores and to lay their cattell on heapes, all w'ch are heigh pvocacōns and open willfull breaches of the former treaties and agreements.

Wherefore you are from M' Winthrope Deputie Gou̅nor of the Massachusets and President of the Comissioners for the vnited Colonies to returne a present long since sent, and left by messengers from Piscus, but not accepted,

1645.

August.
Botes to carry prouision

An ou̅ number of men

The present of Beades, or Wampon'

*53

vnlesse the peace both w⁹h the English and Vncas and other Indians frends to the English might bee entirely kept : but as thinges stand he may no longer keepe the present the Colonies being now forced to other Counsells and Courses.

Yet the English (euen to the Indians themselues if they shutt not their eyes) may cleare and manefest their peaceable disposicōn and just pceedings. You shall let them know that there men already w⁹h Vncas by expresse order haue hitherto onely endeavoured his defence, w⁹hout invadcing, or attempting any thinge against the Narrohigganset Countrey, and if yet they may haue due repairacōn for what is past, and good securyty for the future, it shall appeare they are as desirous of peace and shalbe as tender of the Narrohigganset-

*54   sets blood as euer *Yf therefore Pisscus ℀ Janemo w⁹h other Sachems will (w⁹hout farther delay) come along w⁹h you to Boston the Comission⁹s hereby pmise and assure them they shall haue free liberty to come and returne w⁹hout molestacōn or any just greevance from yᵉ English But Deputies will not now serue, nor may the pᵖaracōns in hand bee now stayed, or the direccōns giuen recalled till the foremenconed Sagamores come, and some further order be taken, but if they will haue nothing but warr, the English are puideing and will proceede accordingly.

BOSTONE, the xviij⁹h of the vj⁹h month. 1645.

post-script.   Yf you cannot conveniently come to speech w⁹h all the foremenconed Sachems You may deliuer the Contents of these Instruccōns to such onely as you haue optunitie to speake w⁹h at the Narrohigganšets especially Pissecus.

Captaine Harding and Mʳ Welborne returneing from the Narrohiggansets Sachems brought back the Present, and acquainted the Comission⁹s, that they found not Benedict Arnold at Providence, and heard he durst not aduenture himself againe amongst the Narrohiggansets Indians w⁹hout a sufficient guard   They also vnderstand that Mʳ Williams sent for by the Narrohigganset Sachems was going thither, wherefore the‸ acquainted him w⁹h their message, shewed him their Instruccōns, and made use of him as Interpretor.   The Narrohigganset Sachems denying some of the passages which Benedict ‸ vpon Oath had formerly certefyed and excuseing others declared that Janemo the Nyantick Sachem had beene Ill diuers dayes, but had now sent six men to pᵖsent his respects to the English, and to declare his assent and submission to what yᵉ Narrohiggenset Sachems and the English should agree vpon whether by their Messengers at the Narrohiggansets Countrey or else where, wherevpon it was agreed That Pisseous cheif Sachem of the Narrohiggansets and Mixano Canowancus his Eldest sonn and others wth full power from the Narrohigganset ₵ Nyantick Indians should forthwth come to Bostone to treate wth the Commissioners for the restoreing and setleing of peace, and what they did conclude should bynd the rest. Captaine Harding ₵ Mr Welborne further acquainted the Comission^{rs} that vpon Mr Williams request they had written to Captaine Mason certcfying him of their hopes of a peace betwixt ye Indians and English, adding in their letter (as they affirme) they did it not to stay any direcc̃õn he had form̃ly receiued.

The Comission^{rs} thanked Captaine Harding ₵ Mr Welborne for their paynes and expedition, but blamed them that they had in seuerall thinges gone beyond their Instrucc̃õns namely in bringing back the Present in vseing Mr Williams but cheefely in writing to Captaine Mason, wch could haue no other end as they supposed but to retard his ꝑceedings and therefore ꝑfessed they thought them worthy of censure and punishment.

Pesseous Mixanno and Witowash three principall Sachems *of the Narrohiggansets Indians and Awasequen deputy for the Nyanticks wth a large trayne of men wthin a few dayes after came to Boston. The Comission^{rs} first acquainted them with the Instruccons sent by Captaine Harding ₵ M Welborne and enquired whether they vnderstood them and came ꝑpared accordingly. They ꝑfessed Mr Williams had not acquainted them wth two waighty passages therein, namely that they must giue satisfacc̃õn for what is past and good securitie for future peace And that they English preparac̃õns and direcc̃õns for invasiue warr might not be stayed or recalled till by treaty some further order were taken.

Herevpon Captaine Harding and m^r Welborne were sent for who therevpon declared that m^r Williams had the Instrucc̃õns in his hand tould them hee had opened all the pticulers therein and by the seũall answers he returned from the Indians they conceiued hee had so done. The Comissioners acquainting the Indian Sagamores that how euer this treaty should succeed. they in their psons and company should receiue noe injurie but should stay and returne in safety (according to the safe Conduct graunted them) entred a Treaty wth the said Sagamors and deputy and first remembred them of seũall agreements made betwixt the English and them both in the Massachusets and at Hartford, by wch they were engaged not to enter vpon any warr either with Vncas or other Indians wthout first acquainting the English wth ye cause thereof: notwthstanding they had this summer at seũall tymes invaded Vncas and had wounded and slayne diuers of his men taken some pris-

*55

August.

oners and brought much dammage vpon him in his estate and had forced the English according to engagement to send their men at sefiall tymes to defend him : And when first ye gefiall Court of the Massachusetts and after the Comission^{rs} for ye vnited Colonies sent vnto them to stay these vyolent and hostile courses and offerred them a faire and a just heareing of all differrenc̷ betwixt them and Vncas : they abused our messengers refused any cessation of Armes reproached and threatened the English Colonies and pfessed whoeuer began the warr they were resolued to continue yt and nothing but Vncas his head should satisfye them.

The Narrohigganset Sachems at first began to charg Vncas wth sondry injuries he had donn them and pticulerly they alleadged his takeing of a ransome for their Sachems life but being tould the Comissioners could determine nothing concerneing these matters in Vncas his absence, ₵ remembred that themselues had hindred his being sent for to answere for himself : they excused themselues concerneing the English, and were loath to acknowledg any breach of Couenant wth them : but after a long debate and some priuate

*56

Some offers of peace for a tyme

con *conferrence they had wth Serjeant Callicat they acknowledged they had brooken pmise or couenant in the afore menc̃oned warrs, and offerred to make another truce wth Vncas either till next planting tyme, as they had done last yeare at Hartford or for a yeare or a yeare and a quarter ; but that not satisfying, one of the Sachems offerred a stick or a wand to the Comission^{rs} expressing himself, that therewth the₍ put the power and disposic̃on of the warr into their hands and desired to know what the English would require of them The Comission^{rs} tould them that the charge trouble ₵ disturbance wch they had brought vpon the Colonies by their vnjust proceedings was greate besides the dammage Vncas had sustayned, yet to shew their moderation they would

2000 fadome of wampen'

require of them but two thousand fathome of white wampam for their owne satisfacc̃on, and that they should presently restore vnto Vncas all Captiues and Canowes they had taken from him wth repairac̃on for his corne spoyled ₵ destroyed in this warr since they were forbidden by the English, referring all other differenc̷ vnto the next meeting of the Comission^{rs}. The Sagamores and Deputy would haue had an abatement in the charge demaunded for the Collonies, and pfessed they had spoyled none of Vncas his Corne that was against the custome and course of their wars but at last craueing onely some ease in the manner and tymes of payment, and that Vncas might restore such

Perpetuall peace concluded.

Captiues ₵ Conowes as hee had taken from them they yeilded that part And the same euening concluded wth the Comission^{rs} a ppetuall peace both wth the English and wth Vncas and all other Indians being frends or subjects to the English and to giue Hostages for the English better securyty, the

Hostages to be giuen.

day being spent in these agitacõns the full yssue was referred to the morneing, then the Comission's againe ppounded to the said Sachems and deputie
the former and other pticulers for setling and establishing a perpetuall peace,
and after a due and serious deliberacõn a full agreement was made and drawne
up as followeth.

> A Treaty and agreement betwixt the Comission's for the
> vnited Colonies of New England on the one part And
> Pessecus Mexanno eldest of Canownacus sonns Jannemo
> (als) Nenegelett and Wipetamock and others Sagamores of
> the Narrohiggansets and Nyantick Indians on the other
> pt made (concluded at Bostone in the Massachusetts the
> xxvij'h of the sixt month 1645.

A warr being raised and psecuted by the Narrohiggansets and Nyantick
Indians against Vncas Sagamore of the *Mohegans contrary to former treaties
and their expresse engagements therein, The English Colonies were first put
vpon charg and inconvenience in sending men for defence of Vncas, then they
sent messengers to the Narrohiggansets (Nyantick Sagamores to stay their
warr till the English according to former couenant and agreement had heard
their greevances, but w'hout successe : And lastly were forced to prepare an
offensiue warr against them. Yet they Comission's before the warr began sent
other Messengers to the Narrohigganset Sagamores to offer them peace vpon
due satisfaccõn for what was past and other just termes for the future.

Pessecus and Mexanno w'h other captaines (Counsellors of the Narrohiggansets and one Deputie for the Nyanticks being come to Bostone, and
joyntly affirmeing they had comission to treate and conclude not onely for the
Narrohigganset(but for the Nyantick Indians, and engageing themselues one
for another were after a larg debate and conferrence about former greevance(
betwixt themselues and Vncas, and a due consideracõn of former Treaties
and agrements w'h the English convinced and acknowledged that they had
broken their Couenants and had thereby not onely endamnaged Vncas but had
brought much charge and trouble vpon all the English Colonies w'h they con-
fest were just they should satisfy.

It was agreed betwixt the Comission's of the vnited Colonies and the
foremencõned Sagamores and Nyantick Deputie That the said Narrohigganset
and Nyantick Sagamores should pay or cause to be payd at Boston to the
Massachusets Comission's the full sum of two thousand fathome of good
white wampom or a third part of good black wampom peage in foure payments
namely fiue hundred fathome w'hin twenty dayes, fiue hundred fathome w'hin

I
*57

Articles of
peace

2

3

foure months, fiue hundred fathome at or before next planting tyme, and fiue hundred w^thin two yeares next after the date of these presents wch two thousand fathome the Comission^{rs} accept for satisfacc̃õn of former charges expended.

4

The foresaid Sagamores and Deputie (on the behalf of the Narrohiggansets and Nyantick Indians hereby ꝓmise and couenant that they will vpon demaund and proofe satisfy and restore vnto Vncas the Mohegan Sagamore all such Captiues whether men weomen or children and all such Canowes as they or any of their men haue taken, or as many of their owne Canowes in the roome of them full as good as they were wth full satisfacc̃õn for all such Corne as they or any of their men haue spoyled or destroyed of his or his mens since last planting tyme And ye English *Comission^{rs} hereby ꝓmise that Vncas shall do the like to them.

*58

5

Whereas there are sondry differrenc℈ and greevances betwixt Narrohigganset and Nyantike Indians and Vncas ℈ his men (wch in Vncas his absence cannot now be determyned) It is hereby agreed that Narrohigganset and Nyantik Sagamores either come themselues or send their deputies to the next meeting of the Comission^{rs} for the Colonies either at New hauen in Septemb^r 1646 or sooner (oopon convenyent warneing) if the said Comissioners do meete sooner fully instructed to declare and make due proofe of their injuries and to submitt to the judgment of the Comission^{rs} for the vnited Colonies in giueing or receiueing satisfacc̃õn, and the said Comission^{rs} (not doubting but Vncas will either come himself or send his deputies in like manner furnished) ꝓmise to giue a full heareing to both pties wth equall justice w^thout any ptial respect according to their allegac̃õns ℈ ꝓmises.

6

The said Narrohiggansett and Nyantick Sagamores and deputies do hereby ꝓmise and couenant to keepe and mayntaine a firme ℈ ppetuall peace both wth all the English vnited Colonies and their Successors and wth Vncas the Mohegan Sachem and his men wth Vssamequin, Pomham, Sokakonooco, Cutchamakin, Shoanan, Passacoñaway, and all other Indian Sagamores and their companies, who are in frendship wth or subject to any of the English hereby engageing themselues that they will not at any tyme hereafter, disturbe the peace of the Countrey, by any assaults, hostile attempts, invasions or other injuries, to any of the vnited Colonies or their Successors or to the aforesaid Indians either in their psons, buildings cattell or goods directly or indirectly, nor will they confederate wth any other against them, And if they know of any Indians or others that conspire or intend hurt either against the said English or any Indian subject to or in frendship wth them, they will w^thout delay acquaint ℈ giue notice thereof to the English Comission^{rs} or some of them.

And if any questions or differrence shall at any tyme hereafter arise or grow betwixt them and Vncas or any Indians before menõoned, they will according to former engagements (w^{c}h they hereby confirme and ratyfy) first acquaint the English craue their judgments and advice therein, and will not attempt or begin any warr or hostile invasion till they haue liberty and allowance from the Comission^{r}s of the vnited Colonies so to doe.

The said Narrohiggansct and Nyantick Sagamores and deputie do hereby pmise that they will forthw^{t}h deliuer and restore all such Indian fugitiues or captiues w^{c}h haue at any tyme fled from any of the English, and are now liueing or abideing w^{t}h or amongst them, or giue due satisfacõon for them to the Comission^{r}s for the Massachusets, And further that they will (w^{t}hout more delayes) pay or cause to be payd An *yearely tribute a month before Indian haruest euery yeare after this at Boston to the English Colonies for all such Pecotts as liue amongst them according to the former treatic and agreement made at Hartford 1638 namely one fathome of white wampam for euery Peacott man, and half a fathome for eich Peacott youth, and one hand length of wampom for eich Peacott manchild And if Weekwash Cooke refuse to pay this tribute for any peacotts w^{t}h him the Narrohiggansct Sagamores pmise to assist the English against him. And they further couenant that ye will resigne and yeild vp the whole Peacott Countrey and euery pt of it to the English Colonies, as due to them by conquest

The said Narrohigganset and Nyantick Sagamores and Deputy do hereby pmise and couenant, that w^{t}hin fourteene dayes they will bring and deliuer to the Massachusetts Comission^{r}s on the behalf of all the Colonies foure of their children viz, Pissecus his eldest sonn, the sonn of Tassaquanawitt brother to Pissecus Awashawe his sonn and Ewanghhos sonn A Nyantick to be kept (as pledges or hostages) by the English till both the foremenconed two thousand fathome of wampom be payd at the tymes aboue expressed, and the differrences betwixt themselues and Vncas be heard and ordered, and till these Articles of agreement be vnderwritten at Boston by Janemo, and Wypetock. And further they hereby pmise and couenant that if at any tyme hereafter any of ye said children shall make escape or be conveyed away from the English before the premisss be fully accomplished, they will either bring back and deliuer to the Massachusett Comission^{r}s the same children, or i they be not to be found, such and so many other children to bee chosen by the Comission^{r}s for the vnited Colonies or their Assignes, and that w^{t}hin twenty days after demaund, and in the meane tyme vntil the said foure children be deliuered as hostages the Narrohigganset and Nyantick Sagamores and deputie do freely and of their owne accord leaue w^{t}h the Massachuset

7

*59

8

1 6 4 5.

August.

Comission^rs as pledges for p^rsent securitie foure Indians namely Witowash Pomamse Jawashoe Waughwamino, who also freely consent & offer themselues to stay as pledges, till the said children be brought and deliued as abouesaid

9

The Comission^rs for the vnited Colonies do hereby pmise and agree, That at the charg of the vnited Colonies the foure Indians now left as pledges shalbe puided for, and that the foure children to be brought and deliued as hostages, shalbe kept and mayntained at the same charg, that they will require Vncas and his men wth all the other Indian Sagamores before named to forbeare all acts of hostility against the Narrohigganset & Nyantick Indians for the future. And further all the p̃misss being duly obserued and kept by the Narrohigganset and Nyantick *Indians and their company ; they will at thend of two yeares restore the said children deliued as hostages and retayne a firme peace wth the Narrohigganset & Nyantik Indians and their Successors.

*60

10

It is fully agreed by and betwixt the said pties that if any hostile attempt be made while this treaty is in hand or before notice of this agreement (to stay former p^rparac̃ons and direccons) can be giuen, such attempts and the consequents thereof shall on neither pt be accounted a vyolac̃on of this Treaty nor a breach of the peace here made and concluded

11

The Narrohigganset and Nyantick Sagamores and Deputie hereby agree and couenant to and wth the Commission^rs of the vnited Colonies, that henceforward they will neither giue graunt, sell or in any manner alienate any part of their Countrey nor any peell of land therein either to any of the English or others w^thout consent or allowance of the said Comissione^rs.

12

Lastly they pmise that if any Peacott or other be found and discoued amongst them who hath in tyme of peace murthered any of the English, he or they shalbe deliuered to just punishment. In witnes whereof the parties aboue named haue interchaungably subscribed these p^rsents the day and yeare aboue written.

The marke
of PESSECUS

the marke of

the mark of
AUMSEQUEN the
Nyantick Deputy

MEEKESANNO

ABDAS ⳨ ⌀ marke

the marke of

the mark ∿∿ of POMMUSII

CUTCHAMEKINS ⌇ marke

WITTOWASH

This treaty and agreement betwixt the Comission^{r}s of the vnited Colonies and the Sagamores and Deputie of Narrohigganset and Nyantick Indians was made and concluded: Benedict Arnold being interpretor vpon his oath Serjeant Callicutt ᘏ an Indian his man being present ᘏ Cutchamakin ᘏ Josias two Indians acquainted wth the English language assisting therein who opened and cleared the whole treaty and euery Article to the Sagamores and Deputy then p^{r}sent.

The Comissioners calling for the number of Males according to the Articles they were brought in from all the Colonies (except from the Massachusets) wherevpon it was ordered, that the number of them be forthwth taken, that the charges of the p^{r}sent expedition against the Narrohigganset ᘏᘏ, And the wampam to be receiued from them may be equally pportioned wch is to be according to the differrent number of males at *present, and not as it may be when the after payments are to be made. The Comission^{r}s also considering the great damnage that Vncas the Mohegan Sachem hath sustayned in these warrs, and that much thereof hath befalne him for want of tymely ayde from the Colonyes, they haue therefore ordered that he shall haue one hundred fathome of wampam out of the first payment to the Comission^{r}s from the Narrohiggansets ᘏᘏ.

*61

100 fathom ordered to Vncas

The Comission^{r}s considering that the Colonies of Conneetacutt and Newhauen, haue expended more then their pportions in the late expedition ᘏᘏ and that they haue beene out of purse a good value a considerable tyme before the other Colonies were at any charg ᘏ about the same, haue therefore ordered that they shall haue the fiue hundred fathome of wampam due vpon the first payment deducting the hundred fathome ordered to be giuen to Vncas.

400 fathom ordered to Conneetacutt ᘏ Newhauen

Whereas the Comissioners were called to Boston vpon extraordinary occasion and the meeting continuing to this day being the first of the seauenth month, so as they cannot assemble at New Hauen at the tyme appoynted in ordinary Course It is therefore agreed and orderred That the next meeting in ordinary course shalbe at Newhauen according to y^e Articles.

September.

The Comission^{r}s haueing occasion to consider whether by vertue of the Articles of confedera$\tilde{c}$ōn they haue not power to censure all such as shall offend in any of the ymployments as messengers of what Jurisdic$\tilde{c}$ōn soeuer they bee, and whether all ministeriall officers be not subject to their co$\tilde{m}$aunds in such service as concernes their authorytie for the ge$\tilde{n}$all affaires of all the Colonies It was agreed that the Comission^{r}s of the se$\tilde{u}$all Colonies should aduise wth the ge$\tilde{n}$all Courts of the se$\tilde{u}$all Jurisdic$\tilde{c}$ōns that such agreements and order may be made therein, as may best conduce to the good of the whole.

Question What power the comisson^r haue to punish messengers ᘏ offic^{r}s offending

Here followeth the Declara$\tilde{c}$ōn before men$\tilde{c}$ōned.

1645.

September.

A Declaraĉon of form̄ passages and pceedings betwixt the English and the Narrohiggansets, wᵗh their confederates, wherein the grounds ℟ justice of the ensuing warr are opened and cleared. Published by order of the Comissionʳs for the vnited Colonies at Boston the xjᵗh of the vjᵗh month 1645.

The most considerable pt of the English Colonies professe they came into these pts of the world wᵗh desire to advance the Kingdome of the Lord Jesus Christ, and to enjoy his p̄cious ordinances wᵗh peace (and to his praise *they confesse) he hath not fayled their expectaĉon hitherto, they haue found safety warmth and refreshing vnder his winges to the satisfacĉon of their soules : but they know and haue considered that their Lord and Master is King of Rightousnes and peace yᵗ hee giues answerable lawes and casts his subjects into such A mould and frame that (in their weake measure) they may hold forth his vertues in their course and carriage not onely wᵗh yᵉ Nations of Europe, but wᵗh the barbarous natiues of this wildernes : and accordingly both in their Treaties and converse they haue had an awfull respect to diuine Rules endeavoureing to walk vprightly and inoffensiuely and in the middest of many injuries and insolencies to exercise much patience and long suffering towards them

The Pecott grew to an excesse of vyolence and outrage and proudly turned aside from all wayes of Justice ℟ peace before the sword was drawne or any hostile attempts made against them, During these warrs and after the Pecott℟ were subdued the English Colonies were carefull to continue and estabish peace wᵗh the rest of the Indians, both for the p̄sent ℟ for posteryty as by seûall treaties wᵗh the Narrohigganset ℟ Mohegan Sagamores may appeare, wᵗh treaties for a while were in some good measure duly obserued by all the Indians, but of late the Narrohiggansets and especially the Nyanticks their confederates haue many wayes injuriously broken and vyolated the same by entertayneing and keepeing amongst them, not onely many of the Pecott nation, but such of them as haue had their hands in the blood ℟ murther of the English seazing ℟ possessing at least a part of the Pecott Countrey, wᶜh by the right of Conquest justly apptaines to the English, by allureing harbouring and wᵗhholding seûall Pecott captiues fled from the English, and makeing proud and insolent· returnes when they were redemaunded, and more lately the English had many strong and concurrant Indian testymonies from long Iland Vnkoway Hartford Kennebeck, and other parts of Myantenomies ambitious designes trauelling through all the Plantacons of the Neighbouring Indians and by p̄mises and guifts laboureing to make himself their vniûsall

*62

Narrohiggan-
sets ℟ Nyan-
ticks vyolated
their coue-
nants.

by harboring
pecots. ℟ keep-
ing part of
their countrey

conspireing to
cut of all yᵉ
English

Sagamore or goûnor, pswadeing and engageing them at once to cutt of the whole body of the English ͵ these parts : which treacherous plotts were confirmed by the Indians geñall preparacõns, messages, insolencies and outrages against the English and such Indians as were subjects or frends to them, so that they English Colonies to their great charge and damnage were forced to arme, to keep strong watch day and night, and some of them to travell wth Convoyes from one plantacõn to another, and when Myantenomy in his circuler trauell was questioned at Newhauen concerneing these thinges, instead of other ꝭ better satisfaccõn hee threatened to cutt off any Indians head that should lay such a charg on him to his face.

English forced to keepe watch and ward.

*The Comission^rs by the p^rmisss obserued Myantenomies proud and treacherous disposicõn, yet thought not fitt to ꝓceede against him in that respect till they had collected more legall and convinceing proofe.

*63

But when these thinges were vnder deliberacõn Myantenomie was brought prisoner by Vncas to Hartford ꝭ the case being opened and cleared as followeth, hee craued the Comission^rs advice how to ꝓceed wth him.

Myantenomy prisoner

It appeared in a Treaty made wth the English at Massachusets 1637 Myantenomy engaged himself not to fight wth any of the Indians and pticulerly not to invade Vncas w^thout the English consent. And after in Tripartite agreement made and concluded at Hartford betwixt Myantenony ꝭ Vncas wth referrence to the English Anno 1638 In wch one of the Articles was that though either of the said Indian Sagamores should receiue injurie from the other, yet neither of them shall make or begin warr vntill they had appealed to ye English and till the greevances were first heard ꝭ determyned, and if either of them should refuse, the English might assist against and compell the refuseing and obstienate pty.

The invade Vncas

Notw^thstanding wch Myantenony and his Confederates haue both secrettly and openly plotted and practised against the life of Vncas, not at all acquainting the English or adviseing wth them, but more especially of late since the foremencõned plotts and designes were in hand.

Practise ag^st Vncas life

First a Pecott Indian one of Vncas his subjects in the spring 1643 aymeing at Vncas his life shott him wth an arrow through the arme, and p^rsently fled to the Narrohiggansets or their confederates, boasting in the Indian Plantacõns that he had killed Vncas, but when it was knowne that Vncas (thoug wounded) was aliue, the Peacott taught (as was supposed) chaunged his note, affirmeing that Vncas had cutt through his owne arme wth a flint and had hired him to say that he had shott and killed him.

Vncas shot in the arme

Myantenony being sent for by the Goûn^r of the Massachusets vpon another occasion brought this Peacott wth him, ꝭ would haue couered him w^th

The pecot that shot him.

the former   but when the English out of his owne mouth found him guilty and would haue sent him to Vncas his Sagamore Myantenony earnestly desired he might not be taken out of his hand(pmiseing hee would send him safe to vncas to be examined (punished. But feareing (as it seemes) his owne treachery would bee discoued in a day or two he stopped the Pecotts mouth, by cutting off his head. But at parting hee tould ye Gouernor in discontent, that hee would come no more to Boston.

Plotts agans^t Vncas by poysoning (sorcery *64 An arrow or two shott at Vncas in Coneetacutt Riuer.

After this some attempts were made (as is reported) to take away Vncas life by poyson and by sorcery, y^t fayleing some of Sequassons company (an Indian Sagamore *allyed vnto an intimate confederate with Myantenomy) shott at Vncas wth an arrow or two as he was going downe Conectacutt Riuer, Vncas according to the foremenconed Treaty 1638 complayned and the English by mediation sought to make peace, but Sequasson expressing his dependence on Myantenony refused, and chose warr, they fought and Vncas had the victory

Myantenomy 900 or 1000 men. Vncas not half so many.

Lastly Myantenomy w^thout any puocation from Vncas (vnlesse the Disapoyntment of former plotts pvoaked) aud sodainely w^thout denounceing warr, came vpon ye Mohegans wth nine hundred or a thousand men, when Vncas had not half so many to defend himself; Vncas before the battaile tould Myantenomy, that hee had many wayes sought his life, and for the spareing of blood offerred by a single combatt betwixt themselues to end the quarrell: but Myantenomy p^rsumeing vpon the number of his men would haue nothing but a battell, the yssue fell contrary to expectacon his men were routed, diuers of his considerable men slayne and himself taken prisoner.

Myantenomy taken prison'

These thinges being duely wayed the Comission^rs judged that Vncas could not be safe whilst Myantenomy liued, wherefore the thought hee might justly put such a treacherous and blood thirsty enemie to death, but aduised him to doe it in his owne jurisdiccon w^thout torture or cruelty. And Vncas haueing hitherto shewed himself a frend to the English and in this and former outrages (according to the treaty) craueing their advice if the Narrohiggansets or their confederates should for his just execucon vnjustly assault him, the Comission^rs for the Colonies pmised Vncas to assist and ptect him.

His death. Pretence of Ransome

Vncas herevpon slew an enemie but not the enmyty against him, the Narrohiggansets soone fell to new contriuements, they p^rtended they had payd a Ransome for their Sachems life and gaue in pticuler about fourty pounds.

This for a while cast an imputacon of foule (vnjust dealing vpon Vncas, but in Septemb^r 1644 the English Commission^rs meeting at Hartford sent for the Narrohigganset Sachems or their deputies desireing they might be instructed to make good their charge.

Vncas came himself, they sent their deputies, but after due examinaćon it appeared that some loose discourse had passed, that for such quantities of Wampam and such pcells of other goods to a great value there might haue beene some pbabilitie of spareing his life, that no such pcells were brought, and the Narrohigganset Deputies did not alleadg much lesse proue that any Ransome was agreed, nor soe much as any serious treaty begun, to redeeme their imprisoned Sachem, and for ye wampam and goods sent as they weere but smale pcells and scarce considerable for such A purpose, so they were disposed by Myantynomy himself to sondry psons for curtesies receiued during his imprisonment and vpon hope of further favour. The Narrohigganset Deputies saw their proofes fell far short of former prtences *and were sylent. The Comission^rs pmised that vpon better euedence hereafter, they should haue due satisfacćon.

Not proued

*65
Further hearing

Wherevpon a Treaty was made, and both pties were engaged that all hostilitie should cease till planting tyme 1645 and after that they would giue thirty dayes warneing either at the Massachusetts or Hartford, before the treaty should cease. Yet in February last the Narrohiggansets by Messengers sent to Boston, declared that vnlesse Vncas would redeliuer one hundred and sixty fathome of Wampam or come to a new heareing w'hin six weeks they would beginn the warr.

Warrs cease till planting tyme.

160 fathome of wampom demaunded.

·This crossed the former agreement and the season was such that neither Comission^rs could be aduised w'h, nor could vncas travell if notice had beene giuen. After wch about or before planting tyme Tantoqueson a Mohegan Captaine who tooke Myantenomy prisoner was dangerously and treacherously wounded in the night as hee slept in his Wigwam, and other hostile acts were on both pts attempted in a priuate and underhand way as they could take advantage eich against other.

Vnseasonable weather

Tantoqueson wounded in his wigwam

But since the Narrohiggansets haue at seůall tymes, openly invaded Vncas, so that Coneetacut and New Hauen, were forced according to engagement to send men, from those Colonies for his prsent defence, but w'h expresse direcćon not to begin any offensiue warr against the Narrohigganset or their confederat{ till further order. In the meane tyme Messengers were sent to the Narrohiggansets from the geňall Court in the Massachusets signifying the Commission^rs meeting, pmiseing their greevances, should bee full and justly heard, and requireing a cessaćon of warr in the meane tyme, but they refused. And heareing pbably that the English from the westerne Collonies were returned, they made a new assault vpon Vncas { haue done him much hurte.

Conneetacutt { Newhauen send forces to ayde Vncas { defend.

Messengers sent to ye Narrohigg^s

The Comission^rs being mett sent Messengers the second tyme both to the Narrohigganset { Mohegan Indians, mynding them of their forṁ treaties {

Messengers sent the second tyme

1645.

September.

A faire answere at first but after retreated

Guides discouraged.

No gulds to be obtayned *66

Messengers abused

The English threatened

Revyleing of Vncas

The messengers derided.

Three Indians w'h hatchets

truce, desireing them to send their deputies instructed and furnished w'h authorytie, to declare and open the grounds of the warr, to giue and receiue due satisfaction and to restore and settle peace.

At first the Narrohigganset Sachem gaue a reasonable ₵ fayre answere that he would send guides w'h them to the Mohegans, and if Vncas consented he would send his Deputies to the Comission's, and during eight dayes hostilitie should cease, but he soone repented of this moderaĉon, tould the English Messengers his mynd was chaunged, sent priuate instrucĉons to the Nyantick Sachem, after the deliuery of w'h, there was nothing but proud and insolent passages, the Indian guides w'ch the English Messengers brought w'h them from Pumham and Sokakanoco were by frownes and threatening speeches, discouraged and returned, no other guides could be obtayned though much pressed, (they knew (as the expressed themselues) *by the course holden at Hartford last yeare, that y' Comissio's would mediate and presse for peace, but they were resolued to haue no peace w'hout Vncas his head, it mattered not who begann the warr, they were resolued to continue it, the English should w'hdraw their garrison from Vncas, or they would take it as a breach of former Couenants, and would pcure as many Mowhauges, as they English should afront them w'h, that they would lay the English cattell on heapes as heigh as their houses, that no English man should stir out of his doore to pisse, but he should be killed.

They revyled Vncas charged him with cutting through his owne arme, and saing the Narrohigganset had shott him, affirmed that he would now murther the English Messengers as they went or returned (if he had optunitie) and lay it vpon the Narrobiggansets

The English messengers vpon this rude ₵ vnciuill vsage wanting guides to pceede and feareing danger returned to the Narrohiggansets, acquainted Pissicus with the former passages, desired guides from him, hee (in scorne as they apprehended it) offerred them an old Peacott Squaw, but would afford no other guides : there also they conceiued themselues in danger, three Indians w'h hatchetts standing behynd the Interpretor in a suspicious manner, while he was speakeing with Pessicus, and the rest frowneing and expressing much distemper in their countenance and carriage. The English Messengers not hopeing for better successe at that tyme depted, telling Pessicus that if he would returne any other answere, he should send it to the English trading house where they intended to lodg that night, In the morneing hee invited them to returne and pmised them a guide to Vncas but would graunt no cessation of armes. When they came to Prouidence they vnderstood that in their absence a Narrohigganset Indian had beene there, and feineing himself

to be of Coneettacut spake in that dyalect, but could not put of the Nar-
rohigganset℄ tone, hee tould Benedict Arnold℄ wyfe (who well vnderstood the
Indian language) that the English Messengers should not passe to the Mohegans, he knew they should haue no guides, but should be destroyed in the
woods as they trauelled toward℄ Vncas.

Thus the English Messengers returned and the Interpʳtor vnder his hand
and vpon his Oath related the former passages (with others (lesse material)
more largely.

Mᵣ Williams by the Messengers wrote to the Comissionʳs assureing
them that the Countrey would soddainely bee all on fire meaneing by warr,
that by strong reasons ℄ arguments hee could convince any man thereof,
that was of another mynd, that the Narrohiggansets had beene wᵗh the
Plantacõns combyned wᵗh Prouidence and solemly treated and setled a New-
trallyty wᵗh them : wᶜh fully shewes their Counsells and setled resolucõns for
warr.

Thus while the Comissionʳs in care of the publike peace sought to quench
the fyre kindled amongst the Indians these children *of strife breath out
threatenings ℘vocations and warr agˢᵗ: the English themselues : so that
vnlesse they should dishonor and ℘voake God, by vyolateing a just engagement, ℄ expose the Colonies to contempt and danger from the Barbarians
they cannot but exercise force when no other meanes will pʳvayle to reduce
the Narrohiggansets and their confederats to A more just and sober temper.

The eyes of other Indians vnder the ℘tection of the Massachusett℄ and
not at all engaged in this quarrell are (as they haue exprest themselues to the
English Messengers) fastened vpon the English wᵗh strict obseruacõn, in what
manner and measure they ℘uide for Vncas his safety : If hee ℘ish they will
charge it vpon them who might haue preserued him, and no Indians will trust
the English if they now broke engagements, either in the pʳsent or succeeding
genⁱations. Yf Vncas be ruined in such a cause, they foresee their heads
vpon the next pʳtence shalbe deliüed to the will of the Narrohiggansets,
wᵗh whome therefore they shalbe forced to comply, as they may for their
future safety, and the English may not trust an Indian in yᵉ whole Countrey.
The pʳmisss being weighed it clearely appeares That God calls the Colonies to
a Warr.

The Narrohiggansets and their Confederats rest on their numbers
weapons and opertunities to do mischeefe as probably as of ould Ashur
Amaleck and the Philistins with others did confederate against Israell : So
Sathan may stir up and combyne many of his Instruments against the
Churches of Christ : but their Redeemer is the Lord of Hostes, the mighty

one in battaile, all the sheilds of the earth are in his hands, hee can saue by fewe ₰ by weake meanes, aswell as by many and great **In him they trust.**

The Comissioners takeing into consideraĉõn the matter concerneing the peace made betwixt the gouerment of the Massachussetts and montseur De Aulney referred to this meeting for confirmaĉõn or abrogation. And such questions and ꝓposiĉõns as haue beene deliũed vnto them, both by the Comissioners for the Massachusets Collonies as also by Mᵣ Saltenstall and Mᵣ Hawtherne ymployed by the geñall Court to enquire about the ꝑceedings of Captaine Haukens and other of the English in ayde of Mounseur De Latore against Montseur De Aulney, and also some questions ꝓpounded by one of the Elders concerneing the same matter, and haueing pused the said Articles of agreement, and all such letters ₰ other writings as concerne the said affaires, haue (vpon mature advice and deliberaĉõn) stated, resolued and answered the said ꝓpositions and questions as here followeth.

*Whether Monsᵣ: Latore being a French man borne, accepting his land from the Canada Company, and of Comission of Leiftennancy of those pts from the King of France, be not concluded thereby (both in facto and de jure) to be a subject of Frauce and to hold all his estate in Accady of the Crowne of France ?

The Comissioners answere affirmatiuely.

Monsᵣ: Latore being knowne and concluded to be subject of the King of Fraunce, and his lands to be accounted (by Custome of all States of Europe) as belonging to that Crowne whether these confederate Colonies of new England (being strangers to that Kingdome of Fraunce and the affaires of that State) may judg of the validitie, of any of the ꝑceedings against Latore there ?

Answered negatiuely.

3

If Monsᵣ Latore his pson, estate and cause belonging to the Jurisdicĉõn, and cognizance of the Crowne of France should be apparently injured, or oppressed by Monsᵣ De Aulney, whether the said Vnited Colonies, haue any lawfull calling to giue assistance to Monsᵣ: Latore against Monsᵣ. De Aulney, holding forth the Authorty of the King of Fraunce for his warrant ?

Answered negatiuely.

- When Monsᵣ: Latore ariued here, in the ship of Monsᵣ: Mooroone, wᵗh

Comission from the Vice-Admirall of France for bringing supply to Latore (stiled therein Leiftennant Geñall of the King of France) and therein required all the Subjects of France and desired all others to yeild him assistance, as occasion should require, whether in this case the voluntaries, might lawfully be pmitted, to goe in ayde of Latore, according to the request of the said Comission?

Answerd That in referrence and respect to the State of France, it might be done, and so it appeared to haue beene allowed in France.

Whether such Volunteers (as were pmitted to goe in ayd of Latore vpon such grounds and intimations as is expressed in the former question) invadeing Monsr de Aulney in his owne habitation &. do by such action lay this Goverment vnder guilt or ptitipaçõn of any hostility, or injurie wch might be comitted thereby

5

Answered. That in referrence to the State of France volunteers going forth as before w'hout Comission or incouragement to do any vnlawfull act the State so pmitting them, doth not fall vnder guilt, vnlesse by some after neglect of Duty.

*Whether Monsr. De Aulney his Intimaçõn of the State of France their satisfaccõn concerneing the Voluntary ayde afforded Latore and the Articles of peace concluded therevpon doe not barr Monsr De Aulney from requireing any further satisfaccõn from this goûment otherwise then in a way of psecution in a course of ciuill justice against pticuler psons intressed?

6

*69

Answered That Monsr De Aulney haueing by his letters Septemb^r 20'h 1644 declared what construccõn the Kinge of France had made of the late voluntary Ayde afforded Latore, chargeing the fault vpon the vice Admirall of France, And ordering that peace should be kept w'h the English, And De Aulney himself by his Agent Monsr De Marie haueing concluded A peace w'h the Goûment of the Massachusets, not excepting nor menconing therein etheir damnage or repairaçõn: wee see not why he should now require satisfaccõn from the said Gouerment for former acts done by the said Volunteers w'hout their Comission or consent.

Whether Monsr De Aulney his seazing the Catch of Joseph Grafton going w'h puisions to Latores fort and refuseing to giue satisfaccõn &c be a breach of the peace on his pte?

7

Answered, negatiuely.

1 6 4 5.

September.
8

Grafton.

Whether the carrying hoame Latores Lady from Boston in the Shipps of Strangers riding in our Harbour, or the attempt of the said Grafton to carry puisions to Latores fort being both donn w'hout the Assistants of this Goûment be a breach of the peace on our pt?

Answered. That vpon consideracõn of the Articles agreed vpon w'h Mons': Marie there appeares no breach of the peace in either.

9

Whether the Mortgage or conveyance made from Mons' Latore to Major Gibbons of his fort (̃ after the Comission of the King of France to Mons': De Aulney was made knowne to vs be of any force against the said De Alncy especially now after the fort hath beene seized into the hands of the King of France by Authoritie of the said Comission?

Answere. Negatiucly. for ought appeares at p'sent vpon what wee haue scene.

I O

Whether the Comission's are to take cognizance of the former injuries offerred to any of the Confederates (as that of Penobscott) (̃. sciug the parties intressed do not now complayne?

Answere. They Comissioners conceiue they neede not expresse their thoughts herein, till the parties interrested shall call for them.

1 I
*70

Whereas some hostile acts appeares to haue beene committed against Mons'. De Aulney in killing some of his men *and destroying and takeing his goods, by some of those English who went forth vnder the Comaund of Captaine Haukins and joyned w'h Mons'. Latore his men therein, whether this act may bee justyfyable in him and the rest of those English, or if they ought not to be called to an account for the same?

Answere. It doth not appeare to the Comission's that Captaine Haukins or any vnder him had any Comission from the goûnor of the Massachusetts or any other to attempt any hostile act agn'st: Mons'. De Aulney, nor to enquire after wronges or require satisfacõn from the one to the other, nor why hee or they should joyne with Mons' Latores men in that way of force after he had receiued Mons' De Aulneys Letter: but Captaine Hawkins being now absent, they leave him to answere for himself.

Whereas the Comission's haue beene further mooued by some of the Court of the Massachusetts to consider of the said hostile act comitted by Captaine Haukins and the English w'h him.

They answere therevnto in effect as before vizᵗ. They conceiue that Captaine Haukins or those wᵗʰ him haue donn seuerall thinges against Monsʳ. De Aulney of weighty concernement (wᵗʰout Comission from hence) wᶜʰ are justly questionable, but the cause depending as they hear in the Court of the Massachusets they referr it to the due course of Justice.

Lastly the Comissionʳˢ vpon serious advice & consideraᵗⁿ doe assent (as is hereafter expressed) to the Articles of peace made betweene the Goũment of the Massachusetts and Monsʳ De Aulney, if hee agree and ratyfye them vnder his hand. The ratyfycaᵗⁿ now drawne vp as here followeth in English (but it was translated into Latine) and vnder the former agreement exemplyfyed &c.

An agreement betweene John Endicott Goũnor of the Massachusets in New England and the rest of the Majestrats there And Monsʳ: Marie Commissioner for Monsʳ: De Aulney Knight Goũnor and Leiftennant of his heighnesse the King of France in Accaday A Prouince of New France made and confirmed at Boston in the Massachusets aforesaid the eight day of the eight month 1644.

The Goũnor and Majestratℓ do pmise to Monsʳ: Marie aforesaid That they and all the English wᵗʰin the Jurisdiction of the Massachusets in New England shall obserue and keepe firme peace wᵗʰ Monsʳ: De Aulney Goũnor &c and all the French vnder his Goũment in Accady and also Monsʳ: Marie pmiseth for Monsʳ: de Aulney that hee and all his people shall keepe firme peace alsoe wᵗʰ the Goũnor and majestratℓ aforesaid, and all the Inhabitants of the said Jurisdicᵗⁿ of the Massachusetts *and that it shalbe lawfull for all their people aswell French as English to trade eich wᵗʰ other, so as if any occasion of offence shall happen, neither of them shall attempt any thing against the other in a hostile way except complaint & manefestaᵗⁿ of the Injurie be first made and satisfacᵗⁿ according to equitie bee not giuen Prouided alwayes that yᵉ Goũnor and Majestratℓ aforesaid bee not bound to restrayne their Merchantℓ from tradeing wᵗʰ the ships wᵗʰ what people soeuer, whether French or others in what place soeuer inhabiting. Prouided also that the full ratifycaᵗⁿ and conclusion of this agreement be referred to the next meeteing of the Comissionʳˢ of the vnited Colonies of New England for the continuance or abrogation thereof and in the meane ⌄ to remayne firme and inviolable.

The treaty of peace wᵗʰ Monsʳ. De Aulney

*71

The Comissionʳˢ for the vnited Colonies of New England haueing pused and considered the agreement and Articles aboue written, and being desireous that a firme & gen̄all peace might be mayntayned betweene the English and all their Neighbours, that euery one might pursue the com̄on intention of subduing this wildernes for the use of man in that way for wch the earth was first giuen to the sonnes of Adam, and for bringing these barbarous people first to ciuilitie (and so by diuine assistance) to the knowledg of the true God and our Lord Jesus Christ It seemes fitt and necessary vnto them, that the agreement & Articles afore specifyed (comprehending therein all the said vnited Colonies) should be confirmed. But whereas there are certaine questions and injuries on both pts alledged and charged, the Comission^{rs} are willing that in due tyme and place ye same shalbe duly heard and composed according to justice, and that peace in the meane tyme, be fully and firmely kept by the English Colonies according to the late Agreement. Prouided that Monsr : De Aulney vnder his owne hand doe confirme and obserue the same.

> These foregoing Conclusions were subscribed by the Comission^{rs} for the seū̄all Jurisdicc̄ōns this second of Septemb^r: 1645.

JOHN WINTHROP Pres^{nt}.	GEO : FENWICK
HERBERT PELHAM	EDWA : HOPKINS.
THO : PRENCE.	THEOPH : EATON.
JOHN BROWNE.	STEPHEN GOODYEARE.

At a meetinge of the Comissioners for the vnited Colonies in New England at New hauen 9ᵗh 7ᵗᵉʳ. 1646.

THE Articles of Confederation being read, an order of the generall Corte of the Massachusets dated the sixt of the third moneth 1646. was presented ℓ read, whereby it appeared that John Endicutt and Herbert Pelham esqʳ, were chosen Comissioners for that Colony for a full ℓ compleate yeare, ℓ were invested wᵗh full power ℓ authority accordinge to the tenure of the said articles, and an order made therevpon at the meeteinge at Boston the 7. 7ᵇᵉʳ 1643.

Mʳ John Browne, ℓ Mʳ Timothy Hatherley presented a like order of the generall Corte of Plimouth the second of the 4ᵗh moneth, 1646, at wᶜh time they were chosen Comissioners for that Colony for one yeare, accordinge to the tenure of the aforementioned articles

A like order of the generall Courte at Hartford for the iurisdicȼon of Connecticut was produced, whereby Edward Hopkins ℓ John Heynes esqʳ were chosen Comissioners accordinge to the tenure of the said Articles for one yeare, wᶜh order was dated the 9ᵗh of the second moneth 1646.

Theophilus Eaton esqʳ. ℓ Mʳ Stephen Goodyeare were chosen Comissioners for the Colony of Newhaven for one yeare, accordinge to the tenure of said Articles, as by an order of that geñall Courte dated the 30ᵗh of the 8ᵗh moneth, 1645. appeared

Theophilus Eaton was chosen President for this meetinge of the Commissioners.

The Comissioners of Connecticute complayned of señall insolencies ℓ iniuries with an high hand lately comitted ℓ maintayned by the Dutch Agent, ℓ some of his family to the disturbance of the peace there ; And a Protest lately sent by the Dutch Governoure against New haven, with the answere returned were read

The Protest was written in Latine, the contents in English was as followeth.

We William Kift generall Director, ℓ the Senate of new Netherlands, for the high and mighty Lords the States of the Vnited Belgicke Provinces, for his Excellency the Prince of Orange, ℓ for the *most noble Lords, the Administrators of the West India Company To thee Theophilus Eaton Governoure of this place, by vs called the Red Hills in New Netherland, but by the English called, New Haven, we giue notice that some yeares past, yours (without any occasion given by vs, ℓ without any necessity imposed vpō them, but with an vnsatiable desire of possessinge that wᶜh is ours, against our Protestations, against the law of Nations ℓ the auncient league betwixt the Kings Maᵗʸ of greate Britaine, ℓ our supiours haue indirectly entred the limitℓ of New Netherland, vsurped diuerse places in them, ℓ haue bene very injurous vnto vs, neither haue they given satisfacčōn though oft required : And because you ℓ yours haue of late determined to fasten your foote neare Mauritius River in this Province, ℓ there not onely to disturb our trade (of noe man hitherto questioned) ℓ to draw it to yourselues, but vtterly to destroy it, were compeld againe to Protest, ℓ by these presents doe protest against you as against breakers of the peace, and disturbers of the publicke quiet, That if you doe not restore the places you haue vsurped, ℓ repaire the losse we haue suffered, we shall by such meanes as God affoords, manfully recouer them.   Neither doe we thincke this crosseth yᵉ publicke peace but shall cast the cause of the ensuinge euill vpon you.   Given in Amsterdam forte. August 3. 1646. New stile.

WILLIAM KIEFT.

The answere was returned in Latine to the said ꝑtest the Contents as followeth.

To the Right Woʳ: William Kieft Gouernoure of the Dutch
in New Netherland.

Sʳ.

By some of yours I haue receaued a Protest vnder your hand Daꞇ Aug: 3. 1646. wherein you pretend we haue indirectly entred the limitℓ of New Netherland, vsurped diuerse places in them, ℓ haue offred you many injuries, Thus in generall, ℓ in reference to some yeare past, more ꝑticularly that to the disturbance, nay to the vtter destruction of your trade, we haue lately set foote neare Mauritius River in that province ℓc

We doe truely professe we know noe such River, nor can conceiue what River you intend by that name vnlesse it be that wᶜh the English haue longe ℓ still doe call, Hudsons River.   Nor haue we at any time *formerly or lately entred vpon any place to wᶜh you had, or haue any knowne title, nor in any other respect beene injurious to you.   It is true we haue lately vpon Pawgusett River wᶜh falls into the sea in the midst of the English Plantations, built a small house within our owne limits, many miles nay leagues from the Manhatteoes from your tradinge house ℓ from any porte of Hudsons River, at which we expect little trade but can compell none, the Indians beinge free to trade with you, vs, Connecticute, Mattachusets, or with any others : nor did we build there till we had first purchased a due title from the true proprietors : what injuries ℓ outrages in our persons ℓ estates at the Manhattoes in Delawar River ℓc we haue receiued from you, our former letters ℓ protest doe both declare ℓ proue to all wᶜh you haue hitherto giuen very vnsatisfyinge answeres : But what ever our losses ℓ sufferinge haue beené, we conceiue we haue neither done, nor returned any thinge even vnto this day, but what doth agree with the law of God, the law of Nations, ℓ with that ancient confederation ℓ amity betwixt our superiours at home, soe that we shall readily refer all questions and differencℓ betwixt you ℓ vs even from first to last to any due examination ℓ iudgemᵗ, either heere or in Europe ℓ by these presents doe refer them, beinge well assured that his Maᵗʸ. our soūaigne Lord Charles Kinge of greate Britaine ℓ the Parliament of England now assembled will maintaine their owne right ℓ our iust liberties against any who by vnjust encrochment shall wronge them or theirs, ℓ that your owne Principalls vpon a due ℓ mature consideration will alsoe see ℓ approue the righteousnes of our proceedings.

NEW HAVEN in New England. Aug: 12ᵗʰ 1646.　　　　　T : E.
　　　　　　　　　　　old stile.

The premises being duely considered both in reference to Hartford ℓ New haven the Comissioners thought fitt to expresse their apprehentions in writinge to the Dutch Gov: in latine but the Contents as followeth.

To the Right woʳ : William Kieft. Governor. ℓc

　　Sʳ

Vpon a due consideration how peace (a choice blessinge) may be continued, we are carefull to enquire ℓ search into those differencℓ ℓ offences soe longe continued betwixt some of our confederates ℓ your selues : It is now neare 3 yeares since the Governor of the Mattachusets by consent ℓ advice of the Counsell of that Colony, did pticularly propounde to your consideration sundry injurious ℓ vnworthy passages done by your Agent vpon the fresh River, ℓ some of his family vpon our brethren at Harford to all *wᶜh you returned an Ignoramus, with an offensiue addiꝯon wᶜh we leaue to a review ℓ better consideration, what inquiry ℓ order you after made ℓ tooke to suppresse such miscarriages for the future, we haue not heard, c̄tainly your Agent, ℓ his

*76

company are now growne to a strange ℞ vnsufferable bouldnes (we hope without Comission) An Indian captiue liable to publike punishment fled from her M^{rs} at Harford is entertayned in your house, at Harford, ℞ though required by the Magestrate is vnder ye hands of your Agent there denyed, ℞ we heare she is either marryed, or abused by one of your men : Such a servant is parte of her Masters estate, ℞ a more considerable part then a beast, our children will not longe be secure if this be suffered : your Agent himselfe in height of disorder ℞ contempt of authority, resists the watch at Harford, drawes ℞ breakes his rapier vpon their weopens and by flight escapes, had he bene slaine in this proud affront, his bloud had beene vpon his owne head: Lastly to passe by other particulars, some of your horses beinge pownded for damage done in the English Corne, your Agent ℞ 4 more made an assault, and stroke him who legally sought justice, ℞ in an hostile way tooke away his teame and laden.

We haue also seene a Protest of yours. Da͞t Aug: 3. 1646 New stile, against our confederat℞ of New-haven with their Answere Da͞t Aug: 12th. ℞ deliuered to lieftenant Baxtey yor messenger: vpon our most serious consideration of the Contents togeither with their title heere held forth we conceiue their Answere fayre ℞ just, and hope it will cleare their proceedings, and giue you full satisfaction, yet to prevent inconveniences wch may grow by any part of the premises, we haue sent this bearer, by whome we desire such a returne as may testify your concurrence with vs to embrace ℞ pursue righteousnes ℞ peace.

Vpon information that the Dutch Governor in a ͠lre to the Governor of the Mattachusets chargeth Mr Whitinge, one of the Magistrates of Connecticut y^t at the Manhattoes he should say, The English were fooles to suffer the Dutch to liue there, Mr Whitinge vpon other occasions beinge now at New haven ye Comissioners enquired of him what had passed *betwixt him ℞ the Dutch Governoure, or him ℞ others at the Manhattoes, ℞ therevpon in English wrote another letter to the Dutch Governoure as followeth.

*77

S^r. since your former dated the fifth of this present we haue spoken with Mr Whitinge concerninge words you chardge him with in yor letter to the Governoure of the Mattachusets, he professeth he neither remembreth nor knoweth any such words spoken by him, ℞ we could wish that all such provokinge ℞ threatninge language might be forborne on both pt℞, as contrary to that peace ℞ neighbourely correspondency wch we desire sincerely to preserue betwixt the 2. Nations. Mr Whitinge complaines of a sentence lately passed against him in his absence at the Manatoes, when he had noe Agent there to pleade to his cause, or to giue in his evidence, ₵ that demandinge a just debt longe since due from some of yours, he receiued neither that helpe of Justice from yoᵣ selfe, nor soe faire an answere as the cause required ₵ he expected, we are assured you will both grante him a review in the form ₵ free passage for recoveringe debt₵ as all the Colonies will readily doe to any of yours in our Court₵, yf in your answere to our former you ~~will~~ please to adde a word or two concerninge the ꝑmisses, it may settle a right vnderstandinge betwixt vs, we rest, Yours, ₵c   September. 7ᵗʰ 1646. old style.

Both these letters were sent by Lieftenant Godfrey a messenger to the Dutch Governoure the same day.

The Comissioners consideringe the treacherous disposition of the Indians, how hard a thinge it is to continue any firme peace with them, how skilfull they growe in the vse of peec₵, powder ₵ shott ₵ insolent thereby, ₵ withall how plentifully those who liue aboute ₵ neare the French and Dutch are (though at high prices) furnished with them, the Traders of both Nations preferringe profitt to their owne ₵ neighboures safety, thought it their duty to reviue ₵ strengthen what former prouision hath bene made, that such disorderly ₵ dangerous tradinge may not onely be straitened, but suppressed in all those Colonies according to their place ₵ trust, they doe therefore confirme the order made at Hartford in Septemb: 1644 hopinge that neither any generall Courte, nor magistrate within those Colonies, will vpon any occasion or for any respect giue license or vse any Coñivance contrary to the scope and true meaninge thereof,   And whereas three of the Colonies haue already made orders to regulate tradinge with others in those *prouisions for war, the Comissioners for Mattachusets, Connecticut ₵ New hauen ₵ the Comissioners for Plimoᵗh in ꝑticular, where for want of such an order some traders haue lately taken too much liberty to carry ₵ sell considerable quantities of powder ₵ shott, or lead to ₵ at the Manatoes wᶜh hath beene as fewell to the fire, a meanes to continue ₵ increase an indirect ₵ hurtfull trade the Dutch haue with the Indians, are intreated to preserue the orders already made, ₵ with due seriousnes to propounde to the seuerall generall Court₵ that speedily some wholesome prouision may be made vnder a weighty penalty, that none within their ꝑticular ₵ respectiue Jurisdictions sell or cause to be sould directly or indirectly any gun or guns of what name or sorte soever, any powder, shott, bullet₵ lead swords or any other weopons or instruments proper ₵ vsed for war to any ꝑson or persons out of these or any of these Jurisdictions without license vnder the hands of two magistrates of the Jurisdiction, or at

*78

1646.

September.

least vnder the hand of one Magistrate & two Deputies intrusted for the pub-licke affaires, And that all & every such license shall from time to time be kept in a booke or memoriall in writinge that all the pcells or particulars with the quantities soe licensed, the persons to whome, & the grounds for w^{ch}, vpon occasion may be considered by the generall Courte or Comissioners for the Colonies.

Mr Hopkins & Mr Heynes acquainted the Comissioners wth a murther-ous plott & designe Sequasson is charged with against themsclues, & Mr Whitinge, that his accuser formerly hired by Sequasson to murther an Indian petty Sachem, offers to witnes this to his face, that the wampan given with Sequassons seuerall false excuses & flight makes the euidence probable, if not certaine, & that Sequasson doth not yet come to cleare himselfe, though twice sent for by Mr Heynes ; The Comissioners consideringe the premises thought fit once againe to send for him with safe Conduct vnder their hands, & accord-ingly gaue instructions to Jonathan Gilbert, as followeth.

•79

You are with all convenient speede to repaire to Warranok or such other place where you vnderstand Sequasson abides, & havinge obtayned oppurtuni-ty to speake with him, you are to giue him to vnderstand that the Comission-ers for all the English Colonyes, (vz§) Mattachusets, Plimouth, Connecticute & New haven who are betrusted *with matters of peace & war in behalfe of all the Colonies, beinge now mett at New haven haue bene enformed y^t he the said Sequasson, & some others are accused by a c̃taine Indian sometimes resid-inge with him, of a plot & conspiracy entered into by them for the killinge of M^r. Hopkins, Mr Heynes & Mr Whiting of Hartford, & that the s̃d Indian was hyred by them for the effectinge thereof, havinge rec^d part of his pay for the same in 3 girdles of wampan wch he hath brought to the English, with promises of a far greater quantity when the designe was accomplished: you are further to acquainte the said Sequasson, that the Comissioners aforesd beinge very desirous to vnderstand the truth or falshood of the premises, doe by you tender to him an open & willinge eare vpon notice hereof, if he forth-with repaire to them at the place of meetinge at New haven readily to heare & imptially to consider what ʌ alleadge & evidence in his owne defence in the presence & before the face of his accuser, who tenders himselfe ready to make good his accusation.

You are for his further encouragement herein to giue the said Sequasson to know, that the Comissioners did promise that he should receiue noe disturba-tion or molestation in his repaire to them from any of the English or any others by their knowledge or consent, & the like free liberty & passage he shall haue in his returne backe whatsoever the discouery of the case shalbe. But if not-withstandinge the aforesd encouragement he refuse psonally to appe before the Comissioners for the clearinge of himselfe, you may let him know, that the withdraweinge of himselfe will much increase the suspition of his guilt to all the English, & induce them to proccede in answereable courses towards him: Yf there be any other Indians at Warranok or thereabouts, whome you know to be accused of the aforesaid plott togeither with Sequasson, you are to re-quire them to repaire hither alsoe in the name of the Comisioners to cleare them selues, if they desire to stand right in the eies of the English & havinge caused them all fully to vnderstand those instructions, you are to take their answere in writing & to returne it to us with all convenient speede.

1 6 4 6.

September.

Jonathan Gilbert vnderstandinge where Sequasson was, went to haue spoken with him, (but as he *conceiueth) the Indians prevented him, & gaue notice to Sequason who therevpon fled & could not be mett with: But a few dayes after Nepinsoyt & Naimataigue two Sagamores with other Indians came to New haven, & informed the Comissioners that they were freinds to Se-quason, & had bene with him at the Mattachuset& & intimated he had pre-sented the Governoure with Wampam, but the Governoure would not accept the present, onely would giue it house roome & wished them to attend the Comissioners at this meetinge, & if Sequason cleared himselfe then he would tell them more aboutes the present, they alsoe professed respect to the English & said they had brought down Sequason to cleare himselfe, that one of them held him by one arme, & the other by the other, yet when he was neare New haven, almost at the towne fence, he brake from them & made an escape, they added alsoe that he was ashamed to come because he had brought no present. The Comissioners tould them they intended Sequason no hurt, but desired to bring him & his accusor face to face, that he should haue a iust hearinge in their presence: But as they were assured y° Governor of the Mat-tachuset& would returne his present, if he did not cleare himselfe, soe the Comissioners would neither accept any present if tendered, nor should the want of it preiudice his cause. The Comissioners were by some other Indi-ans informed, that Sequason was wth in a mile of New haven & it was consid-ered he would gladly make his peace some other way then by a due examina-tion & tryall. The two Sagamores said he was afrayd & durst not come, though he confessed it was iust he should come & cleare himselfe if innocent, all wch being considered the Comissioners conceiued, that Sequason whither guilty or afrayd of the English, would be plottinge against them, and soe

*80

proue dangerous, wherefore they thought fitt ₵ ordered, that all iust ₵ prudent meanes should be vsed (his life preserued) to bringe him to tryall that the matter might some way be ishewed.

In the meane time they thought fitt to examine Wotchibrok a Potatuke Indian Sequasous accusor, who waited to giue euidence against him, he beinge warned by Thomas Stanton the Interpretor to speake nothing but truth, affirmed that beinge this last springe in a wigwam with Sequason

*81   at Warranot ₵ ready to depart, Sequason perswaded him to *stay three daies, thence he drew him to the Falls abouc Mr Pincheons, when they had bene there fowre dayes, Wontibrou would haue bene gone to   ˄ to see some freiuds, Sequason tould him it was dangerous to trauell that way he would be killed, walked along with him to a springe, ₵ there tould him that if euer he would doe him the said Sequason a kindenes now was the time, he was almost ruyned, ₵ the English at Harford the cause of it, he should therefore go to Hartford ₵ kill Mr Hopkins, Mr Heynes or Mr Whitinge ₵ he would giue him a greate rewarde, ₵ therevpon pluckt out of his bagg, three girdles of wampan ₵ gaue them to him with a peice of a girdle to play and promised him much more. Watchibrok tould him it was dangerous to kill an English Sachem, they would finde out the murtherer and pursue him to death, what wōld then wampam doe him good. Sequason said he had store of wampan, when the thinge was done, they would fly togeither to the Mowhaukes, But in the way when they came to the Wampog Indians, he should giue it out that Vnkus had hired him for so much wampam ₵ that would sett the English against Vnkas, ₵ then he the said Sequason should rise againe, ₵ he further tould this examint Naimetaigue one of the forementioned Sagomores that came on the behalfe of Soquason ₵ his father knew ₵ approued the said murther. Wotchibrough further saith that having taken the aforesd wampam he remembred that himselfe had taken formerly Busshege ₵ brought him to the English who for a murtherous attempt at Stanford, was put to death at New hauen, that if he should kill any English by such meanes, he should goe in feare of death all the dayes of his life, ₵ that for bringinge in Busshege he had a gratuity from the English, ₵ for discovery of the plot he should finde favor ₵ he thought the favoure of the English with security would be better to him than Sequasons wampam with feare ₵ danger, he therefore came first to Tuncksus ₵ the next day to Hartford ₵ discouered Sequasons practise, he saith further that Sequason hearinge of the discovery spake to Rominot an Indian, ₵ he sent 6d by another Indian to this examinant, desiringe him to conceale ₵ hide as much as he could of the plot ₵ not to lay

all open, but he in anger *bad the said six pence hold his peace, he had discouered it ₵ would hide nothinge.

Two petitions were presented to the Comissioners from John Griffin, Edward Elmar ₵ others, complayninge that some Indian or Indians had wilfully
₵ malitiously burned some quantities of Pitch ₵ tar of theirs togeither with
beddinge, a Cart ₵ its furniture with heapes of Candlewood, tooles
₵ work for greater quantities of pitch ₵ tar in value (as they expresse it)
aboue 100ᵗ ₵ pticularly they complayned of Wahannos a Waranot Indian as
guilty therein as by sufficient euidence they thought they could proue, that
he had since avoyded all the English plantations, and that he beinge sent for
by a warrant from some of the Magistrates of Connecticut fled, but beinge over-
taken ₵ seised by one of the English he was rescued by Indians, ₵ the English
by them jeared ₵ abused, ₵ pticularly by Chicwallop, Sachem of Nowottok,
wherevpon Jonathan Gilbert ₵ John Griffin with others were sent with
instructions from the Comissioners, as followeth.

> Instructions for Jonathan Gilbert ₵ John Griffin sent by the Co-
> missioners of the vnited Colonies to Chickwallop Sachem at Na-
> wattock and Manahcuse an Indian, abidinge in those pt₵ the
> 5. Sept. 1646

You are with all convenient speed to repaire to Newattock ₵ havinge
informed the Sachem there of the meetinge of the Comissioners for all the
English Colonies at New hauen, you may give him to vnderstand that the
said Comissioners haue beene enformed of some late practises of Manahauces
an Indian, now or lately residinge with him, in burninge the pitch ₵ tar
of some inhabitant₵ of Windsore vpon Connecticut, ₵ of some resistance
made by himselfe agꝟt some English sent by order from the Magistrates, vpon
the Riuer of Connecticute to bringe the said Mahanose to a due tryall of the
said charge layd against him. You are further to let him know that the said
Comissioners not beinge willinge to condemne any before they heare them,
doe by you tender them an impartiall hearinge of what they can alleadge in
their owne defence, if they presently vpon notice hereof repaire to them at
the place of their meeting in New haven, wᶜʰ you are in the Comissioners
*name to require of them, And for the encouragemᵗ of the said Sachem   *83
herevnto, you may let him know that the Comissioners doe promise he shall
receaue no disturbance nor molestation in his repaire to them or returne from
them from any of the English or any other with their consent or knowledge,
But in case they refuse to attend the advise of the Comissioners herein, you

shall enforme him that such refusall will much increase the suspition of their guilt, ℭ induce the Comissioners to proceed in answerable courses towards them; when you haue caused them fully to vnderstand these instructions ℭ that you pceiue they are resolued not to make their apparance here, but to withdraw themselues from the way of righteous proceeding℄ therein propounded to them, Yf vpon a prudent consideracõn of the strength you haue with you in reference to the nomber ℭ strength of the Indians that may oppose you, you doe iudge your selues able with safety to yoᵗ psons to bringe away Manahanoes in a forcible manner then you may constraine him to come alonge with you, Provided you can do it without preiudice to his life.

At their returne they informed the Comissioners that they could not meete either with Chickwallop, or wᵗʰ Manahanoes, they conceiued the Indians had carryed away Manahanoes, but the Sagamors ℭ Indians at Waranoco carryed it insolently towards the English vauntinge themselues in their armes, bowes ℭ arrowes, hatchets, swords, some with their guns ready chargd before ℭ in the presence of the English messengers, they primed ℭ cocked them ready to giue fire, ℭ tould them that if they should offer to carry away any man thence, the Indians were resolued to fight, ℭ if they should stay but one night at the English tradinge house, neare all the Country would come in to rescue any such Indian seised. Yet the next morninge the Sachem with some others offered the English messengers 8 Fadome of wampam towards satisfaccõn ℭ promised to provide more. The messengers not havinge any thinge to that purpose in their Comission advised the Sachem to send to the Comissioners but he refused.

*Herevpon Noynetacha one of the Sagamores of Waranaco, who as before came on Sequassons behalfe, was questioned by the Comissioners aboute those proude affronts to the English, at first he denyed pt of what he was charged, ℭ excused some pte, but one of the English messengers beinge present, ℭ he hearinge the rest should be sent for, fell vnder most of the chardge professinge he intended noe harme to the English.

The Comissioners seriously consideringe the pᵐⁱˢˢℭ thought, that if such wilfull ℭ hostile practises against the English, togeither with the entertayninge, ptectinge or rescuinge of offenders were suffered, the peace of the Colonies could not be secured, it was therefore concluded, that in such cases the magistrates of any of the iurisdictions, might at the plantifs chardge send some convenient strenth of English, ℭ accordinge to the nature ℭ value of the offence, ℭ damadge seise ℭ bring away any of that plantation of Indians that shall entertaine, ꝑtect, or rescue the offendor, though it should be in another_s iurisdicc͠on, when through distance of place, counsell, or direcc͠on cannot be had, after notice ꝗ due warninge given them as abettors or at least accessory vnto the Iniury and damage done to the English, onely woemen ꝗ children to be sparingly seised, vules knowne to be some way guilty. And because it wilbe chargeable keepinge Indians in prisone, and if they should escape, they are like to proue more insolent, ꝗ dangerous after, it was thought fitt, that vpon such seasure, the delinquent or satisfaction be againe demanded, of the Sagamore or plantation of Indians guilty or accessory as before, and if it be denyed, that then the magistrates of the Jurisdicc͠on deliuer vp the Indians seased to the pty or pties indamaged, either to serue or to be shipped out ꝗ exchanged for Negroes as the cause will iustly beare. And though the Comissioners forsee that such severe (though iust proceedinge) may ꝓuoke the Indians to an vniust seasinge of some of ours, yet they could at present finde noe better meanes to ꝑserue the peace of the Colonies (all the forementioned outrag̀ ꝗ insolencies tendinge to an open war considered) onely they thought fitt, that before any such seysure be made in any plantac͠on of Indians the ensueinge declaration *be published ꝗ a copy of it given to the pticular Sagamo^{rs} ꝗ accordingly copies were given to Nipnesait, Namatayhue the 2 before mentioned Sachems. Dat. 7^{ber}. 15. 1646.

1646.

September.

*85

.

The Comissioners for the Vnited Colonies consideringe how peace wth righteousnes may be pursued betwixt all the English ꝗ the seuerall plantatious of the Indians, thought fitt to declare ꝗ publish, that as they will doe noe iniury to them, soe if any Indian or Indians of what plantac͠on soeuer, doe any wilfull damadge to any of the English Colonies, vpon proffe they will in a peaceable way require satisfaction, accordinge to the nature of the offence ꝗ damadge, but if any Sagamor, or plantac͠on of Indians after notice ꝗ due warninge entertaine, hide, ꝑtect, keepe, convey away or further the escape of any such offendor or offendors, the English will require satisfacc͠o. of such Indian Sagamore or Indian plantac͠ons, ꝗ if they deny it, they will right themselues as they may vpon such as soe maintaine them that doe the wronge, keepinge peace ꝗ all tearmes of amity ꝗ agreement wth all other Indians.

A letter from m^r Peeters, ꝗ another from William Morton one of the plantac͠ons at Pequatt were reade, wherein they complaine against Vncus for a plott ꝗc ꝗ for some iniurious ꝗ hostile insolencies comitted by him ꝗ his brother against Notewas Cooke ꝗ his man at the English plantation to the disturbance of the peace {c And by advice of the Comissioners, answeres were returned that Vncus was expected, if they sent any instrucc̄o̅ns to chardge him they should be heard. Vncus came and stayed certaine dayes before any of the English came or sent from Pequatt, wherevpon after inquiry { a large debate with Vncus the yssue was drawne vp in the ensueing writinge and vnder the Comissioñs hands given to Vncus.

Septemb: 14. 1646.

Whereas seuerall compl^ts haue beene made against Vncus for an assault made vpon Neckewash Cooke { his company at or neare the English Planta̅c̅o̅n at Pequatt, concerning wch with some other accusations not onely w^m Morton but m^r Peeters wrote lately to one of the Comissioners { by way of answere were acquainted that Vncus within 4. or 5. dayes was expected at New hauen vppon other occasions, { then the case might be heard betwixt them, Vncus came accordingly, but none *either from Nameoke or Seabrooke, The Comissioners therefore questioned Vncus in all the pticulars expressed in w^m Mortons letter : he acknowledged some miscarriages in vindicatinge his owne right soe neare the English plantations, { complayned of seuerall wrongs he had receiued, namely that diuerse of the Pequat{ formerly graunted him, were drawne from him vnder colloure of submitting to the English plantation at Pequat that Neckwash Cooke vpon some countenance { incouragem^t given by the said English, hunted within his proper limit{ without his leaue. And that Neckwash Cooke (the Narragenset and Nyanticke Indians not havinge pformed their Covenant{) should without the Comissioners knowledge be entertayned and maintayned against him as a freind to the English.

These things beinge considered, though the Comissioners would receiue nothinge against the English plantation in their absence, yet desiringe to prouide for their future peace { withall to maintaine Vncus in his iust right by Thomas Stanton the interpreter expressed themselues as followeth.

I   First that it was an error in Vncus to begin any quarrell with Neckwash Cooke to the disturbance of the publicke peace without consent of the English.

2   2.^ly that to doe it neare the English plantation was an offensiue affront and blameworthy : and the Comissioners required him to acknowledge his fault to that plantation (as he did to the Commissioners) { by promise to secure them from any such disturbance for the future.

3   Whereas compl̴t{ are brought against Vncus his brother for some insolent expressions or carriage, but neither the accusers or accused beinge

present the Comissions only advised Vncus that he take due order
therein.

The Comissioners acquainted Vncus with a declaracōn wᶜh they intend
to make to the Indians, that in case of any wilfull damadge done to any of
the English in these Colonies by any Indian or Indians vppon proffe they
will in a peaceable way require iust satisfaction But if any Sagamore or
Plantation of Indians after notice ℓ due warninge entertaine, hide, protect,
keepe, convey away, or further the escape of any such offendor or offendoʳs,
the English will require satisfaction of such Indian Sagamoʳs or Indian plantations, ℓ if they deny it, they will right themselues (as they may) vpon
such as so maintaine them who doe the wronge keeping peace ℓ all tearmes
of amity ℓ agreemᵗ with all other Indyans, wᶜh Vncus approued.

*The Comissioners assured Vncus that he pforminge the covenantℓ con-
cerninge the Pequatℓ, they will neither take any of them from him, nor allow
that they be withdrawne by any of the English plantacōns, till they haue
some further iust groundes, ℓ acquainted him therewith.

That the Comissioners haue not yet graunted any license to Neckwash
Cooke or any other of the Narragensett or Neanticke Indians to hunt
within his prop limitℓ, nor will they allow any English plantacōn to countenance any such disorderly huntinge, till vpon a due hearinge the Comissioners set some order therein.

6

The Comissioners thought it disorderly ℓ vnwarrantable for any English
plantation to entertaine Neckwash Cooke or any of the Narragenset or Neanticke Sagamors or their companies into a league, protection, or submission
vntill they haue fully performed all their covenantℓ with the Colonies, and
that the Comissioners haue considered ℓ ordered some thinge therein.

The 16. Sept: William Morton ℓ 3 Pequatℓ Indians came from mʳ
John Winthrops plantacōn, Vncus dismissed from the Comissioners, but not
gon from Newhaven was sent for, sundry questions were propounded and Iniuries chardged, but the Comissioners fownde noe cause to alter the former
writinge given him, onely a plott mencōed by mʳ Peeters was by wᵐ Morton chardged vpon him, namely that for some pcell of wampam, aboute 15.
fadome he should hire Wampushet a Pequat powowe now present, by himselfe or some other with a hatchett to wounde another Indian ℓ to lay it
vpon Neckwash Cooke, the Indian was accordingly hurt and Neckewash
Cooke at first chardged with it, but after the Pequatℓ Powow troubled in
conscience could haue no rest till he had discouered Vncus to be the author.
Wᵐ Morton being asked what witnes he had against Vncus answerd that an

Indian wooman had spoken as much, but whither she had heard it from Vncus, or onely from the Pequatt Powow he could not say: being further asked to whome the Pequat powowe had first chardged Vncus as guilty in the plott, he said it was to Robin an Indian who had serued Mr Winthrop, the whole euidence for ought appd, restinge vpon Waupushett. The Comissioners by Tho: Stanton required him to relate the story, wch he did but contrary to the expectation of William Morton (of the 2 Pequat(wch came with him, he cleared Vncus (cast the plott (guilt vpon Neckwash

*88

Cooke, (Robin *Mr Winthrops Indyan, (though Thomas Stanton had repeated to him all he had sayd, (the Comissioners ppounded seuerall questions, and wm Morton by order from the Comrs did the like, (though the other two Pequat(, whereof the one was Robins brother seemed much offended, (after sd Vncus had hired him to withdrawe (alter his chardge, yet he psisted (said Neckewash Cooke (Robin had giuen him a payre of breeches, (promised him 25. fadome of wampam to cast the plott vpon Vncus, (that the English plantacon (Pequat(knew it. The Comissioners abhorringe this diuillish falshoode (advisinge Vncus if he expected any favoure (respect from the English to haue no hand in any such designes or other vniust wayes, dismissed wm Morton (the Indyans.

Vncus now beinge gon (nothinge yet heard from the Narragenset (Nyanticke Indyans accordinge to theire covenant(, the Comissioners did seriously consider what course should be taken with them, they called to minde their breach of covent(in all the articles, that when aboue 1300 fadome of Wampan was due they sent (as if they wold put a scorne vpon the   ^   ) 20 fathome (a few old kettles.

That the Narragensets chardged the Nyanticks, and they the Narragensets, but both delude the Colonies. That the Nyantick(had sent 100. fathome of Wampam as a psent to the Governoure of the Mattachusets, promisinge to send what was due to the Colonies very speedily. Mr Winthrop would not accept the present, tould them they might leaue it with Cuchamakin, (when the covent(were fully pformed he would consider of it. But no payemt nor any thing tendinge to satisfaction since tendered, the Comissioners were alsoe informed, that the sd Sagamo's had taken contribuçön of wampam from their men, (by good euidence it appeared, that by present(of wampan they are practisinge with the Mohawkes, (with the Indyans in those part(, to engage them in some designe against the English (Vncus. All wch beinge duly considered with the former passag(mentioned in the printed declaraçön the last yeare, (the chardge they putt the Colonies to before these articles of peace were concluded, the Comissioners haue a cleare way open

to right themselues accordinge to iustice by war, yet to shew how highly they
prize peace with all men, ℭ pticularly to manifest their forbearance ℭ long
sufferinge to these Barbarians, it was agreede that first the forementioned present should be returned, ℭ that after that againe before any thinge should be
attempted against them a declaration *by some fitt messenger should be sent
from the Mattachusettℭ vnder the hands of all the Comissioners as followeth.

A declaration or instructions for

sent by the Comissioners of the Vnited Colonies, vzϡ, the Mat-
tachusettℭ, Plimouth, Connecticut ℭ Newhaven to Pessicus
Canonicus Janemo ℭ other Sagamors of the Narragensett ℭ
Nyanticke Indyans.

First you shall enforme the Sachems aboue menℭoed that the Comissioners from all the English Colonies who mett at Newhaven expected them
or their Deputies accordinge to an expresse article in the coven^ts made at
Boston the last yeare fully instructed to meete with Vncus that all differenceℭ
betwixt them might be fully heard and iustly ordered and yssued. Vncus
attended diverse dayes but none at all came from them, though they haue the
Articles by them ℭ though from the Mattachusettℭ they haue bene mynded of
the time soe that Vncus was forced to depart vnsatisfyed.

That in noe other parte they haue obserued the Covenantℭ wch solemnly
ℭ with much deliberation they made with the English Colonies . as .   **2**

Though they left hostages at Boston to bringe 4. of their children, yet
they neither brought any of their children within the time limited, nor haue
yet brought the right children named ℭ agreede.   **I**

whereas towards the greate chardge they had put the Colonies vnto in
defence of Vncus against their hostile assaultℭ vnjustly made, they should
haue paide 500 fadome of wampam in Septem: 1645. 500 fadome in De-
cemb : ℭ 500 fadome in May, they haue yet paid but 170 fadome in all.   **2**

They haue neither returned to Vncus the captiues, ℭ Canooes vnjustly
taken the last yeare, nor made him any satisfaction for his corne spoyled as
by coven^t they are engaged.   **3**

They haue not restored the Indyan fugitiues ℭ captiues fled from the
English, nor giuen any satisfaction for them, nor haue they paide the tribute
due for the Pequatℭ, who liue amonge them, nor any parte of it.   **4**

Lastly as appeares by good euidence, by presentℭ of wampam, they
haue beene practisinge with the Mohawkℭ ℭ other Indyans contrary to their
Covenantℭ; soe that the premises to all the Comissioners and Colonies doe

justly render them a pfidious ℓ treacherous people, and *accordingly in their owne season they should proceede against them, ℓ what ever the consequencℓ proue, themselues are the authors of it.

Sept. 15ᵗʰ lieftenant Godfrey returned from the Manattchoes ℓ brought 2 letters from the Dutch Governoure, the one in latine, the other in English, the latine translated hath these contents.

> To the most noble ℓ worthy Comissioners of the federated English met togeither at the Red Mounte, or New haven in new Netherlands, wᵐ Kieft Director ℓ the Senate of new Netherland doe send many salutations.

Yours dated the 5th Septemb: old style we receaued the 21. new style by your messenger to wᶜh we thincke sufficient to giue this shorte answere.

That the Inhabitants of Hartford haue deceiued you with false accusations as were easy to be euidenced by vs if it were now seasonable to produce our allegations wᶜh we can proue to be true by diuerse attestations as well of your owne Country men, as ours, togeither with other authenticke writinge, but that we may not seeme to be willing to evade you with vaine words, we shall at this time present you a few particulars, out of soe greate an heape, whereby, as by the claw you may iudge of the talants of the lyon, ℓ therfore passinge by their vsurpinge of our jurisdicčõn, ℓ of our proper grounde against possession solemnly taken by vs, ℓ our ꝑtestačõns formerly made, we doe say, that the bloude of our country men wrongfully shed by the inhabitantℓ of Hartford, and the sellinge of our domesticke beastℓ by them, doe sufficiently testify the equity of their proceedings ℓ therefore your prejudgemᵗ supported by this oath Creto Cextius, as if you should say Amen, Amen, seemes wonderfull to vs, ℓ done contrary to the modesty requisite in such an assemblie, who should allwaies keepe one eare for the other party.

,Soe far as concernes the Barbarian handmaide although it be apprehended by some that she is no slaue but a free woeman, because she was neither taken in war, nor bought with price, but was in former time placed with me by her parents for education, yet we will not suffer that she be wrongfully detayned, but whither he shall pay the damadge to her Mʳ. or she shalbe restored to him we will not suffer him that desires her for his wife to marry
*91   her, vntill she be lawfully babtised. *Concerning the breakinge in of our Agent vpon the watch at Hartford we truely conceiue that watches are appointed for the defence of townes against the violence of enemies, ℓ not for the hinderinge of freinds returne to their owne houses, ℓ therfore least

mischeifes happen, it were good to committ such a trust to skilfull men, ȝ
not to ignorant boyes who when they once finde themselues loaden with
armes, thincke they may alsoe lawfull cry out, etiam nos poma natamus.

Certainly when we heare the inhabitants of Hartford complayninge of
vs, we seeme to heare Esops wolfe complayninge of the lamb, or the admo-
nition of the younge man who cryed out to his mother chideinge wth her
neighboures, oh mother revile her, least she first take vp that practise against
you : But being taught by pcedent passages we recciued such an answere to
our Protest from the inhabitants of New hauen as we expected, the Eagle
allwaies despiseth the Beetle fly, yet notwithstandinge we doe vndauntedly
continue in our purpose of pursueinge our owne right by just armes and
righteous meanes, ȝ doe hope without scruple to execute the expresse
comands of our superiours.

To conclude we protest against all you Comissioners mett at the Red
Mounte as against breakers of the comon league, ȝ alsoe infringers of the
speciall right of the Lords, the States our superiours, in that ye haue dared
without expresse ȝ speciall Comission to hould yor generall meetinge within
the limitȝ of New Netherlande, these things are spoken from the duty of
our place, in other respectȝ we are yours.

WILLIAM KEIFT, by the Comaunde
of the Lord Director ȝ Senate
CORNE : TINHAVEIUS.

Amsterdam fort in
New Netherland the
22. Sept. 1646.

The other letter wrote in English was as followeth.

Worthy Gent.

Yo^{rs} of the 7^{t}h Septemb: I haue rec^d wherein you are pleased to
mention yor speakinge with Mr Whitinge concerninge some words spoken by
him ȝ mentioned in my letter to my honoured freind Mr Winthropp Gov-
erno^r: of the Mattachusetts, what I haue there chardged him with I haue it
vnder good testimony of his owne country men however, I shall rather ym-
pute it to his present passion then any pmeditated resolucõn ȝ alltogeither
forgett it. *Yo^r hono^{ble}: desires that all occasions of Discontentm^{ts} may be
remoued by the forbearinge of all threatninge ȝ pvokinge language on both
sides, ȝ that the sun of peace may more clearly shine amonge vs, I both
applaude ȝ desire.

*92

Whereas likewise you mention Mr Whitinges comp^{lt}: concerning a sentence of Corte passed here against him in his absence ȝ without any Attorney

to pleade for him, I cannot but apprehend it as a greate injury to my selfe in pticular, but cheifly to you, gent; that he should soe misinforme you, for in the first place he left Mr Dolling for his Agent, who pleaded his cause for him, ℓ what pces was then and there adwarded with the reasons ℓ groundℓ inducinge vs, if he had produced the Copy of the Sentence of Corte vnder our Secretaryes hand, I suppose you would haue beene very well satisfyed. Yet if he can further cleare the said cause by better Euidence I shall willingly graunte a review, ℓ doe that wch is just accordinge to that light God giues me.

    Concerninge debts due to him from any here, I shall according to justice ℓ the law of our Country doe him right

    Whereas I vnderstand there is somethinge ꝑtended to be due to him from our Agent Mr Dauid Provost, I suppose our ꝫd Agent shall giue such fayre satisfaction to m^r Hopkins, or Mr. Haynes in the said cause, that it wilbe clearly demonstrated to them, that it is more pretence then a just due. soe Gent. I shall take my leaue of you ℓ rest

Yo^rs in all officℓ of loue.

Fort Amsterdam 22th of   W^m. KEIFT.
Sept. 1646. S. N.

    To these letters the Comissioners thought meete to returne this ensueing answere.

    S^r. we haue lately rec^d by our messenger, 2 letters from you, the one in English, the other in Latine, of the forṁ though we close not in each pticular, we can in the generall make a further construcꝯon, in the latter we must professe our selues much vnsatisfyed, some pticulars, or the weight in them, you leaue vntouched in some you are misinformed : the Indyan mayde was taken in war ℓ for late miscarriages of a publick nature, was subiect to the justice of the *of the place, she flyes is receaued at your house ℓ detayned both from her m^r, ℓ from the magistrate, as by a writinge vnder the hands of your deputyes may appeare, ℓ from yor Ageut we are . informed that one of yours hath abused ℓ defiled her, such a practise we should condemne in one of ours with any vnmarryed, much more with an vnbabtised Indyan : what order you haue taken that she be returned, what satisfaction you   ^   for this wronge we heare not, We conceiue waches are in all places set to prevent inconveniencℓ ℓ mischeifℓ wch may be done by enemies, or disorderly persons, ℓ in all places a sober ℓ comely answere

*93

expected, he that shall draw and breake his weopen vpon a watch, neither attends his duty nor safety. Yo^r Agent ꝯ 4. more came in an hostile manner assaulted, strike ꝯ take away the teame ꝯ ladinge from a man peaceably following his occasions, who had onely legally sought satisfaction for damadge, to this you returne no answere, Vpon our second thoughts we conceiue these things to be vndoubtedly true, ꝯ to be vnsufferable disorders, we thougt you ouerstraine in exceptinge against that phrase (most certainely) ꝯ that without wronge to yo^{r}selfe you might haue spared that chardg of ymodesty, we conceiue you will hardly proue either by witnesses or writinge that our Confederats of Hartford haue deceiued vs by false complᵗts, for your other expressions, proverbs or allusions, we leaue them to yor better consideraꝯon you might indeed expect a faire ꝯ iust answere from our confederats of New haven wch we did ꝯ doe hope will giue you satisfaction, either here or in Europe, but we shall waite the yssue. Your conclusion though it seeme harsh to vs, agrees with your premises, ꝯ that we say no more, we haue more cause to protest against yor ꝑtestation, then you haue to be offended at o^r bouldenes in meetinge at Newhaven, ꝯ for ought we know, may shew as good Comission for the one, as you for the other, But our iust liberties being ꝑseru\ed we rest Yours ꝯč.

An English plantation being lately begun by Mr John Winthrop Junior at Pequat, a question grew to wch Colony the Jurisdicꝯon should belonge. The Comissioners for the Mattachusets ꝑpounded an interest by conquest the Comissioners for Connecticut, by patent, purchase ꝯ conquest. It was remembred that in a treaty betwixt them at Cambridg 1638. not perfected. A proposition was made that Pequat river in reference to the conquest, should be the bounds betwixt them, but Mr Fenuick was not then there to pleade the pattent *neither had Connecticute then any title to those lands by purchase or deed or gift from Vncus. But the plantaꝯon is on the west side of Pequat, and soe within the bounds at first propounded for Connecticut. The Com^{r}s joyntly agreed, that an English plantation there being well ordered may in sundry respectꝯ be of good vse to all the Colonyes, ꝯ thought fitt it should haue all encouragem^t, onely they conceiued, vnles hereafter the Mattachusetts shew better tytle, the Jurisdiction should belonge to Connecticute.

*94

A question beinge propounded aboutꝯ the interpretation of a passage in the Comissioners conclusions at Boston 1643. the Comissioners for Connecticute ꝯ New hauen joynctly (Mr Eaton ꝯ Mr Hopkins being present at those agitations) conceiue the sense is cleare, that all tracts or ꝑcell of lands are

P. 18.

thereby preserued to the Colony of Plimouth, except that possessed by the English or Indyans, who had then submitted to the Mattachusetts, but vpon what grounds it was done, vnles to ease Plimouth of chardg in Gortons businesse, or for that they thought the land questionable, or of smale value is not now remembred.

A question was ppounded by the Comissioners for Connecticut concerning an imposition layd on goods passinge by the Rivers mouth to sea, wch all the plantations on Connecticut River pay, cheifly to maintayne the fort for security & conveniency, onely Mr Pincham & Sprinckfield who haue in their pportion the same benefit refuse. The Comissioners thought it of waighty concernm^t to the plantations aboue, that the mouth of the River be secured : but Mr. Pincham being absent, & noe instruccons given from the generall Corte in the Mattachusets, the yssue and determination was respited till the Comissioners next meetinge.

Mr Pelham on behalfe of Richard Woddy and Mr Pincham by letter complayned of some theft& Comitted by some of the Narragensett Indyans, the like compl^t was alsoe made by Mr Browne in the behalfe of Wm Smith of Rehoboth but in the absence of the Indyans nothing could pcede.

According to former orders the nomber of males should now haue beene brought foorth from the seuerall Colonies & a true accounte should alsoe haue beene brought of all expenc& in the scuerall expeditions for the publicke safety, but the Mattachusetts & Plimouth being defectiue in one or both, nothing could be yssued with full *satisfaction, onely it appeared that Conecticute & Newhaven Collonies haue expended more then their pporcōns, namely Conecticut. 162^t. 3^s. 1^d at least, & Newhaven 71^t. 8^s. 7^d at least, as the accompts were represented with some disadvantage to them, wch monies shoulde haue beene p^d vnto them by the other Colonies some time since, It is therefore ordered that the Mattachusetts forthwith pay to Conecticute or their assignes. 136^t. 19^s. 11^d. & to New haven or their assignes 71^t. 8. 7^d, & that Plimouth pay vnto Conecticute or their assignes. 25^t. 4. 0^d. And that against the next meetinge the accompts be better ppared & brought in. And vpon consideration of souldiers dyett & other expences in wine, hott waters, powder & shott wherein any of the Colonies may either be puident or remisse to their owne or their neighboures damadge, it was now ordered, that no Collonies for such expenc& bring to acc°. aboue 6^s. a man p weeke according to the nomber of souldiers, onely meetings of service a due consideration may be had of the expenc& of powder & shott, & in this accompt boate hyre not to be included. And that no Colony bringe to accompt for the wages of any souldier aboue 6^s. p weeke, for officers not aboue the rate followinge vz&, a

Corporall 8ˢ. p weeke, a sergeant 10ˢ. an Ensigne 15ˢ. lieftenant 20ˢ. & for the Captaine not aboue 30ˢ p weeke.

Vpon serious consideration of the spreading nature of Error, the dangerous growth & effects thereof in other places & pticularly how the purity & power both of religion & of Ciuill order is already much complayned,* if not wholy lost in a parte of New England, by a licentious liberty graunted & setled, whereby many casting off the rule of the word, pfesse & practise what is good in theire owne eyes : And vpon information of what petitions haue beene lately putt vp in some of the Colonies, against the good & straite waies of Christ, both in the Churches & in the Comon Wealth, the Comissioners remembring that those Colonies for themselues & their posteritie did enter into this firme & perpetuall league, as for other respects so for mutuall aduise that the truth & liberties of the gospell might be preserved, & ppagated, thought it their duty seriously to Comend it to the care & consideration of each generall Corte within these Vnited Colonies that as they haue layd theire foundations & measured the temple of God, the worship and worshipps by that *straight Reed God hath putt into their hands, soe they would walke on & build vp (all discouragemᵗˢ & difficulties notwithstandinge) with an vndaunted heart & vnwearied hand, according to the same rules & patternes, That a due watch be kept & continued at the doores of Gods house, that none be admitted as members of the body of Christ, but such as hold foorth effectuall callinge & thereby vnion with Christ the head, & that those whome Christ hath receaued, & enter by an expresse covenᵗ to attend and obserue the lawes and dutyes of that spirituall Corporation, that Babtisme, the seale of the Covenant be administred onely to such members & their ymediate seed, that Anabaptisme, familisme, Antinomianisme & generally all errors of like nature wᶜh oppose, vndermine & slight either the scriptures, the Sabboth or other ordinanc& of God, & bring in & cry vp vnwarrantable Reuelations, inventions of men, or any carnall liberty, vnder a deceitfull colloure of liberty of conscience, may be seasonably & duly supprest, though they wish as much forbearance & respect may be had of tender conscienc& seeking light as may stand with the purity of religion & peace of the Churches. (The Comissioners of Plymouth desire further consideration concerninge this advise given to the generall Cort&.)

And lastly that some serious pvision be speedily made against oppression whither in Comodities, or wages, against excesse & disorder in apparrell, drincke & all other loose and sinfull miscarriages not fitt to be named amongst Christians, by wᶜh the name of oʳ holy God is much dishonoured, & the

[*Corrupted, Mass.Arch ves, vol. 2, 3 9.]

*96

1 6 4 6. Churches of Christ in those part℈ much reproched, as if they were strict in
their formes onely, or had respect onely to one of the tables of Gods law,
September. their fruites in reference to the other, beinge nothinge better then the wild
vines or brambles in the wildernes. Yf thus we be for God he will certainely be with vs, And though the God of the world (as he is stiled) be
worshipped, and by vsurpation sett vpon his throane in the maine ℈ greatest
pt of America, yet this small parte ℈ portion may be vindicated as by the
right haud of Jehovah, ℈ justly called Emmanuells land.

*97   *The foregoing conclusions were agreed vpon by the Com⁷³. of the vnited
Colonies. 18. Sept. 1646, ℈ subscribed.

New Hauen. 24. Sept. 1646

Concerninge the Narragensett ℈ Nyanticke Indyans when first the
present is returned ℈ in a fitt season after the declaration drawne by the
Comissioners sent ℈ interp̄ted to them, yf yet they attend not the Colonies
iust satisfacc̃on or if by any insolent ℈ hostile carriage they giue further
pvocation, It is now agreed, that in May, or any other fitt season vpon
convenient warninge from the Mattachusetts, with the consent of the Comissioners for Plimouth all the Comissioners for the Colonies doe meete at Plimouth to consider of some further course to secure our owne peace ℈ to bringe
the Narragensetts ℈ their confederates into a better frame.

Whereas the Colonies at present affoorde some help towards the maintenance of some poore schollers in the Colledge at Cambridge in the Mattachusetts, It was propounded ℈ thought fitt that some course be taken with the
parent℈ ℈ wᵗh such schollers themselues (as the case may require) that when
they are furnished with learning, in some competent measure, they remoue
not into other Countries, but improue their pt℈ ℈ abillities for the service of
the Colonies, ℈ for this purpose the Comissioners for the Mattachusetts were
desired to advise with the generall Courte ℈ Elders there for the orderinge
such a course, ℈ how such schollars may be imployed ℈ incouraged, when
they leaue the Colledge either in New plantations, or as schoole mᵗs. or in
ships, till they be called and fitted for other service.

Whereas our good God hath from the first done great thing℈ for his
people in these Colonies in sundry respect℈ worthy to be written in our
heart℈ with a deepe ℈ charected impression not to be blotted out ℈ forgotten
℈ to be transmitted to posterity, that they may know the Lord, ℈ how he hath
gloryfyed his grace ℈ mercy in our foundations ℈ beginnings, that they also

may trust in him, and walke with a right foote before him with out warping (declining, It is desired by the Comissioners, that all the Colonies (as they may) would collect (gather vp the many speciall puidenc(of God towards them, since their arrivall (setling in these part(, how he hath made roome for them, how his hand hath bene with them in laying their foundations in church (comon wealth, how he hath cast the dread of his people (weake in themselues) vpon the Indians *scattered their counsells, broken their plotts (attempts (continued our peace (notwithstanding their insolencies rage and malice) made gratious pvisions for vs, (in all respect(hath bene a sun (shield to vs, and that memorialls beinge made, they may be duly comunicated (seriously considered, that no thinge be mistaken, but that history may be compiled according to truth with due weight by some able and fitt man appointed therevnto.

THEOPH: EATON president.

HERBERT PELHAM.　　TIMOTHY HATHERLY.

JO: ENDECOTT.　　JO· BROWNE.

STEPHEN GOODYEARE.　　JO: HEYNES,　ED: HOPKINS.

ℭAt a meeting of the Comissioners for the vnited Colonies of New England held at Boston 26. July 1647

an order of the generall Corte of the Mattachuset℥ da℥ 26. of the third moneth 1647 was presented, whereby it appeared, That Thomas Dudley ℓ John Endecot esq᷍s were chosen Comissioners for that Jurisdiction for this present yeare, ℓ weer invested with full power to treate ℓ conclude of all things according to the tenure of the Articles of combination concluded at Boston. 19th of the third moneth 1643.

A like order for the Jurisdiction of New Plimouth dated the first of the 4th moneth 1647. was read investing mʳ William Bradford ℓ Mʳ John Browne with like power as Comissioners to treate ℓ conclude accordinge to the tenure of the said articles.

An order of the generall Corte of Connecticute was alsoe presented ℓ read da℥. 28th. of the 4th moneth 1647. appointing Mʳ Edward Hopkins ℓ Cap℥ John Mason to the foremenₒ̃ned service ℓ investing them with full power according to the Articles of Confederation.

A like order for the generall Corte of Newhavens Jurisdiction da℥ 27. October. 1646 inuesting Mʳ Theophilus Eaton, ℓ Stephen Goodyeare with the like power according to the tenure of the said articles for the yeare ensueing was now alsoe read.

Thomas Dudley Esqʳ. was chosen President for this meeting.

The Comissioners by experience findinge that the occasions of the Colonies some times require their meeting℥ ℓ consultations before the ordinary time appointed by yᵉ articles of Confederation in the 7th moneth   And that at such times the ordinary meetinge in Sept: may well be spared (the generall occasions of the Colonies being dispatchid) wᶜh yet seemes by the Articles ought necessarily to be attended euery yeare, it was agreed, that it be propounded to the seuerall generall Court℥, that it may be left to the liberty of the Comissioners for the time beinge to order the time of meetinge, as the occasions of the Colonies may require : And to forbeare the ordinary time of the meetinge in Sept. as they see cause, Provided there be a meetinge once every yeare.

Consented vnto

*And whereas the Articles of combination seemes to require the meeting togeither of the whole nomber of the Com̃ʳs. before they can consult or conclude of any occasions wᶜh concerne the Colonies, wᶜh may be very p̃iudiciall to the publike weale, not onely the liues of men after they are on their journeys (beinge lyable to hazzards) whereby their meeting with the rest may be p̃vented, but other occasions may alsoe intervene to hinder the same, It was agreed that it alsoe be recomended to the generall Cortℓ that when any meetinge is agreed vpon, whither ordinary or extraordinary (all the Comissioners chosen by the seuerall jurisdic̃c̃ons having had seasonable notice thereof,) yf no more then 6. come, they may meete consult, ℓ in (case •they all agree) conclude such things as concerne the seũall Colonies, as if the whole nomber were togeither.

One principall cause of the Comissioners meetinge togeither at this time being to consider what course should be held with the Narragansett Indyans, ℓ their confederatℓ who haue not onely broken their Covenᵗℓ, solemnly made at Boston in Aᵒ. 1645. But as the Comissioners haue bene enformed credibly, haue bene plottinge ℓ by p̃sents of wampam, ingageinge the Indyans rounde aboute to combine with them against the English Colonies in war. It was thought fitt to send Thomas Stanton, Benedick Arnold, and Scargeant Waite, as messengers to them, And that there might be better assurance of a true returne the Comissioners gaue Thomas Stanton as interpreter the oath ℓ instructions followinge.

> You shall fully ℓ truely according to the best of your abillities ℓ knowledge in the Indian language expresse the message now sent by you to Pessackℓ ℓd from the Com̃rs of the vnited Colonies, and in like manner make returne of what answere you receaue from them or other considerable passages you meete with according to the instruc̃c̃ons here given you this 27. July. 1647.

Tho: Stanton you are hereby desired to goe with what speed you may, to Pessackℓ the cheife Sachem of the Narragensetts, as alsoe to Nenegrate ℓ Webetamuk ℓ deliver to them in reference to themselues ℓ all their confederatℓ in the Indyan tounge (as neare as may be) the message hereafter written, in the words *wherein it is expressed, as sent vnto them from all the Comissioners of the Vnited Colonies now mett at Boston in the Mattachusetℓ, And you are to bring backe to vs with all conuenient spÆede their answere ℓ resolu̾c̃ons with what other considerable passages you meete with either from Pessackℓ or any other considerable Sachem Counsellʳ, Captaine or Indyans.

1 6 4 7.

July.

The vnited Colonies haue now neare 2 yeares waited for the pformance of the Covenᵗ made at Boston by the Narragensett Sachems in the seuerall partᶜ concerninge the English ᶜc but haue founde hitherto nothing intending to satisfaction. The last yeare they should haue mett the Comissioners at Newhaven, Vncus then attended, but they neither come nor sent. The Comissioners therfore now assembled at Boston expect them all with full satisfaction to the seuerall foremen∞ed ingagemᵗᶜ, Vncus is appointed to meete them here ᶜ expected daily, For their incouragemᵗ the Comissioners hereby ꝑmise full safety that they shall come ᶜ returne without danger from the English Colonies yf they refuse or delay, they intend to send no more, but to proceede hereafter as they shall see cause.

The 31ᵗʰ. July Tho: Stanton returned with Pessackᶜ answere as followinge. Pessackᶜ being charged for not meetinge the Comissioners at New haven the last yeare, his answere was, he had no warninge. It is true said he I haue broken my Covenᵗ these 2 yeares, ᶜ it is ᶜ hath bene yᵉ constant greife of my spirit. 2ˡʸ. the reason why he doth not come at this time is, because he hath beene sick ᶜ is now sick, had I bene but pretty well (said he) I would haue come to them. 3ˡʸ. he saith he hath sent his full minde by Nenegrate ᶜ what Nenegratt shall doe concerning his businesse he will stand to it : he saith alsoe, that he hath sent Powpynamett and Pomumskᶜ to goe ᶜ heare ᶜ testifie that he hath betrusted his full minde with Ninegratt. 4ˡʸ. he doth say when he made his covenᵗ he did it in feare of the Army that he did see, and though the English kept their covenᵗ with him there and let him goe from them, yet the Army was to goe to Narragensett ymediatly ᶜ kill him there, Therefore said the Comissioners sett to your hands to such and such thinges or els the Army shall goe forth to the Narragensetts.

Mcyanno answered that at this springe he did deliver his minde to Nenegrett, ᶜ what he did or doth he will stand to it.

*102

*alsoe he said if Nenegrett shall make any other or new Covenᵗ or agreemᵗ with the English Sachems he will stand to it.

    THO: STANTON.   BENEDICT ARNOLD.

In which answere the Comissioners founde seuerall passagᶜ of vntruth ᶜ guile ᶜ were vnsatisfyed.

First Mʳ Pelham ᶜ Mʳ Hopkins by Benedict Arnold at the latter end of the third moneth 1646 minded Pesseckᶜ ᶜ his company of the meeting at New haven, ᶜ the time when the time should be, ᶜ they promised to come or to send their messengers thither.

Thomas Stanton vpon his best observation could not discerne any sick- 2^{ly}
nes, or other indisposition of body to hinder his trauell.

after covenants haue bene soe solemnly made ℓ hostages given, ℓ a   3
small pte of the wampam payd, ℓ all the rest due, now to pretend feare is
a vaine ℓ an offensiue excuse.

August. 3ᵈ. Ninegratt with some of the Nyantick Indians ℓ two of
Pessacks men came to Boston, ℓ desiring Mr John Winthrop that came from
Pequatt plantation might be present, they were admitted.   The Comissiõns
asked Ninegratt for whome he came whither as a publick pson on the behalfe
of Pessacks and the rest of the Narragensettℓ confederates, or onely for
himselfe as a pticular Sagamore, he at first answered, that he had spoke with
Pessacks. but had no such Comission from him, he added there had not
beene so good agreemᵗ betwixt Pessacks ℓ himselfe as he desired, but by
Mr John Winthrops testimony, by the answere Tho: Stanton ℓ Benedict
Arnold brought from Pessackℓ ℓ by the witnesse of Pessackℓ two men, it
appeared to the Comissioners, that what ever formallity might be wanting in
Pessacks expressions to Ninegratt, yet Pessack had fully ingaged himselfe to
stand to whatsoever Ninegratt should conclude.   The Comissioners therefore
asked Ninegratt, whence it proceeded that the Narragensett confederates (of
wᶜh him selfe was one) had neither paid the wampan to the English Colonies,
nor pformed any other of their Covenᵗℓ, either with the English or with
Vncus.   Ninegratt first pretended ignorance as if he had not knowne what
covenantℓ had beene made, he was tould that one of his men, as his deputy
was *present at the treaty ℓ vnder writ the Covenantℓ that Pessackℓ ℓ   *103
Canonicus sonne with the rest affirmed that what they ℓ his agents did conclude, Ninegratt had promised to stand vnto, That they had a Copy of the
Covenantℓ in parchmᵗ, ℓ had or might haue Mr. Wᵐs help at all times to
interprete them, there could therefore be no truth in his answere.

Ninegratt asked for what the Narragensettℓ should pay so much 2^{ly}
wampam, he knew not that they were indebted to the English, he was
answered that the Narragensetℓ had greatly broken their former Covenantℓ
with the English, ℓ contrary to their agreemᵗ ℓ engagemᵗ, they had made war
vpon Vncus, wounded and slain diuerse of his men, taken captiues, seased
some of his Conooes, and spoiled much of his Corne, by wᶜh hostile outrages they had constrayned the English at their great chardges to send men
for Vncus defence.   That the Comissoners for all the Colonies meetinge at
Boston on this occasion sent messengers to the Narragensett Sachem, But
instead of iust satisfaction, their messengers were slighted, ℓ yll vsed, ℓ
Ninegrate himselfe vsed threatninge ℓ insolent language, he tould the mes-

sengers that by the meetinge at Hartford they knew the Comissioners would endevoure to compose matters, ҁ to setle a peace betwixt them ҁ Vncus, but they were resolued to war, nor would they enquire who began war, they would carry it on. ҁ nothing but Vncus head should end it, ҁ if the English did not withdraw their garrisons from the defence of Vncus, they would heape vp their Cattle as high as their wigwams, ҁ an Englishman should not step out of the doores to pisse, but they would kill him.   Ninegrat not able to deny this charge, pretended that the English messengers provoked him, but that appeared a false ҁ weake excuse, he lastly affirmed that the some was soe great, that the Narragensetts had not wampam enough to pay it, but that satisfyed not, it being well knowne to the Comissioners, that the Narragensetts are a greate people, ҁ can raise a greater quantity of wampam vpon a shorte warninge when they please : Ninegrate herevpon asked, what wampam had beene already p^d, vpon the Coven^t ҁ ҁ how the reckoninge stood, he was answered that Pessacks first sent 170 fathome of wampan wch was rec^d in part of payem^t, after he sent some kettles ҁ aboute 15. fathome of

*104

wampam wch beinge *a contemptible some was refused, ҁ that the narragensett messengers had sould the kettles to Mr Shrimton a brasier in Boston at

The value of wampam.

12^d p ₺, they weighinge 285^t. came to 14^t. 5^s but the Indian messenger presently rec^d 20^s in pt, the rest with the mentioned wampam amountinge to 4^t. 4^s. 6^d the left in the brasiers hand, in all amounted to 17^t. 9^s. 6^d. wch hath beene since attached by Richard Woddy for goods stollen from him by a Narragensett Indian.   Ninegrate was not satisfyed with the attachm^t, ҁ affirmed that neither the kettles nor wampam did belonge to Pessacks himselfe, nor to the Indian that had stollen the goods, ҁ y^t they were left for the Comissioners in pt of payem^t ҁ so must be reckoned,   The Comissioners thought it not fitt to presse the attachm^t, but reckoned the kettles ҁ wampam at 70 fathome ҁ acknowledged the receipt of 240 fathome, besides a pcell of Wampam sent by Ninegrate himselfe to the Governoure, whither as a present to him, or in pte of payem^t to the Colonies, he was wished to expresse, togeither with the quantity he sent, because the said wampam then apprehended to be a present was not accepted by the Governoure : But in trust left in the hands of Cutchamaquin who vpon a message from the Comissions had lately brought in 2 girdles with a string of wampam all wch himselfe rated at 45 fathome, affirminge he had rec^d no more except 8^s. wch he had vsed, ҁ would repay.   Ninegrate tould the Comissioners that he had sent 30 fathome of black and 45. fathome of white in value togeither 105 fathome, that he left it to the Governoures discretion whither he would take it as a present, or as pte of the debt : but being pressed to cleare the question himselfe, he answered his tounge should not belye his heart, let the debt be satisfyed as it may, he intended it as a present to the Governoure, He alsoe affirmed he sent no girdles, it was all in strung wampam white ℰ black in different ꝑptions as before. Herevpon Cutchamaquin was sent for ℰ before Ninegrate questioned for his vnrighteousnes and falshood, he at first psisted, ℰ added to his lyes, but was at last convinced by Ninegrate ℰ his messengers who then brought the present, ℰ was now heere that the wampam for the Governoure was 105. fathome, besides wᶜh Ninegrate had sent Cutchamaquin. 10. fathome for himselfe.

These things being largly debated, Ninegrate was wished to consider ℰ advise with the Narragensettℰ deputy ℰ to giue their full answere the next day *according to wᶜh the Comissioners would resolue ℰ ꝓceede. The next day Ninegrate with the deputies for Pessack appeared, Ninegrett tould the Comissioners that before he came he doubted the burthen of the busiuesse would lye vpon him, Pessackℰ having fayled him in what he should haue done ℰ now he fownde what he feared yet vpon due consideration of former passages with the Covenᵗℰ made at Boston Aᵒ. 1645. he was resolued to giue the Colonies due satisfaction in all things, adding that he would forthwith send some of his men to the Narragensett ℰ Nyanticke Indyans to gather vp the residue of wampan yet behinde, that in 3 dayes he hoped to haue an answere what they would doe ℰ in 10 dayes at furthest he conceiued the wampan might be here, that himselfe resolued to stay at Boston till it came, And soe he would ꞓtify the Narragensett confederates : But if the collection of wampan should falle shorte of the whole some due, he desired some for-bearance, assuring them the residue should be shortly payd, ℰ they should see his reallity in keepinge Covenᵗℰ ℰ tearmes of amity with the English : where-with the Comissioners were well satisfyed for the present, hopinge they should finde answerable pformance ℰ Ninegrate sent away his messengers.

*105

Whereas a question propounded the last yeare at New haven concerninge an ymposition laide vpon goods passing through the mouth of Connecticute river to sea was respited to this meeting, the Comissioners for Connecticute desired the same might now be considered ℰ yssued. And the Comissioners for the Mattachusettℰ did therevpon deliuer in writinge certaine reasons from the generall Corte of that jurisdiction against the said imposition wᶜh were as followeth.

At the generall Corte at Boston. 4ᵗʰ. 9. moneth. 1646 the Corte having considered the controuersy betwixt the Jurisdiction of Hartford vpon Conecticute ⁅ the inhabitant⁅ of Sprinckfield vpon the same River touchinge either the purchase of the Fort ⁅c at the Rivers mouth, or the payem⁴ of such Customes as is or shalbe imposed vpon them towards the maintenance of the same, doth declare its judgem⁴ as followeth.

First they conceiue that the Jurisdiction of Hartford hath not a legall power to force any inhabitant of another Jurisdiction to purchase any forte or other lands out of that Jurisdiction without their consent.

2ˡʸ
*106

*They conceaue that it were injurious to require a custome to the maintaining of such a forte, wᶜh is not vsefull to such of whome it is demanded.

3

They thincke it very vnequall for them to impose a custome vpon the freinds ⁅ confederates, who haue not more benefit of the Riuer by exporting and importinge of goods, then strangers of another nation where there they liue wᵗhin Hartford Jurisdicⁿ pay none.

4

The propoundinge ⁅ standinge vpon an imposition of Custome to be paid to the Rivers mouth by such as were, or are within our Jurisdiction, hindered our confederation aboue 10 yeares, And there was never any paid to this day, now to impose it vpon any of ours after our confederation will putt vs to new thoughts.

5

It seemes to vs very hard that any of our Jurisdicⁿ should be forced to such a disadvantage as will necessarily in thrall their posterity by imposing such rates ⁅ customes as will either constraine them either to departe their habitations, or weaken their estates, especially when as they with the first tooke possession of the River, ⁅ were at greate chardge at buildinge ⁅c wᶜh if they had foreseene would not there haue planted.

6.

Yf Hartforde Jurisdiction shall make vse of this power ouer any of ours, we conceiue we haue the same power to imitate them in the like kinde wᶜh we desire may be forborne on both sides.

p the Corte.

INCREASE NOWELL secr:

Vnto wᶜh Mʳ Hopkins (some respite beinge given him to consider of the same) delivered in writinge the answere followinge.

A shorte answere to the reasons propounded by yᵉ genñall Corte of the Mattachusetts for Springfield not payinge of the imposition at Seabrook forte presented to the Comissioners of the Vnited Colonies. 27. July - 1647.

The first argument seemed (at least to vs) to laboure of a greate mistake in reference to the case in hand (to omit all other iust exceptions that *might be made against that affirmation) and doth not touch the present question, wch is, whither such an imposition be lawfull ⟨ regular, bottomed vpon a foundation of equity ⟨ righteousnes, ⟨ not to what vses ‸ imþuem^t, the meanes raised vpon the imposition is put, for if there be sufficient grounde ⟨ reason for the imposition, that it transgresse not a rule of righteousnes in regarde of the thinge itselfe, not exceeding a rule of moderation in regarde of the quantity it concernes not the pty that payes to inquire after, or call to acc^o. for the imployem^t of the monies raised by ye imposition therefore the further answere it might be absolutely denyed that wch is imposed to be p^d by Springfielde as they passe, is to purchase lands or forte.

The second, as it is a position in itselfe nakedly considered seemes at least to lay most of the goverm^t of Europe vnder the guilt of injustice, yet because it hath an appearance of an equitable consideration in it, we are content the yssue of the present difference may lye there, for we affirme the forte mentioned hath beene for nigh 12 yeares past, is at present, ⟨ may be still for the future, vsefull to that plantation, ⟨ yet not j^d p^s by them towards it to this very day.

The third is but a presumption, ⟨ if it had any cleare foundation, yet the comparison is not equall.

The fowrth ever since the first readinge of it hath beene a reall troble to our thought⟨, labouringe of so apparant mistakes, both in the one pte of it ⟨ in the other, wch makes vs hartily wish that we may be all conscientious carefull that our publicke record⟨ may carry such euidence of truth, that those who desire to take advantages may not haue any just occasions given them, for whereas it is said the combination was hindred aboue 10. yeares by the meanes þpounded, if a due consideration be had of it, it will appeare, it was not aboue 5. yeares from the mentioned agitation for combination, ⟨ the conclusion of this present confederation the one beinge in June. 1638. the other agreed vpon in May 1643. ⟨ whereas it is affirmed that the þpounding and standing vpon an imposition of custome at the Riuers mouth hindered the combination soe many yeares, *it shall (if need) be made appeare by the oath of those who were imployed in that service, that they were soe far from stiffly standinge vpon such an imposition, y^t they did not soe much as propounde it, as it is there expressed, nor could they in reason doe it, the townes haueinge no interest in, nor relation to the forte at that time.

The fifth carrieth not y^t strength of reason with it as to compell our vnderstandinge to fall in therewith for what inthralement such an imposition season, that whatever conference hath formerly passed about the custome or imposition at Seabrooke, there never was any setled or demanded of any of the plantations, till now of late, ℓ from the first day that any of the plantations vpon that Riuer haue paid it, hath vpon the same grounds beene demanded ℓ expected of ℓ from Springfield, That it is no impeachmᵗ of any liberty granted by patent to the Mattachusettℓ that Springfield seated vpon the River of Conecticut, doe beare a moderate ℓ equall pt of charges whither of scouring any parte of that River, or Rivers mouth (if there should be occasion) or in making or maintayninge such a forte as is in question to secure the passage to and fro, that the imposition in question is but the payemᵗ of 2^d p bushell for corne, and about jᵈ p ⁱ for beaver passing out through yᵉ *the* mouth of that River, and therefore seemeth a moderate charge in reference to the custome propounded, ℓ no matter of iust greiuance or discouragemᵗ to the plantations themselues, ther setled

*The ℘misses being weighed ℓ considered with all due tendernes ℓ respects to the ~~induceinᵗ~~ᴵⁿᵗʳᵉˢⁱᵉⁿˢℓ the s̄d Comissiofs for Plimouth ℓ New haven doe conceiue ℓ conclude   *110

First that Springfield doe henceforward from time to time giue in to Connecticute or the Agent or agentℓ a true note or accompt of all Corne, ℓ beaver they or any of them ship, or carry out through the mouth of that Riuer to sea, to pay or desposet into their hands after the rate of 2^d. p bushell for corne, ℓ 20ˢ p hogshead for beaver soe exported.   I

that the mentioned imposition be neither at any time hereafter raised, nor increased vpon any of the inhabitantℓ of Springfield, without just ℓ necessary cause to be first approued ℓ allowed by the other Colonies, nor continued longer then the forte in question is maintayned, ℓ the passage as at present thereby secured.   2

That at the next meetinge of the Comissioners any Deputy from the Mattachusetts Colony, or from Springfield plantation, shall haue liberty further to ℘pound or obiect as they see cause against the present imposition, wᶜh according to the nature ℓ prop weight of the matter alleadged, shalbe duly heard ℓ considered without any disadvantage from the conclusion now made in the premisses.   3

A petition was presented by Mʳ Henry Dunster ℘sident of Harvard colledg to the Comissioners wherein he desires their resolution in these ensuing querees.

Whether you be willing to submitt the youth of your Colonies that be   I

1647. or shalbe students so far to the Colledg Discipline administred by the President ℓ fellowes ℓ in cases arduous, by the advice of the ouerseers, that what-
July. soeuer punishm^t shalbe inflicted for the demerits, according to the lawes of
the said Colledg shall no waies infringe any priuiledge or honourable exhibition from your Colonies to the Colledg, ℓ whither you doe not giue your
approbation to the said lawes.

2   2ly. whereas vpon the seasonable motion of Mr Tho: Shepheard, the seū-
all Colonies agreed firmely to contribute to the furtherauce of learning in the
*111 Colledg, the disposall whereof hath wholy beene *left to me hitherto, wherein
I haue allready fownde some cases difficult to my selfe, ℓ wch may be dangerous in time ensueing to others, vnles by your counsells they be regulated,
therfore haue I thought it necessary to propound to yor wisedome these
following questions.

I   whereas that way is by free contributions wherein euery Colony, Towne,
ℓ family take themselues to be at liberty to giue or withould, yf therfore some
Colonies or townes in them shall giue nothinge, yet out of the said places
well deserving schollers shall come, whither then these shalbe as capable of
the s̄d contributions, as such as come from other Colonies that doe contribute
liberally and consequently, if these supplies shalbe extended to schollars coming from forraine places, as old England, Virginia and the like.

2   2^{ly}. whither in any case you giue way that any of the s̄d supplies be
diverted from the Society for the maintenance of schoole schollars, ℓ if soe in
what cases.

3   3^{ly}. whither we shall haue respect in the disposall of the said contributions to all the schollars in geñall, (as by maintenance of Comon officers or
the like) or especially to such as are poore pious ℓ learned the three vsuall
qualifications looked at in such cases, and whither any scholler discontinuinge
from the Colledg aboue a moneth shall haue his exhibition continued.

4   4^{ly}. whither any schollers that haue had these exhibitions, shall accounte themselues soe ingaged to stay in the Country, as that they may not
goe away without offence, ℓ if soe, then what way they may disingage
themselues.

5   5^{ly}. seeing the contributions of the Colonies haue already amounted to
aboue 50^t. p annū. And if the first proposition of j s. a family were attended,
they would amounte to much more, whither therefore if the said exhibitions
were collected by some faithfull officers, counstable or the like ℓ p̃sented to
the generall Cortes, or their betrusted in the said Colonies, ℓ thereof a fitt
*112 p̃portion as themselues shall see good, allotted to the colledge 8^t. *p Añ for a

schollarshipp ℓ 16.ᵗ p añ for a fellowship ℓ the rest for the maintenance of
schollars at the grammar schoole in the plantaãõns where these collections are
made the said course would be more honourable ℓ orderly to the Collonies ℓ
colledge ℓ more satisfactory to the people, when they shall see how their giftℓ
are bestowed ℓ how themselues may reape the fruite of them both at home
ℓ abroade.

Sixtly whither it is expected that pious dilligent and learned Graduatℓ   6
should be elected fellowes, as emergent occasion shall require, ℓ that then
they should haue for their encouragemᵗ the stipend due from such schollars as
are vnder their tuition, wᶜh for the present is a considerable parte of the
Presidents maintenance. therfore we humbly entreate you to state, what you
thincke to be a meete allowance for the President ℓ whence it shall arise.

Seaventhly seing from the first euill contrivall of the Colledg buildinge   7
there now ensues yearely decayes of the rooff, walls ℓ foundation, wᶜh the
study rentℓ will not carry forth to repaire, Therefore we present it to your
wisedome to propounde some way to carry an end to this worke.

Eighthly seinge the publicke library in the Colledg is yet defectiue in all   8
manner of bookes, especially in law, phisicke, Philosophy ℓ Mathematickℓ,
the furnishinge whereof would be both honourable and proffitable to the
Country in generall ℓ in speciall to the schollars, whose various inclinations
to all professions might thereby be incouraged ℓ furthered, we therfore humbly entreate you to vse such meanes as your wisdomes shall thincke meete
for supply of the same.

Ninthly seing it wilbe of concernemᵗ ℓ incouragement to the Studentℓ,
that the degrees here taken may be so accounted in England ℓ we are informed of the readines of some Masters of Colledges there to entertaine ℓ
pmote such a motion, we therefore desire yoʳ advise and furtherance in this
matter. So prayinge for the blessing of the Lord vpon all your consultations for the welfare of the vnited Colonies I humbly take my leaue ℓ rest

Yoʳ willing servant

HENRY DUNSTER.

*The answere of the Comissioners to the former petition ℓ queres so   *113
far as concernes the Colonies in joynct respects.

First they conceiue that all who send any youthes to the Colledg doe,
Eo facto, submit ℓ leaue them to the Colledg discipline, as is vsuall in such
cases in all placℓ in Europe.

2ⁱʸ. they apprehend it very equitable, that those Colonies ℓ places wᶜh
doe contribute or are most inlarged therein, should be first attended, when any

of theirs are equally capable of the releife affoorded thereby w^{ith} others, though they would alsoe that deserving youthes from other places (recommended from such Colonies that doe contribute) b*ut* not neglected.

3^{ly}. they doe not thincke it fitt that any of the s̄d supplies be diverted to the maintenance of Grammar schoole schollars, the seuerall plantations making ꝑvision in those kindes within the seuerall Jurisdictions.

4^{ly}. The supplies graunted by the seuerall Collonies were first intended for the support ꝑ encouragem^{t} of poore pious ꝑ learned youthes, and it is desired these ends may cheefly be attended in the disposall thereof, onely if no such youthes be present, it may be imployed for the Comon advantage of the Colledge, ꝑ if any schollar shalbe absent in a disorderly way aboue a moneth at one time they iudge   ˄

5^{ly}. It is apprehended by the Comissioners that those who haue benefitt by the contributions of the Collonies should be engaged to attend the service of ye country vpon tender of imploym^{t} ꝑ maintenance sutable to their condition ꝑ the state of the Country, but such tender being made in case they doe not acquiese in what is presented, but for greater outward advantagꝑ or other respectꝑ chuse to depart, they should be engaged in convenient time to repay what they have rec^d, from the Colonies.

6^{ly}. The Comissioners ꝑmise with concurrent endeavours to promote the contributions accordinge to the former ꝑpositions, but doe not iudge it meete to put it into any other frame.   The other ꝑticulars *mentioned belonge properly to this Jurisdiction wherein the Comissioners will not intermeddle, but referr the consideration thereof to the wisedome and piety of the generall Corte for this Collony.

> The question concerninge the Jurisdiction of the English plantation lately setled on the west side of Pequatt River was againe taken into consideration by the Comissioners.

Mr. John Winthrop now present exprest himselfe as more indifferent, but affirmed that some of the plantation sate downe there in reference to the goverment ꝑ in expectation of large priviledges from the Mattachusetts ꝑ should be much disappointed if that plantation fall and be setled vnder any other jurisdiction.

The Comissioners considering what passed at New haven last yeare ꝑ that in all the Colonies though title to land may be seuerall waies aquired, yet Jurisdiction goeth constantly with the Pattent, they tould Mr John Winthrop that they doubted not, but Conecticute would tenderly consider ꝑ affoord

such priuiledges as may suite a plantation soe remote, but concluded that the
Jurisdiction of that plantation doth ℓ ought to belonge to Conecticut.

A Petition in the name of many Pequattℓ was p̃sented by M^r
John Winthrop to the Comissioners as followeth.

The humble petition of Casmamon and Obechiquod in the name ℓ
behalfe of other Pequatts now dwelling at Namyok, humbly sheweth.
That whereas our Sachems ℓ people haue done very ill against the English form̃ly for wch they haue justly suffered ℓ beene rightfully conquered by
the English, we yor humble petitioners, who had no conseut nor hand in shed-
ding the English bloud, but by the advise of Necquash fled from our country,
being promised by Necquash that the English should not hurt vs if we did
not ioyne in war against them, doe humbly beseech the Com̃^{rs} to take vs
vnder the subjection of the English, and appointe vs a place where we may
liue peaceably vnder the goûm^t. of the English. Casmamon and the Pequatts
present gaue in the names of the Pequatts *ℓ Nyanticke Indians to the n^o. of
62. on whose behalfe the petition was presented, the p̃ticular names are
vnder written ℓ left with Mr Hopkins.

*115

The Comissioners not having form̃ly heard either from Necquash while
he liued, or by any other meanes since of any such innocent Pequats who
fled from their country to decline that vniust war against the English, w^{ch}
the rest of their Countrymen p̃secuted. By enquiry from Thomas Stanton
from Foxon one of Vncus his men ℓ at last by confession of the Pequats
present fownde, that some of the petitioñs were in Misticke fort in fight
against the English ℓ fled away in the smoake. That others of them were in
other places to fight against the Narragensetts ℓ Moheygens then assisting the
English, so that the grounde of their petic̃on proued false ℓ deceitfull. It
apped further vp̄ enquiry that these Pequatts, or most of them though they
might haue beene entertayned by other Indian Sachems, yet vpon the psua-
sion of Necquash ℓ p̃mises of good vsage from Vncus, they submitted to
him, ℓ haue beene reckond amonge his men, p^d him tribute, ℓ assisted him
in his war ever since, onely they complaine of sundry oppressions and out-
ragℓ wch they haue suffered from Vncus, some concerning p̃ticular psons,
others of a more generall consideration, in wch the body of the Pequats seeme
interessed.

Obochiquod complayned that Vncus had taken away his wife, defileth
her, ℓ keepeth her away p force. Foxon being present (as Vncus deputy)
was questioned aboute this base and vnsufferable outrage, he denyed that

Vncus either tooke, or kept away Obochiquods wife p force, ₵ affirmed that Obochiquod withdrawinge with other Pequat₵ from Vncus, his wife refused to goe with him, ₵ that amonge the Indians it is vsuall when a wife soe desert₵ her husband another may take her, Obochiquod affirmed that Vncus had defiled her before, ₵ still kept her against his will.

The Comissioners though not satisfyed in pointe of proff w'h Obochiquods relation, yet abhorringe y' lustfull adulterous carriage of Vncus, as it is acknowledged ₵ mitigated by Foxon ₵ conceiuinge that he that abusinge another mans wife havinge *power in his hands, his life either by force or desert to depriue the complayninge husband of his life, ordered ₵ concluded that Vncus restore Obochiquods wife, that Obochiquod himselfe haue his liberty to sitt downe ₵ settle either at Nameoke vnder the English, or els where as y̆ English shall appointe, ꝑuided that he assist Vncus in his wars, soe oft as the English shall direct.

*116

Sanaps another of Vncus his men, but a Conecticut Indiã ₵ no Pequat vpon the reporte of a Sachems squaw (since dead) complayned, that Vncus had abused his wife, he affirmed that after she was soe defiled, she grew froward, ₵ he had little peace with her, he added that Vncus had since taken away his corne ₵ beanes p force ₵ had engaged himselfe ₵ attempted (as he conceiues) to take away his life. but the Comissioners founde noe proff first or last of these chardges, ₵ for the corne Foxon conceiues, Vncus seised it, because Sannap w'h the Pequat in a disorderly manner withdrew him selfe from Vncus, vnder whome he had liued seûall yeares. they conceiued therefore that Sannop might either returne to Conecticut, or liue at Nyanticott, or that some ꝑvision be made for his safety ₵ peace at Mohegon, ₵ that Vncus vpon Euidence restore what corne or beanes he hath taken from him in an vnrighteous manner.

In generall the Pequatts complayned, first of Vncus his vnjustice ₵ tyranny, drawinge wampam from them vpon new pretenses from time to time, they say they haue given him wampam 40 times since they came vnder him, ₵ that they haue sent wampam by him to the English 25 times, but know not whither all, or any pt of it was rightly deliuered. 2ˡʸ. that in their play if a Pequat win of a Mohegen, he caunot get payemᵗ. if he complaines, Vncus carries it ꝑtially to the Mohegens ₵ threatens the Pequats. 3ˡʸ. when Vncus had a child dyed, he made an offeringe ₵ gaue his wife a gift, ₵ comanded the Pequats to doe yᵉ like. They being affraid collected 100 fathome of wampan ₵ gaue it as a present, wᶜʰ pleased Vncus, ₵ he promised thenc forward to esteeme them as Mohegens, yet a few dayes after, Vncus brother came ₵ tould them that Vnõ ₵ his Councell, had determined

is or can be to the Inhabitantȼ there, as to cause them to forsake their habitations vpon that grounde, our thoughts reach not, especially consideringe if
that Jurisdiction grow exorbitant in their taxes, there is a remedy provided in
this combination to rectify any such deviations, but if weakninge of estates
be a sufficient plea to free men from payinge of taxes, we know not, who will
pay, for all such payemᵗȼ doe weaken mens estates.   What is meant by
taking *of* possession of the River (wᶜh was possest by the other townes a
considerable time before the foundation of that plantatiō was layd) ȼ the
greate chargȼ in buildings we vnderstand not, for we are wholy ignorant what
expences they haue beene at in that kinde,   But for their owne pticular private advantages, nor can we yeeld a ready beleife to what is affirmed, that if
they had forseen the^or present imposition would haue been required, they
would not then haue planted for the thing carryeth that euidence of equity
with it that Mʳ Pincheon whiles he looked vpon him selfe as a member of
that Jurisdiction, acknowledged the same ȼ yeelded vpon a motion made by
himselfe to Mʳ. Fennicke (as we haue it from his testimony deserving credit)
that the trade of beaver vpon the Riuer, wᶜh is the greatest thing now stuck
at, ought in reason to contribute to the chardg of the forte : besides the
incouragemᵗ given by Mʳ Pincheon vnder his owne hand, by others to the
gentlemen interested in Seabrooke forte, wᶜh might well draw out from them
an addition to the former expencȼ, there seemes to deserue some weight of
Consideration in the present case.

6

*109

      To the sixt we willingly assent, ȼ in parallel cases *shall readily submit.

      Wᶜh Argumᵗȼ ȼ answeres being read ȼ a further debate betwixt the
Comissioners of the Mattachusetts ȼ Conecticute had ȼ Mʳ Pincheon then in
Boston being sent for, and desired to add what further reasons he could
against the imposition in question, he wholy referring to what the generall
Corte had done, it appeared to the Com̄ʳˢ for the other two Collonies vpon
their most serious consideration, that it was of weighty concermᵗ to all the
plantations vpon the River of Conecticute that the mouth of the Riuer ȼ the
passages of goods through it to and fro (though at some chardg) be ꝑserued
ȼ secured to them, that though the forte at Seabrooke be not of force against
an enemy of any considerable strength, yet an English plantation being now
setled there, it may more easily be ꝑserued, ȼ may in a comfortable measure
secure the passage aforesd for the conveniencȼ of all the plantations, vpon
that River, of wᶜh benefite Springfield doth share with the rest, That though
nothinge be as yet demanded from the Dutch house within Hartfords limitȼ,
yet this imposition with other differencȼ, are like to be considered in a fitt

to kill some of them, wherewith being much amased they consulted, ₵   **1647.**
resolued to with draw from Vncus, ₵ to submitt ₵ subject themselues to the
English. 4ˡʸ. That desiring favoure of the English they purposed to collect   **July.**
wampam from amonge themselues *and to present it to them ₵ by some of   ***117**
their old men acquainted Vncus therewith, yet the next morninge he came
with his men armed to the forte, called for those who promoted that businesse,
threatninge to kill them but they escaped out of the forte, went to Conecticut
₵ complayned. 5ˡʸ. that though Vncus seemed glad that Mʳ John Winthrop
came to settle an english plantation at Pequat, ₵ ꝑsented him with wampan,
yet without cause (as they conceiue) he quickly tooke offence, fell to outrages,
first Vncus having a man wounded at long Iland, had occasion to goe thither
₵ required Robin alias Casmamon with other Pequats to goe with him, Robin
alledged that he had ingaged himselfe with some others to Mʳ Winthrop,
who was his former Mʳ, to build him a wigwam, the rest not knowinge any
cause why Vncus should take so many men with him, excused themselues,
yet ꝑmised if any should shoote an arrowe against him vpon notice they
would come over ₵ assist him. Vncus was not satisfyed, threatned to be
revenged ₵ did cut all their netts. 2ˡʸ. Mʳ Tho: Peeters beinge ill ₵ others
in the plantation wanting provision, wished Robin to goe a huntinge, Robin
ꝑfessd he durst not, Vncus would be angry, Mʳ Peters told him he should
goe, as in or from an English plantation, Robin replyed we are but 20 men,
we cannot driue the woods, wherevpon Mʳ Peters by a warrant sent for
Weekwash Cooke to goe with him, ₵ they hunted on the East side of Pequat
vpon this occasion, Vncus made the assault of wᶜh the Comissioners heard
the last yeare at New haven, ₵ Mr. Winthrop hath now further to complaine. Foxon being present gaue answere to the aforesaid charges as followeth.

First he beleiueth the Pequat₵ haue for tribute and vpon other occasions   **I**
at sundry times pᵈ wampam to Vncus but denyeth that they in pticular had
given him any for the English, but the Moyhegens ₵ they had sometimes
joyned togeither to giue in wampan wᶜh had beene sent as a ꝑsente twice into the Mattachusett₵, ₵ sometimes to Mʳ Heynes at Hartford, but he thinckes
the nomber of 25. times to be alltogeither false.

2ˡʸ he conceiues that the Pequat₵ being an vnder people might haue   **2**
some wrong from the Mohegens in play ₵ durst not presse for their right, but
denyeth that Vncus had any hand therein.

3ˡʸ. he acknowledgeth that the Pequats did bring in 100 fathome of   **3**
wampam at the death of Vncus child ₵ were ꝑmised favoure as is expressed,
but the latter was onely a trecherous plott of Vncus brother ꝑswading

*the Pequats to withdraw from Vncus into their owne country, ℓ there he would come vnto them, And to ꝑvoke them therevnto he tould them (though falsly) y^t vncus had determined to kill some of them.   4^{ly}. though Vncus at first apprehended noe inconvenience in such a ꝑsent to be sent by the Pequatts to the English, yet being after informed that it was a plott, or a fruite of crooked counsell given them by Tassaquanott Sassacus his brother, who had suggested vnto them, that most of the cheife Sachems were cutt off, Vncus to them but a stranger, why should they serue or giue wampam to him, they should rather send presents to the English, withdrawe from the Mohegens, ℓ settle in their owne Country, herewith Vncus was iustly offended.   5^{ly}. he acknowledgeth that Vncus was glad at M^r. Winthrops setlinge at Pequatt ℓ presented him with 25. fathome of Wampan, but he was after troubled when Robin ℓ other Pequatts his men refused to goe with him to long Iland.   Foxon added that he had heard some of the Mohegens tooke fish from them, but knoweth not that he cutt their netts though he cannot deny it.   Lastly he confesseth that Vncus and his men were foolish ℓ faulty in that rash assault wch they made vpon the Pequatts ℓ Neckwash Cookes men at Nameok especially in the Euglish plantation, to the affrightm^t of the woemen ℓ children there ; But saith, Vncus ℓ his men were troubled, that Mr Peters should not make vse of them who would willingly haue hunted for him ℓ the English, but they were much ꝑvoked y^t Neckwash Cooke, a professed enemy to Vncus, ℓ one who stands in tearmes of *of* possession ℓ had broken all Coven^{t}ℓ with the English, should be soe entertayned ℓ imployed by Mr Peeters, he added that Vncus had a right on the East side of Pequatt from his father, from his mother, ℓ from his wife ℓ had leaue to hunt there from the English wch Neckwash Cooke never had till now.

The Comissioners considering the ꝑmisses as far as they conceme the Pequattℓ interested in the petition ordered, that Vncus be duly reproued for any passage of tirannicall goverm^t ouer them, soe far as they may be proued, ℓ seriously enformed that the English Colonies cannot owne or protect him in any vnlawfull much lesse trecherous ℓ outragious courses, but they are not so far satisfyed in those Pequat complaintℓ, as to iustify their disorderly

withdrawinge, ℓ whereas Mr John *Winthrop spake of a resignation made by Vncus of those Pequats to him, wch yet he insists not on.   The Comīrs doubt, whither there were not some misinterpretation ℓ soe misvnderstandinge therein, but however remembring the proud wars some yeares since made by the Pequatts, and the just resolutions of the English that (though after the warre they spared the liues of such as had noe hand in the bloude of the English, yet the remnant of that nation should not be suffered (if the

English could help it) either to be a distinct people, or to retayne the name of Pequatt{, or to settle in the Pequatt country, but that they should all be devided betwixt the Narragensett { Mohegens Indians, { that vnder a tribute to the English, they concluded that neither the Narragensett Sagamořs nor Vncus had power to resigne them or any of them to any English plantation or Jurisdiction without the consent of the Comissioners, { ordered those Pequatt{ foorthwith returne a due subjection to Vncus, that he receaue them without charge or revenge for this disorderly withdrawinge, or the complaintes they haue now made { in all respect{ to governe them with due moderation as he doth the Mohegen Indians (the tribute to the English onely excepted) yet they thought fitt that the old men who were at Namecke before Mr Winthrops cominge, should continue there, or be soe provided for as may best suite the English plantacõn at Pequatt, but vnder subjection to Vncus, as the rest.

Mr John Winthrop on the behalfe of the Nepnet Indians complayned, that Nowequa (Vncus brother) came vpon them the last yeare with 130 Mohegens { plunderd them, takinge from them 35 fathom of wampan, 10 copp kettles, 10 greate hempen basketts, many beare skins, deere skins { other things to a greate value.

Foxon being questioned affirmed, that Vncus with his cheife Counsellors { Capt{ were at New haven with the Comissioners, when his brother thus plunderd in pticular he knoweth not what wampam or other goods were taken away, but affirmeth that Nowequa at the same time robbed some of Vncus his owne men, neare adjoyuinge, but Vncus neuer rec^d any of the spoile either of the one or the other.

Mr Winthrop { some with him complayned further, that Nowequa with 40 or 50. Mohegens lately goeing oũ to Fishers Iland, did staue a Canoo, freighted the Indian that was there with his man, that his man without some puision against such outrages would be vnwilling to stay { himselfe should suffer in his occasions there. It was alsoe testifyed by an English man of Mr Winthrops plantation, that Nowequa returning thenc hovered against the English plantation in a *suspitious manner with 40. or 50. men, many of them armed wth guns to the affrightm^t, not onely of ye Indians on the shore (soe that some of them began to bring their goods to the English houses) but of diuerse of the English themselues.

*120

The Comissioners considering the sundry comp^ts now brought against Nowequa (Vncus brother) confirmed by Foxon his acknowledgm^t { testimony by enquiry of doing that the Nepnat Indians having noe Sachem of their owne are at liberty pt of them by their owne choice doe apptaine to the Narragensett Sachem, ꝑ pte to the Mohegens, soe that when the covenants betwixt the English Colonies ꝑ the Narragensett confederatꝑ come to be considered, satisfaction for the outrages comitted by Nowequa wilbe expected, ordered that Vncus from them be fully informed, that he must either regulate ꝑ continue his brother in a righteous ꝑ peaceable frame, for the future vndertakinge ꝑ providing that vpon due proff due restitution be made to such as haue been wronged by him, or els wholy disert ꝑ leaue him, that the Narragensett ꝑ others may require ꝑ recouer satisfaction as they can. They also thinck it fitt ꝑ just that with the Canooe split ꝑ broken by Nowequa due consideration be had of returninge the gun taken from a Mohegen by the englishman at Fishers Iland, as the case vpon examination shall require.

Mr Winthrop and his servant Robin als Casmamon ꝑsented sundry complꝑtꝑ against Vncus importing that though at first he seemed glad to entertaine the English plantation at Pequat, yet his carriage hath bene such since, as if he intended by alarums and affrightmentꝑ to disturb ꝑ breake that plantation. but that which appeared to the Comissioners most cleare ꝑ weighty was an hostile assault the last yeare made vpon Neckwash Cooke ꝑ the Pequats now petitioning, neare or within the English plantation, in wch some of the Indians invaded were wounded, all of them plundered, the english disturbed ꝑ affrighted, their cattle driven away ꝑ they sustayned much losse in seüall respectꝑ.

Two petitions from sergeant Mynott ꝑ Wm Morton were read, wherein they desired satisfaction, the one for a curtaine or bead coveringe taken away (as he saith) worth 2 fathome of wampam, wch it seemes he had lent Neckwash Cooke: the other for charges of a journey he made the last yeare to complaine against Vncus at Newhaven, ꝑ the complainte of one Stibbins for corne taken away or spoiled was heard, all wch being duly considered, the insolency ꝑ outrage of Vncus ꝑ his men appeared much more *heinous then the complꝑt at Newhaven the last yeare impted. The Comissioners (havinge the last yeare ordered that Vncus should acknowledg his fault to the English plantation, wch they heare he pformed in Capt Masons presence) thought fitt now to add that vpon the returne of the Pequats to his subjection, Vncus foorthwith pay into the hands of M^r Jo. Winthrop, to be by him disposed ꝑ diuided to the English ꝑ ould Pequats ꝑ other innocent Indians towards the repaire of their losses in ꝑportion as he shall finde cause 100. fathome of wampan.

Mr John Winthrop did further informe the Comissioners that he vnderstoode from the Mowhaset Sachem of long Iland, that after the Pequats wars he had by Vncus sent 60. fathome of Wampam as a p̃sent to Mr. Winthrop Gove.ʳ: of the Mattachusetts, ℓ had alsoe then given to Vncus. 20. fathome for himselfe, but vpon enquiry he findes that Vncus did never deliuer the s̃d present. The Comissioñs thought fitt ℓ concluded, that if vpon inquiry ℓ examinac̃õ it be fownd, Vncus hath receaued ℓ vnjustly detayned this wampam, he be required forthwith to make payem.ᵗ to him the Governoure.

Mʳ John Winthrop maketh clayme to a greate quantity of land at Nyanticott by purchasse from the Indians, gaue in to the Comissioners a petition in those words.

Whereas I had the land of Nyanticott by a deed of gift ℓ purchasse from the Sachem before the wars, I desire the Comissioners wilbe pleased to confirme it vnto me, ℓ cleare it from any clayme of English ℓ Indians according to the equity of the case.

Mʳ John Winthrop havinge no writinge from the Indian Sachem concerning these lands presented to the Com̄.ʳˢ the testimony of their Indians as followeth.

We Tromatuch Wambarsquaske Antuppo doe testify vpon our knowledg before the wars were against the Pequats, Sassious our Sachem of Nyantick did call vs ℓ all our men togcither, ℓ tould that he was resolued to giue his Country to the Governours sonne of the Mattachuset̃ who liued then at Pattaquassat alias Conecticut Rivers mouth, ℓ all his men declared themselues willing therewith, Therevpon he went to him to Pattaquassett̃ ℓ when he came backe he tould them he had granted all his Country to him the said Governours sonne ℓ said he was his good freind, ℓ he hoped he would send some English thither sometime hereafter, Moreover he told him he had receaued coates from him for it, wᶜʰ they saw him bring home.

*122

*We vnderwritten doe testify that we heard these Indians testify the aboue written testimony concerninge the graunte of the land of the Nyantyk̃. Tho: Stanton, Cary Lathome, Tho. Mymat, Wm. Burdman.

I doe remember that Sasyous Sachem of the Nyanticot̃ did giue Mʳ John Winthrop his country of Nyanticut before the Pequats wars, myselfe being interp̃tor in that businesse, at the Rivers mouth.

p me.   THO: STANTON

This testimony was taken vpon oath before me

JO: ENDECUTT.

The Comissioners for Conecticut vpon the readinge of Mr Winthrops petiĉõn, desired to be satisfyed vpon what grounde the Comissioners could take the determination of the case in question concerninge Nyanticut land℥ into their hands, vnles it be by the mutuall consent ℥ desire of both parties, wch seemed to clame interest therein, ℥ for themselues, though they could in their owne pticulars submit to their judgm^t yet they humbly conceiued it was beyond their Comission to refer any such thinge to be determined at this time, nor are they ƥpared to make a full answere to Mr Winthrop for the right he challengeth in those lands, onely they ƥsent to the Comissioners consideration, that the gift or purchase ƥtended by M^r. Winthrop beares not date, nor is lymited w^thin any precise bownd℥, nor doth it yet appeare, whither the Indian mentioned to giue the s̄d lands had any reall or true interest in them himselfe, And the ƥtended graunte is onely verball noe Recorde by writinge appearinge of any such thing wch intimates, that what ever it was, it was looked vpon as a transient airy passage. Besides Mr Winthrop was then ymployed by Gentlemen interessed in Seabrooke ℥ whither the lands mentioned were not procured by him for them, ℥ by him with their meanes doth not appeare, how ever it seemes somewhat vncomely (at least) for Mr Winthrop, who was acquainted with their great ingagem^t℥ in the place to purchasse land for himselfe, beinge their Agent, soe neare the cheife place of their intended Residence. But if all that is answered satisfy not, yet they humbly conceiue the land was iustly conquered before Mr Winthrop made any clayme therevnto, wch makes his dormant title (if it may be so called) altogeither invalide.

The Comissioners for the Colonies duly consideringe the ƥmisses, though they desire the English plantaĉõn at Pequatt may haue all comfortable ℥ requisite *accomodations, yet they see no grounde for themselues to intermeddle or determine any thinge concerninge the clayme ℥ title in question.

*123

Vpon occasion of the former debate some of the Comissiofis acquainted Mr Winthrop wth some report℥ they had heard that he was aboute a purchas of land℥ at longe Iland, he was desired to take knowledg that longe Iland (for a considerable some of money p^d) is vnder engagem^t℥ to scũall psons of Conecticut ℥ Newhaven, ℥ that any title wch may be ƥtended from M^r. Cope will be fownde weake, as himselfe a little before his death had acknowledged.

Mr Elliott on the behalffe of an Indian called Todorsway complayned that one of the Mohegens called Cogeleys belonginge to Vncus his brother, ℥ knowne by Mr Pincheon did owe him . 6. beaver skins, ℥ desired some meanes might be vsed for Recouery of the same, The Comissiofis thought fitt that enquiry be made, ℥ satisfaction required if the debt be fownde just.

According to agreem^t ⸤ order made the last yeare at New haven the nomber of males w^{t}h the chardg⸤ pp^r. to the combination expended by the seûall Colonies were now brought in, by w^{c}h it appeared that the Mattachusetts w^{t}h Mr Dunsters bill, ⸤ a gratuity given to Maior Gibons had expended —475^t. 01^s. 6^d. Plimouth with 3^t. 10^s. for bread—101^t. 10^s. 0^d. Conecticutt as p acc^o. last yeare 296^t. Newhauen as p acc^o. 170^t. 18^s. 7^d. of w^{c}h some of 1043^t. 10^s. j^d. as the accompt was cast vp both by ye Comissioñs. ⸤ by the auditor for the Mattachuset⸤, the Mattachusetts are to pay 670^t. 03^s. 4^d. Plimouth 128^t. 13. 4^d. Conecticut 140. 2. 5. Newhauen 104^t. 11. 0^d. By w^{c}h it appeares that the Mattachusetts were to pay to Conecticute 128^t. 14. 3^d. ⸤ to Newhaven 66^t. 7. 7^d. w^{c}h is in all 195. 01. 10^d. ⸤ that Plimouth is to pay to Conecticut 27^t. 3^s. 4^d.

And because the weighty concernem^t⸤ of the Colonies may sometimes call for a meetinge when yet the Comissioñs (as hath beene formerly founde) are not ꝑpared, to giue in the nomber of their males, It is now thought fitt ⸤ ordered, that it be ꝑpounded to each generall Corte that after the ꝑportion now setled in this ꝑsent acc^o, the Colonies shall hereafter beare their seûall ꝑt⸤ of all chardge disbursed, for the publicke till some inconvenience arise or appeare by a considerable increase or decrease in some of the Jurisdictions, ⸤ that in such case any of the 4 Colonies callinge for it, the males be againe brought in, ⸤ chardges borne according to the first importe of the Articles.

Not to be alterd

The Comissioners vnderstanding that the Indians are plentifully furnished w^{t}h English guns, powder ⸤ shott (notwithstandinge seûall orders made by them *(and as they hoped confirmed by the generall Court⸤ in the seûall Colonies to suppresse a trade of such a dangerous consequence) vpon enquiry finde that a considerable pt of this Inconvenience doth arise from warrants ⸤ dispensations graunted, either by the generall Cort⸤ or by some magestrat⸤ of the Mattachuset⸤ to shop-keeps, or others to sell, lend, or furnish some Indians either because they are confederates, or vnder the governm^t of that Jurisdiction, or vpon some other respect, w^{c}h cannot secure the Collonies frō danger: For the publicke safety they desire therefore y^t all such warrants formerly granted may be speedily called in, ⸤ due care taken, that no guns, swords, rapiers, or rapier blades, powder, lead, shott, or other instruem^t⸤ or furniture for war, be sould, given or lent, or by any other meanes directly or indirectly be passed over into the hands or power of any of the Indians vpon any ꝑtence or respect whatsoever, And they conceiue it worthy of the most serious thought ⸤ consideration of the Collonies how the like disordered trade may be suppressed at Roade Iland ⸤ their confederates,

*124

ℓ of all other English plantacõns ℓ if possible it may be alsoe restrayned in the french ℓ dutch Jurisdictions.

The Comissioners having waited many dayes for a retorne from the Narragansetℓ Indians ℓ their confederats, the 16ᵗh of August Ninegrett ℓ Pessacks deputies acquainted thē that the messengers were now returned, but had in noe measure answerd their expectation, they had onely brought .200. fathome of wampam. The Comissioners by Tho: Stanton their Interpretor asked what the reason was, that soe much being due soe little was brought, ℓ from whome this .200. fathome came. Ninegratt ℓ the rest could giue noe satisfaction to the former question, onely Ninagrett p̃tended that his being from home had hindred the gathering ℓ sendinge of the wampam, for the latter he said 100. fathome came from Pessacks, ℓ 100. fathome from himselfe, he added that since they fell soe far short in the payemᵗ of their debt, he would order that the 105. fathome intended for a p̃sent to the Governoure, should goe towards satisfaction of the Collonies, ℓ desired respite for the rest, vntill next spring, ℓ then if it were not fully paid, the English should take his head ℓ seise his country.

The Comissioners not thinking it meete to begin a p̃sent war if satisfaction (though with a little forbearance may be had otherwise) by their interpretor acquainted Ninegratt, that since he p̃tended the wampam had bene gatherd ℓ pᵈ if himselfe had bene at home, they would giue him free leaue to returne, ℓ 20 dayes more from hence to collect ℓ send the residue yet behinde ℓ tho: 500 fathome of the wampam now due should fall *short in his payemᵗ 20. dayes hence, they would forbeare it till next planting time, ℓ in the meane time accept both the 200 fathome now brought, ℓ the 105 fathõ intended for a present in pt of payemᵗ, but if they brought not, 1000. fathome more within 20 dayes, the Comissioners would send noe more messengers, but take course to right themselues, as they· see cause in their owne time. And if they be forced to seeke satisfaction by armes, he ℓ his confederatℓ must not expect to make their peace as lately they had done by a little wampam. In the meane time though for breach of Covenᵗℓ they might put their hostages to death yet the Comissioners would forthwith deliver the children to Ninegratt, expecting from him the more care to see ingagemᵗℓ fully satisfyed. And if they find him reall in his pformance, they will chardg all former neglectℓ vpon Pessacks, who hath not attended Covenantℓ ℓ in such case they shall expect from Ninegratt his best assistance, when he shall be required to recover the whole remainder from him. All wᶜh Ninegrett cheerefully accepted, and pmised to pforme accordingly.

This 200. fathome of wampam being thus rec^d from Ninegrett, the Comissofis fownde the acc° to stand thus

Mr Pellham rec^d allmost 2 yeares since aboue what was given to Vncus———————————————————————	70. fath
left by the Narragansett{ in M^r shrimptons } hands in kettles { wampam —————————— }	70. fath
In Cutchamakins hands by Ninegrett ————————	105. fath
Rec^d of Ninegratt 16. Aug. 1647 —————————	243½. fath.
The some is ———————————————	448½ fath.

of wch as the Comissioners { Auditor for the Mattachusetts cast it there is

due to ye Mattachusets ———————————————	288. fath 4^d
to Plimouth ——————————————	55. fa: 1^s. 6^d
to Conecticute ————————————	60. fa. 1^s. 1^d
to New haven ——————————	44. fa. 4^s. 7^d.
wch was accordingly devided	447.fath.7^s. 6^d

A writinge being p̃sented by Sergeant Collicut { others to the Comissioners in the nature of a petition wherein they complaine against the Dutch { Sweeds for seuerall greevances { in pticular for high Customes imposed vpon them at the Mauatoes, { for a disorderly trade in selling guns powder { shott to the Indyans {^{c} The Comissioners thought fitt to write to the duch Governoure as followeth.

*Honoured S^r.   *126

We joinctly congratulate yor arivall { enterance to the goũm^t at Manatoes {c hoping all the English Colonies shall enioy w^{t}hin yor limit{ all the fruites of a neighbourly { freindly correspondency in a free concourse and intercourse as yo^{r}s haue { shall doe in all our port{ { harbors: some thing{ p̃sented to vs we shall p̃sent to your consideration. first we heare of a dangerous liberty taken by many of yours in selling guns, powder, shott { other instruem^t{ of warr to the Indians not ouely at yor forte Aurania (though we conceiue that trade there driven is very vnsafe both for yor selues { vs but at long Island within the River of Conecticut, at the Narragansetts { other places within the English Jurisdictions, And though possibly you haue good lawes to suppresse soe mischeevous a trade, yet soe stronge is the temptation by an excessiue gaine arising thence that w^{t}hout a constant care { severe execution (as we finde by daylie experience) the inconvenience cannot be

removed, but the meanes we leaue to yor owne wisedome ₹ iudgm^t.   Secondly
we heare of an high Custome, excise or recoguition demanded ₹ taken for
all goods sold within yor Jurisdictions, not onely of yor owne people, but of
the English, with heavy fines, ₹ seisures for omissions or misse entries to the
hinderance of trade ₹ the discouragem^t of our marchant₹, whereas hitherto all
our harbours haue beene open ₹ free to yours without any such burdens ₹
hassards, We entreate from you therefore in a few lines a pfect information of
what Customes ₹c you require with the grownds of the same both for goods
imported ₹ sould, ₹ for beaver, Mouse, ₹ for other comodities exported, and
in what cases you impose fines ₹ make seisures, that we may enforme our
marchants, ₹ steere our course accordingly, with our due respec:₹ to yo^rselfe
₹ the late governoure Mounsier Keift we rest.

yor lovinge Friends the Comissioners of the
vnited Colonies.

Boston in the
Mattachusetts. the.
17th of 6. moneth. 1647.

The foregoinge conclusions were agreed ₹ subscribed by the Comissioners the 17th of the 6. moneth. 1647.

EDWARD HOPKINS	THO : DUDLEY ℘sident.
JOHN MASONE.	JOHN ENDECOTT
THEOPHILUS EATON	W^M BRADFORD
STEPHEN GOODYEARE.	JOHN BROWNE

At a meteing of yᵉ Comisioᵣˢ: for yᵉ vnited colonyes of New England: held at New Plymñ: yᵉ 7ᵗh 7ᵗh 1648

an order of yᵉ Genᵣall Courte of yᵉ Masachusetts Dated yᵉ 10ᵗh of yᵉ 3 mᵒ 1648. was presentᵈ. whereby it appeared yᵗ John Endicott: Esquire ꝝ Mᵣ· Simon bradstreete were Chosen comisoᵣs for yᵗ· Jurisdictiŏ for this p̃sent yeare: ꝝ were invested wᵗh full pwer to treate ꝝ conclude of all things: according to the tenᵣ: of yᵒ articles of combinacĩ: Concluded at Bostŏ: yᵉ 19ᵗb of yᵉ 3 mᵒ 1643:

1648.

September.

A Licke Order from the Jurisdictiŏ of New Plymñ Dated yᵉ 7ᵗh 4ᵗ. 1648: was Reed investeing Mᵣ Wᵐ Bradford: ꝝ Mᵣ John Browne wᵗh yᵉ Licke pwer: as Comisionᵣs: to treate ꝝ Conclude according to yᵉ tenᵣ: of yᵉ saide articles

An order of yᵉ: Genᵣ. Court of coniticott: was alsoe p̃seuted ꝝ Reede Dated the 18 may 1648 appwoynteing Mᵣ. Eđ. Hopkins: ꝝ Mᵣ. Rogger Loodloe: to yᵉ formencĩ seruice ꝝ investing them wᵗh full power: according to yᵉ articles of confederatiŏ:

a like order from the Genᵣ Courte of New hauens Judictiŏ. Dated yᵉ 3ᵗh· may 1648: Investing Theoph: Eaton Esqᵣ ꝝ Mᵣ. John astwood wᵗh the Licke power according to yᵉ tenᵣ of yᵉ saide articles for yᵉ yeare insewing was Now alsoe Reed.

Mᵣ· Wñ Bradford Esqᵣ: was Chosen p̃sident of this meeteing:

It was p̃pounded for the avoydeing of ofenc̃: and the carefull pᵣsᵣvaciŏ: of Loue ꝝ amety: betwixt the vnited Colonies and theire comisioᵣs: that a dew order might bee settled and obserued: by theiᵣ comisoᵣs: as in theire Subscriptiŏs· soe alsoe in theire tackeing płce at all publique meeteings, Dewering the time of theire *Seuᵣall sesions, wᶜh vpŏ dew consideracions was thus Agreed, that the Comisioᵣs of the masachusets shall haue the first płce at all such meeteings, ꝝ accordingly the Comisionᵣs of the othᵣ Colonies in such order as they are Named in the articles of confideraciŏ: vizſ: Plymᵗh Conitacott ꝝ New hauen, Onely it is p̃vided that any Comisioᵣ may manifest such psononall respects as in his owne discretiŏ hee Judges meete to any of the rest of the comisᵣs in any of the foremeñ pticulers, notwᵗhstanding this conclusiŏ

John dislił. pp'siŏ for takeing pl'ce in publiqᵘ meeteings as thinkeing it contrary to Scriptᵣ rules

*128

Mʳ: Wiłł Cottington & Captain Patridg of Roade Iland pᵉsented this insewing request to the Comisioʳs in Wrighting.

Oʳ Request & mociõ is in the behalfe of oʳ Iland: that wee the Iland's of Roode Iland may be Rescauied into combinacĩõ wᵗh all the vnited colonyes of New England in a firme & pp̃tuall League of Friendship & amity : of ofence & Defence Mutuall advice and succoʳ vp̃õ all Just occasions for oʳ Mutuall safety & wellfaire, & for pᵉserueing of peace amongst o'selues: and pᵉventeing as much as may bee all occasiõs of warr & Diference, and to this oʳ mocion wee haue the consᵗ of the maioʳ pt of oʳ Iland:

WILŁ COTTINGTÕ

ALICXSANDER PARTRIDG

To wᵇich mocion: the Comisʳs returned this answer vnder all theire hands:

Mʳ. Cottington & Captaine Parᵗ the Comisʳs for the vnited Colonies haue Considered what youe haue pᵖounded Eithʳ by speach oʳ wrighting & finde yoʳ pᵉsent state and condiciõ full of confusion and Dangʳ haueing much Disturbanᵈᵉ amongst yoʳ selues and noe security from the Endians they desier therfore in seuᵉrall Respects to aford both advice and helpe. but vp̃õ the pᵉusall of the antient Patent graunted to New Plymᵗʰ they finde Roade Iland vp̃õ wᶜh yʳ plᵃntacions are setled to fall wᵗhin theire line & bounds, wᶜh the honourable comittie of parlement thinke not fitt to Straighten oʳ infringe: nor may wᵉ if therefor yoʳ selues and the Inhabitants oʳ the most and most Considerable pt of them ; vpon a dew Considʳ of Plymᵗh Patent and Right, accknowledg yʳ selues within that Jurisdictiõ wee shall consider and advize how youe may bee accepted vpon Just termes and wᵗh tendʳ *Respectꜱ to yʳ Conveniencie : and shall after aford yᵘ the same advise, protectiõ And helpe wᶜh other Plantations wᵗhin the vnited Colonies Injoye, wᶜh we hope in sondery respects may tend to yᵒʳ Comfort and safety.

*129

Y· 7ᵗʰ 8ᵗ 1648

Henery Bull of Newport vp̃õ Roode Iland pᵉsented a p̃ticiõ to the Comision'rs informeing, that som Narragansett Indians had beaten him & othʳ wise done him Iniury: desiering the Comision'rs to send to the Sachem of the Narragansetts to send the saide Indians that Satisfactiõ might bee giuen him for the wronges hee hath sustained :

To wᶜh the Comision'rs Returned this answer: that they much pittied his Condicĩ and were viry senceable of the wrongs hee hath sustained, but forasmuch as it is a pᵗiculer cace & belongs pp̃ʳly to Roade Iland wheare he liues to Releaue him the Comisoʳs could not see a faire and Convenient way to answer his desier but Refered him for further answer to the advice giuen to the Iland in Gen'all wherby both hee and oth'rs that are oppressed may com to Rescaiue dew satisfactiõ and for his future security gaue him a wrighting vnder the Comisio'rs hands of the same Contents w'ch they gaue to houlden ℄ Warn'r w'ch heraf'r Folow'th.

Wheareas there was p̃sented a wrighting vnto vs from the towne o'r plantaciõ of Warwicke: as they call it, by theire Meseng'rs M'r. Randall houlden ℄ M'r John Warn'r subs̃b'd By M'r John Smith assistant in the behalfe of the whole towne Dated the 4th of y'e 7'th m'o 1648 wherein they compl̃ne Amongst oth'r things of diu'rs Inguryes Insolencies and afronts off'red them by the Indians that are aboute them and neere Inhabitants to them as namely: killing theire Cattell about a hunderd hoggs: abuseing theire seruants when they take them alone: and som times makeing violent enterance into the howses and strickeing the mast'rs theareof: Stealeing and ployneing their Goods And hereupon doe ernestly desire to know y'e mindes of y'e comisioners herein and to receiue aduise from them. Whearevpõ the Comision'rs for theire future Security gaue them this Insewing wrighting:

To all Indian Sachems whome it may Concerne: Inhabiting within the Narragansett Bay and pl̃ces adiacant:

The .Comision'rs for the vnited Colonyes of New England haueing Rescaiued informã'c of seu'rall outrages comited vp̃ the psons and Cattells of the English in Seu'rall pl̃ces *Canot but looke vpõ such p̃ctizes as tending to the disturbance of the p̃blique peace : and therefore adviz that dew care may bee tacken by the seu'rall Sachems and all oth'rs whome it consernes to p̃vent and abstaine from all such miscarages for the future and if any off them Rescaiue any Iniury from the English: vpõ Complainte in dew pl̃ce and order: satisf' shall bee Indeuo'red the'in according to Justice: as the Licke will bee Expected from them: Plym'th this 10'th of y'e 7: 1648

*130

Wheareas by order of the Comiso'rs the Last yeare it was p̃vided that the peaquats Resideing neere to the English Plantaciõs Settled at Nameach should Returne to their former Subiectiõ to Vnquas: as may more fuly appeare by the acts of that meeteing which was made knowne ℄ signified to them both by the Comisiõs themselues at boston ℄ by Mr. Hopkins allsoe Att Peaquatt: but noe Conformety hath hith'rto beene yealded Thearevnto by y'm it was Now thought fitt and concluded that M'r John Winthrape bee informed of the continued mindes And Resolucions of the Comis'rs for theire returne. and desiered To further the same but in case a Reedy atendance

1648.

September.

bee not forthwith yealded hearevnto, Vnquas shall haue order, ℓ Li𝖇ᵗ by Constrainte to Inforce them ; ℓ it is desiered that the Goᵣment of Conitacott will pvide hee bee not therein opposed by any English Nor the Peaquats or any of them habored or shiltered in any of theire howses: whiles noe Just offence is giuen them by him or any of his in theire pᵣpᵣ Conscrnmᵗs.

Vpon the Informaciŏ˄ Complainte of Mᵣ Will Westerhowse a duch mᵣchant (Liueing at, and a planter in New hauen) Conserueing the duch Goᵗnᵣs tackeing away his shippe from him, whilest shee was Rideing at Anckec in New hauen Harbour) Intreateing advice of and helpe from the Comisionᵣs thearein : this insewing Answer was Returned:

Mᵣ William Westerhowse:

*131

The Comisionᵣs for the vnited Colouies, haue Considered what you haue propounded, by way of advice and helpe: Conserneing yᵣ shippe and goods Seized by the duch Goûñ in New hauen harbour: *But they doe not yet heare, what the duch Goûfi can Chardg: Nor vpon what grounds hee made that seizure : if hee haue nothing to pretend or aledg But that New hauen is pt of or within the New Netherlands the Inglish Colonies must and doe protest against it, and according to theire deuty by all ~~dew~~ Just means aserte the English Right Both to New hauen Lands and harbours, Aud to all English plantacions from Cape Cood both one the maine and Ilands that are posessed by the English, at present vnder theire Goûmᵗ as anciently Grãnted by the kings of England to theire subiects, sence purchased by the English from the Indians, the trew propriatᵣs of the Land : and for diuers yeares peaceably possesed and planted by them without any Question or demãnd by the Dutch or any for them, And shall accordingly Expect to bee Righted Both for the Injury and afront In tackeing a shipp out of one of theire Harbours vpon such Chaleng ℓ titles to the place vniustly claimed without Purchas posesion or any other Considerable Ground:

Vpon which occasion Mᵣ Eaton acquainted the Comisionᵣs what had passed bettw̃ the dutch Goûnᵣ and New hauen Colonoꞑy, and sundery Lettᵣs from the dutch Goûꞙꞑ was Reed, and theire Answers returned to Agnst the 28. 1648. all wᵣh being dewly Considered, the Comisionᵣs did first inquire of Mᵣ Wⁱᵐ Westerhowse, whoe In the dutch Goûnᵣs Last Letter was accuzed of a ireguler trade with the Indians, what gunãs and powder hee had brought And how hee had disposed the same.

hee Answered with much confidence, that he had not Brought at most aboue ten Guns In all, and not aboue a thousand weight of powder, of which the dutch Goûꞙfi had seized in the forementioned shippe about fiue hundered pound$_s$, hee had sould three 100 pounds to Newhauen Colony, or Plantacion, and most of the rest by pounds to Newhauen planters, and others within that Jurisdiction, but absolutly denyed that euer hee sould gun or guns or any powder to any Indians, or any dutch man or if the dutch Gou'ñ or any other could proue to the Contrary hee professed himselfe willing to Submit, to the seuerest Sencure, as being fully Informed by the Gouñ of New hauen, that all such tradeing, without express Licence from som of the magistrates was vnlawfull, and they further thought fitt by way of ꝑp'racion Either to a meeteing with the duch Gouñ or provision for theire owne safety and Con-venienceie to wright to the Duch Gouñ as followeth:

Hon'ed Si'

It is now more then a full yeare sence the Comisioners desiering to cõtinew and Confirme a Just and ꝑfitable peace betwen the English Colo-nyes and the duch plantacions in these ꝑts wrought vnto yo'' & ꝑsented what they had heard : first Conserneing a daingerous Liberty tacken by yo''s to sell guns powder and shott, and other Instruments of warr to the Indians Both at Orrania forte And other places within the English Jurisdictions, a trade damnable as yo' selfe calls it, sertainly vnsafe, and like to ꝑue of mischeuous Consequence both to the English and Duch, Secondly Conserneing a high Cvstom of Regunicion with other burthens, and Incon-uenient Imposisions Layed not onely one yo' owne people but one the Eng-lish m'chants Tradeing at or som time In theire returne, but pasing by the Manatas; but to this day wee heare not of any inquiry Prohebicion or sesation of the foremeneioned Trade at the Orrania forte, Nay wee heare that the Mowhakes and other Indeans Liueing neere that place, are soe furnished with guns, Powther *And shott, that they growe bould, and dareing & may proue daingerous to vs all, nor doe wee finde any abolishon or moderač in the saide Customs and grieueances Imposed at the Manatoes, Nay wee haue not rescaiued any answer, not soe much as a ꝑticuler Informacion as wee Re-quested, of what is required and expected That wee might Informe o' m'chants, to ꝑ'vent future fines & Seasures

*132

M' Will Westerhowse one of yo' Contry men, but at p'sent a planter at New hauen, Informeth vs and Complaineth of his owne And p'en-cipalls greate loss, and damage by y' seasing his shipp, and goods within New hauen harbour, hee professed hee would haue Cleared himselfe at the Man-otoes of being either Rebell or fugatiue To or from his natiue Cvntry, that hee paide Cvstoms at his Comeing forth In reference to Virginia and the English Colonyes: But not admiting him thither : It seemes yo' Refered

1648.

September.

him to the Expected meeteing at Conitacott. heerevpõ wee haue prvsed and considered yoᵣ Claime to all the Landᵉ Riuers Streames ℰℯ: from Cape inlopen to Cape Cood, with yᵣ pretest, and Lettᵣˢ Both Dated Octoᵇᵣ the 12. 1647 Noua Stilla wherein wee finde Sondery vnsatisfiing pasages: wee haue alsoe scene diuers other Letters which yoᵂ haue sent to the Goûñ of Newhauen with his seuᵣall answers To agust the 28. 1648: old Stile : by all which wee finde much Cause of meeteing to settle a Right vnderstanding betwixt the English Colinies ℰ yᵣ selfe, which hath beene by yoⁿ propounded in sondery of yᵣ Lettᵣˢ And was desiered and intended by the English Colonyes : though vpõ nessesary Consideracons Defered to a fitter season In the meane time Some passages in yᵣ Lettᵣ by way of ℗ᵣacion had neede to bee Cleared in yᵣˢ (of the 25 of June 1647) to the Gõᵣnᵣ of the Masachusetts : yoⁿ desier that himselfe and som others. of the English may bee deligated, ℰ that they will bee pleased to giue yoᵂ a meeteing, to agiatate past ocasiõˢ, to Reconsile the ℗sent and to preuent all future occasions of Contestaciõ, but yᵣ Closse seemes then to Importe, that all this is but to ℗pare things that yᵣ or oᵣ Lords and Masters, may more easy determine, in yᵣˢ of Nouemᵇᵣ the 15ᵗʰ 1647 to the Gõᵣnᵣ of New hauen Mencioning the meeteing by yoᵂ ppounded, yoⁿ ℗fesse yᵣ Resoluciõ to giue pregnant testimony to the world of yuᵣ Rediness for a fayer and Neighbᵣly Composeure of diferences, but in yᵣ Lettᵣ to mᵣ Goodyer deputy Goᵣnᵣ at New hauen Dated the 13ᵗʰ December 1647 yoᵂ express yᵣ selfe more doubtfully, if yoᵂ meete in the spring with the Goûñ of the Masathusetts ℰ Plymouth, yoᵂ hope yoᵂ shall Indeuᵣ Reconsciliaᵗ, but to put any thing to them as arbitratoᵣs yoᵂ were not then Resolued, wᶜh in som of vs suspended all formᵣ thoughts of a meeteing till the mater againe was Reuiewed, by yᵣ seûall Lettᵣs to the Goᵣñ of Mathatusets and plymouth ℰ New hauen Whearein desiefg A meeting at Conitacut yoᵂ express yᵣ selfe, as not Doubting but Mutuall satisfaction wilbee giuen to one and othᵣ In euᵣy respect ; that past diferances and agreiueances shall bee forgott, future preuented, and a happy vnion firmely established, the ℗mises considered wee

*133

disier *To bee Informed whither yoᵂ haue Comision from yoᵣ ℗insipalls to make a Reference to whome because som tyme yoᵂ mencioned the two Gouᵣnᵣs of the Mathatusetts and Plymouth and som time the Comission's, and what yoⁿ propose to Referr, whither title to Land or other Questions and diferances, as the Goûñ of New Hauen did som time ppound (Nouemᵇᵣ the 16ᵗʰ 1647) If yoᵂ please heerein to express yᵣ selfe, wee shall the bettᵣ vnderstand oᵣ way and accordingly as the Case may Require further the meeteing with the first oppertunity: in the meane tyme with hartᵉ Inclined and Ingaged to all Councels treatyes and wayes of a wholesom and just

peace, ꝑ wee shall ꝓpound vnto yoᵂ such Consideraĉs as wee suppose yᵣ
selfe will judg Eaquall, and till diferences bee jseued or som speedy Cource of
settlemᵗ agreed, nessesary, vidaƷ that the traders within any of the dutch
plantacions, or vnder the dutch Goûꝓ whither mᵣchants or mariners may
expect noe more Liberty within any of the harbours belonging to the English Colonyes Either in pwoynte of anchering Customs Scarching fines
Seizvres ꝑĉ, then the English Colonyes and theire Mᵣchants ꝑ Marriners Inioy
at the Manatoes: or within yᵣ Jurisdictiõ, Secondly that if vpon sẽrch wee
finde in any of yᵣ traders vesels, within the English Jurisdiction any quan-
taty of guns powther shott ꝑꝶ fitt for that mischevous trade with the Indians
and soe tending to the publique damage of both the English and dutch, wee
shall make stay of them vntill further Inquiry: and satisfaction bee made
and giuen. Thirdly that what Restraints, penaltyes and Confiscacions yoᵘ
put vpon the English Colonyes and theire mᵣchants for tradeing with the
Indians within yᵣ Jurisdictiõ: The same the Colonyes must put vpon yᵣs
within the English Limits: fourthly Refering what is past to the mecteing
ꝑpounded if hearafter youe tacke and Carry away any shipp Vessell or
goods out of any harbour within the English Jurisdiction or Elce wheare
seize any vesell or goods Belongeing to any Marchant or marriner either English dutch or other nacion Admited to be planters or Inhabitants within any
of the vnited Colonyes yoᵂ will nesesitate vs to vindicate the English Rights
And to Repaire such damages, by all suitable and Just meanes. Wee shall
add noe more, but to preuent mistackes, ꝓfesed, and desĩ yoᵂ will beleue
that wee shall neither ꝓtect or Covntenance any vnrighteous cource in any
of ouᵣs to your ꝑivduce nor Impose oᵣ any way inovate Either in pwoynte of
Customs: or in the Liberty of oᵣ harbouᵣs, or otherwise till wee doe or might
vnderstand yoᵣ minde and resoluciõ in the former pticulers The vtmost of oᵣ
aime being but to remoue what might hinder or slacke the peace and that
neighboᵣly Corespondancie that wee disier intierly to ꝑseȓ betwixt the English Colonies and the dutch plantaciõ in these ꝑts, but if yoᵘ Refuse or delay
either to retourne ã answer or to giue dew and meete Satĩfaction in the
ꝓmises yoᵣ selfe will hinder the mecteing wᶜh wee all desier from which wee
may doe and hope we expect reall and Lasting fruite and will not then
blame vs if by all just means, wee seasonably ꝓvide for our owne safety and
Conveniency: Thus desiering yoᵂ will bee ꝑtsed with yᵣ first opertunity to
returne yoᵣ minde and answer hearein to mᵣ Eaton Gouᵣnᵣ of New hauen
Colony from whome that our counscells and Cource bee accordiñg ordered, we
expect the Isew and result of these our ꝑposcalls wee tacke Leaue ꝑ rest

    Plym̃   Septemb̃ᵣ 16ᵗʰ 1648)   Yoᵣ Loueing Friends

*Septemb^r the 12th the Comissioners Rescaued a packat brought by two Indians, whearein they found Lett^{r}s from Mr John Wintherope, from Captaine Mason and Mr Williams (with a retou^{r}ne from Tho: Stanton) by all which together with the Informat̃ formerly brought into the Colonyes by the Indians aboute them it appeareth that the Naragansetts and Nianticke Indians in Steed of paying the wampom longe dew to the Colonyes by theire Covenants made at Boston in Ano 1645 they haue by wampom hired the Mouhackes the Pocontock Indians aud others to cut of Vnquas and his people, and in case the English defeud him, then to fight with the English, wch Councell of theires was soe farr Ripned And p̃pared for execut̃ That Thõ Stanton and others sent as Mesengers from Conectacutt to inquire into (and if it might bee) to stopp such proceedings found the Indians mett at pocomquatuk as at theire Randivoze: whoe accknowledg they had rescaued Wampom ᵽc̃ from the Narragansets to invade Vnquas, that they were mett for that purpose: and expected both the Mohackes and other Indians to macke vpp theire full numb^{r}s : but partly by a reporte they had hearde That twoe Mowhacke Sachems were killed by the french or Easterne Indians or partly vnderstanding by Thom̃ Stanton that the English were a just and warr-licke people would defend him, they would stopp the intended invasion of Vnquas for this time, And further they were Informed by Mr. John Winth^p That the Narraganset and Niantique Indians were with draweing theire ould men theire weomen and childeren into Swampes, hideing theire Corne ᵽc̃, and soe prepareing to meete the Confeiderates the Mowhaukes, and with Eight hundered men to invade Vnquas and the Mowhackes were discribed by theire armes, as haueing fower hundred guns ᵽ for each gunñ three pownde of powther, and answerable shott: with a p̃visiõ for theire brests to secure them in the fight, and that Ninegratt in p̃ticuler Had inquired whither the English would defend Vnquas expressing himselfe that if they did, they Could soone burne the houses att Conectacutt ᵽc̃, that Weaquash Cooke and the Pacatucke Indians, had retired themselues to a pwoynte of Land, and disclaimed any adheareing to the Narragansetts in the foremencioned designe, all which beeing Considered the Comissioners returned thankes to Mr John Wintherope Captaine Mason, ᵽ Mr Williã desiering them if they heard any thing further Conserneing thee Indians Designes, either against the English or Vnquas they would as ᴧ Case might require giue speedy noatis thereof, both to the Matathusetts and Conitacott that from thence the other Colonyes, might vnderstand the dainger, and provide for theire safety, and vpon further Consideraciõ of the Narãgansetts and Niantiques breach of Covenants and trech-erous p̃seedeings, they thought fitt and desiered that the Comison^{r}s for the

Matathusetts, with theire first Conveniencie send sixe horce men with an able Intarpriter to the Narragansett & Niantique Sachems with the Instructions Foloweing ; giueing the Intarpriter an ōth trewly to express their minds and to make a trew Returne of the Sachems Answers : the Instructions were as Followeth,

Instrūtions For   Sent by the Comissione^{r}s of the vnited Colonies to Peasacus &c.

*Youe shall with ye first Conveniency goe to Narragansett and Niantique and if it may bee pcure a meeteing with all the Chefe Sachems, and giue them fully to vnderstand, that the Comission^{r}s of the English Colonyes Lately mett at Plyñ, haue dewly Considered what hath formerly passed betwixt the English and they the saide Sagamores and theire people, and more pticulerly, what had past att boston the last yeare, that vpō Ninecritts promis and Ingagemt they not onely gaue further tyme that the wampom long sence deue might bee fully brought in but gaue backe the Indian Hostages then in theire hands, whom they might for breach of Covenants iustly put to death the Comission^{r}s therfore hoped that at length the Narragansett Sachems in Gen^{r}all and Ninagratt in pticuler, would haue Considered and pvided for theire peace, by giueing dew Sattisfaction to the English Colonyes, but they finde to the Contrary, the whole Narragansett Carrag being full of guilefull delayes as if they would proclaime themselues a false Trecherous people not to bee trusted or treated with, Secondly you shall acquainte the said Sagamores or soe many of them as yo^u haue opertunity to speake with, that the English Comissioners from seuerall places and Sondery psons of Crediott: haue full Informacion of their latte Trecherous designes in hireing the Mowhaukes the pocantack Indians and others to asault and Cutt of Vncus and his people whearein the Comissioners canot but tacke knowledg of theire direct breaking the peace settled three yeares sence at Boston, with theire proude and insolent threttnings against the English, together with the mad and outragious Carrag of waopen homein one of the Narragansetts Captains who as a fier brand is still kindleing discontents and ofences, as if hee would drawe one a warre & soe the effusion of much bloode wch the English would spare :

Lastly: yo^w shall lett them know that the saide Comissioners haue sent yo^w to the saide Sagamores and theire people, to vnderstand theire purpose and resolucion, and if they Intend to Inioye the fruites of theire agrem^t Made at Boston in Ano 1645 they doe without further delayes bring in the rest of the wampom yet vnpayed, that som dew Cource may bee tacken with woapinhawmin, that hee disturbe not the publique peace and that dew pvision bee made for the security of Vncus and his people, whome the English are bounde to defend ₵ preserue while hee Carieth himselfe fairely or as the Cace may require mackes dew satisfaction for iniuryes, and yoᵂ shall tacke theire answers pticulerly and fully wᵗʰ such dew Consideracion that if there bee Cause for the Satisfaction of the Comissioners and Colonyes yoᵂ may returne it vpon oath,

The foregoeing Message beeing sent and the mesengers retū⁴ it is desiered that the Comissioners of the Matathusetts giue speedy noatis to the Comissioners of the other Colonyes what returne is made thearevnto by the Narragansetts ₵ Niantiques Sachems, that if noe Satisfaction bee giuen them in the ꝑmises, but they ꝑcede in theire Continened ꝑvocacions, a meeteing of the Comisiouᵣs may bee hasteued before the ordinary time in Septemᵗʳ (in the most Convenient Season) to pvid for the safety of the Colonyes, and vindicat̃ the houᵣ of the English in pᶠormance of theire Covenants to Vncus whose Ruin hath beene soe often atempted by them, and it is Conçaū the most Convenient ptᶜᵉ for a meeteing in the foremeuc̃ed Case to bee at Boston and the time the 16ᵗʰ day of July that all things may bee ordered in the fittest Season, and best maner for the atainemᵗ of our ends in the publique wellfaire wᶜʰ they recomended *To the seuerall Generall Coᵗᵗs to Consider of and pvide for accordingly and because it is vnsertaine what asaults may bee made vpon vncus and wayes tacken for his ouerthrowe, before the Comissioners Can meete it is Left to the Comisioners for Conitacutt and New hauen to aford such assistance to him from these twoe Colonyes as they shall judg the nesesety of his Cace maie require, vntill further ꝑvision bee made for his safety by the Concurant advice of all the Comissioners at theire meeting.

the Comissioners for the Matathusetts ꝑsented to the Comissioners of *of* the other Colonyes a writeing from a Comitee of theire Genᵗall Coᵗᵗe desiering that a dew Consideraciõ may bee had thereof, ₵ answer to the Seuᵗall pticulers, the wrighting is as Followeth.

Bostõ iu Suffolke

Att a meeting of the Com̃ity opwoynted by the Last Genᵗall Courte (vizṣ) the Goᵣnoᵣ Deputy Goᵣnᵣ Mᵣ Belingham Mᵣ Hibins Mᵣ Simons, Captin Caine, Captain Artherton Captaine Hawthorne the Suv̆ Genᵗall, and Mᵣ Jackson, the 19ᵗʰ of the 4ᵗʰ Mᵒ and adiournied to the 26ᵗʰ of the 5ᵗʰ month, it was agreed and ordered that the ꝑpsisiõ̃s heere Folowing should be Comended to our Comissioners for the vnitel Collonyes, by them to be propounded to the rest of the Comissioners at theire next meeteing,

*136

Wheareas the intencion of the United Colonyes in o^r Confederacio̅ was to p̃serue and ppogate the truith and Libertyes of the Gospell, and to pvide for Meutuall safety against enemies and p̃sernacion of peace amongst o^r selues, (Comon wellfaire, as by the Second and Eight Article (c̃, soe as the Comissioners Power should not extend to Limitt or Interupt the Siuell Go^{r}m^t or Church affaires within any of the Colonyes within it selfe According to the entent of the third article and the pviso in the sixth article, it is desiered that the Comissioners would please to make a more full and Cleare explainac̃ of those articles, and of the said pviso, according to the ppsisions here Foloweing vidz̃. by safety in the second Article to bee intended onely safety from an enemye, Not from Comon pvidences, as Famin pestolence (c̃, the same of Comon wellfaire,

The scope of the Eight Article to extend onely to Causes which Conserne diuers of the Colonyes (not any one in itselfe) or som one or more of the Colonyes, and som neighbo^r Plantacions, not within the Confideracio̅

and by Indians to bee ment Indian Straingers or such Neighb^r Indians as are not in Subiection to the Gou^{r}m^t of any of the Colonyes

In such Cases of Ciuell nature w^{t}her the Comissioners may haue power to make orders (c̃, yett not to haue power to make Gen^{r}all officer of a Ciuell Nat^r to execut such orders, but the same to be executed by the Officers of such Jurisdictions as shallbe Conserned therein, and if such Jurisdiction or Colony shall not Submitt and pforme (c̃, After dew admo̅ then to be Responcall to the rest of the Colonyes for breach of League and Couenant, and to be declared what further power the Comissioners haue in such Caces or what willbee fitt to be don in case any Colony should Chang theire Religion pfessed ec,

*Wheareas in Cace sixe of the Comissioners shall not agree the Cause is to be refered to the fouer Gen^{r}all Courtes, and by theire Joynte agrem^{t}s to be determined (c̃, to be Considered of it were not more expedient to bee determined vpo̅ the agrem^t of any three of them pvided it bee in such Cace, whearein the Comissioners haue to dcalle.

If the anuall meeteing were not beter to be triauuall, exept occasions require any meeteing in the intreuall, and the Comissioners at such occasionall mecteings to haue power to put of the next Triannall metings if they see Cause.

Wheareas by y^e .6. Article each of the Colonyes is to haue two Comissioners, and the Colony of the Matathusetts beares almost fiue for one in the proportio̅ of Charge with any one of the rest, they desier to haue one Comission^r more or otherwise they shall be content that any other of the

1

2

3

4
*137

Not allowed

5

6

Colonyes shall haue the same p̄viledg to haue three Comissioners to the other twoe, if such Colonyes will beare the Licke p̄porcion of Chardg with the Matathusetts,

It is desierd it may bee Considered if that way of yᵉ p̄porcioning the Chardg in the 4ᵗh Article, by Numbering of people bee Convenient (if Lawefull or safe in Regaurd of the Frequencie of it) or equall in regaurd of the diferant Condicions of som of the Colonyes; oʳs being many pore laboʳoʳs and artificers, som of the other all men of ability well stoct (c̄, if it bee found soe, then some other more safe (̧ equall Cource to bee agreed vpon

Wheareas ther bee diuers orders made by the Comissioncrs (as aboute admission of Church members, maintainance of scolers at Cambredg, about a Genʳall trade (c̄. as in the booke of Records of the Comissioners Acts doe more fully apeare, all which orders are oncly by way of advice, to the Genʳall Courts of the Seuʳall Colonyes yet for as much as orders by way of aduise are in som cases introductions to orders of power where the advice is not Followed it is to bee p̄pounded if it were not seasonable to be declared that in such Cacos, if any of the Colonyes shall not thinke fitt to Folow such advice, the same not to be accoumpted any offence or breach of any article of our Confederacion or to giue power or occasion to the Comisioners to p̄sede to any act of athority in such Cace

Wheareas by order of the Comisioners at theire last meting at Boston Sprinkefield is Inioyncd to contrebute towards an Imposision for the maintainance of Sea brooke forte (as the order seemes to Intend with Liberty for the Matathusetts (c̄,) to p̄pounde and obiect (c̄, at the next meteing of the Comissionʳs (c̄, as in the same order doth more fully apeere, according whervnto wee doe p̄pounde, to the honored Comissioners the obiections and arguments heere following :

First wee obiect that our Reasons formerly deliuʳd in to the Comissioners haue not Resc̄aiued a full answer from our breatheř of Conectacut, nor can wee pscaiue that the p̄amble to theire saide order *Doe make any suply of such defect in our bretherens answer Or is a suficient grounde of the saide order for yᵉ saide Contribucion (c̄ : as wee hope to make euident by pticulers,

> 1 Reasō, oʳ First reason was drawne from the defect of power in one Jurisdiction to contribut towards the purchas of Lands, tenem̄ᵗs (̧ other hereditamᵗs or Libertyes whatsoeuer.

>> Answer. The answer is that the question is mistacken which should haue bēne whither the Impo-

sision be Lawefull or regular, not to what vse ℈. ℈
Conclude that in such Case the pty is not to Inquire
After the Imploym^t of the means soe Contributed
℈ with deniall of pwoynte of Imploym^t for purchas

To this answer wee reply, 1 : the answer is not to the argum^t. but to an Reply
other thing. 2ly. that the question (as we Consċaiue) is not mistacken for
which we refeer our selues to M^r hopkins owne Lett^r, and Mr Fenwix intrest
in the Imposisiō for if he hath sould the forte and yet haue sole (or any)
right to the Imposision for maintainance of it, then it must needes bee for
the purchas, and if hee bee nŏt to Imploy what he resċaiues For the maintainance of the forte, then it must bee for the purchas, or for som other
Consideraċ which will not answ̄ the entent of the order, and to bee forced to
contribute to a purchas and yet to haue noe share in the thing purchased
seemes not just : 2ndly wee deny the argum^t to bee good : at Least not to
    ₐ in o^r Case for Sprinkefeild is not in Subiectiō to the Jurisdiction at
Conectacut soe as to resċaiue any of theire Imposisions w^thout Quesť ℈. as
if the Comissioners vpon noatis of a foraigne enemy should raise a Thousand
pounds to maintaine a man of warre vpon the Coast, and in steed thereof
should raise a fort at the enterance of one of o^r harbō^rs, the Colonyes might
Justly question this Impm^t ℈.

2 Reasons, *our first*

> o^r second reason is vpon that maxem which wee Cōscaiue
> to be the sole grounde of the Comission^rs order vidz℥ Qui
> senti Comaudvm sent tire debit et tonas ₐ Converco ℈ :
> but Sprinkefield hath noe benifit ℈ therfore it ought
> not to be Chardged.

The Answer to this is i. that such oposision would reflect vpō most of Answ
the Gou^rm^ts of evrup, secondly a reference of the Cause to be jsewed vpon
Sprinkefields hauing benifitt or not ℈.

Wee Reply to the first it is noe good argum^t to say most of the *Gou^rm^ts Reply
of euroup doe thus, therfore it is Lawefull noe more then if wee should say   *139
most of the Gou^rm^ts ℈. opress both Subiects ℥ Straingers ergo opresion is
Lawefull : 2ndly Let any such example be prodused (as Comonly allowed)
wheareby a suitable benifit is not held forth or at Least ꝓtended. 3dly vpon
all Imposisions vpon straingers, if they Licke not to pay them they haue
Libertie ℥ opertunity to avoyde them, they may keepe from vnder Comānd

wheareby to be compelled, but Sprinkfīld had noe such Liberty before the Imposision Raised nor can haue any such opertunity for the avoydeing   After Beeing Imprisoñd by the Scituaciō of the habitatiō, to the Second if wee might conclude of fuiture time by what is past wee might Joyne jsew vpō this pwoynte, but when a meere p̄sibility is to bee determined by mens various sirmises it Canot bee safe to referr maters of weight to such vnsertaine jsew, but Let it be graunted, that Sprinkfeild may haue benifit by Sea brooke fort: yet not being nessesaryly, but continge^t onely, they are noe more bound to Contribute in that respect, then New hauen ᵱ wee are bound to contribute to the maintainance of Hartfō^d Bridges or theire high waies : which we haue more sertaine benifitt by for though they might Impose a toale for the maintainance of a bridg (not soe in an anciant high waie) yet men were at Liberty to pass ouer the ancient fords if they Like it not to pay theire Toale and we desier noe more at Seabrooke, but to pass as allwayes wee ᵱ others haue done ; but if wee com to Ancho^r for refuge vnder y^r forte or volontaryly will macke vse of ye Chardg, wee will not refuse to pay for our benifitt as if Conectacutt wilbee at Chardg to Clence the Chanell for pasage of greate shippes : and therevpō lay a Impost vpon all of such a burthen as could not haue passed otherwise then if Sprinkefield will make vse of it for shipps of such burthen it is reason they should pay the Impost:

> 3 Reasō o^r Third Reason was from a grounde of equity for if som Straingers which dwell vp the Riuer be sparred the burthen will lye more heauy vpon the rest.

Answer

The Answer to this is first ; that it is but a p̄sumption ᵱᵈ. secondly the Comp^{is} is not equall.

Reply wee Reply (if it will not bee Confessed ᵱᵈ,) then vpon our first paym^t wee may disier an accoumpt of what hath beene rescaiued ᵱᵈ wch Canot bee denyed vs, secondly, we Confess the Comparison is not of things every way a Licke, but the diferance makes the more for vs for they being more strainger̃ (wee less or not at all,) being Now vnited Tribut should bee demãnded of them rather then of vs :

4 Reasons, our fourth Reason Consisteth of twoe branches 1 tacken from the Longe time that this Confideracion was hindered by the propoundeing and standing vpon such p̄posisiō ᵱᵈ.

The second from our p̄roscription of Imvnyty: ᵱᵈ.

*To which they answr by discouering theire greife at or Mistacke as they terme it, and Implisitly taxe vs with Neglect of Evident truith, in or publique Records : 2ndly by Laying open or mistacke in maner folowe- ing : viz. wheareas wee say that this Combinacion was hindered for aboue x. yeares by the means ppounded, They say it will bee founde that it was Not full fiue yeares From the mencioned agitaciō for a Combinacion (the con- clusion of this prsent Confederacion, the one being in June 1638 and the other Agreed vpon in may 1643 and whereas it is afirmed (ð, it shall if neede bee be made apeare by the oath of those whoe were Imployed in that seruice, that they were soe farr from stifly standing vpon such ane Imposision as they did not soe much as propounde it as it is heere expressed, nor Could they in Reason doe it the townes haueing no intrest in, nor relacion to the forte at that tyme.

To this wee reply 1. wee must Confesse theare is a mistacke in the Reply words as for wante of one monosillable which the necesitie of the aprehendiñ the trew meaneing might haue helped without any greife or trouble, for it being knowne to them and vs, that from the first Establishing the Gourmt of Conectacott to the pfiting of our Confideracion there Could not bee aboue seauen yeares, it must needes bee Either ā expression against or meaneing to put in ten for foure or sixe, or elce it must bee a huperobolicall speach, as is not rare, either in humaine or deuine wrightings, to expresse a less Number by ten as Jacob saide to Laban thoue hast changed my wadges ten times ; but wee shall not neede to vse any figur to helpe or expressions if the word since had beene aded according to the trew meaneing of some that had ane hand in the passing the reasons, (ð. for wee can make it apeare, that the not consent- ing to free passage in the Riuer of Conectacotte had hindered the combinañ ten yeare sence or neere theareaboutes, at the time when those Reasō were drawne vp, (howsoeŭ som of the Comission rs, then Imployed at Cam- beridg may haue forgotten, yet it is sertaine to vs (for Littera scripta manete) that ye Article for the free passage vp and downe the Riuer was then stood vpon by vs, and they afirmeing that the riuer (ð did belong to the Lords (ð — (onely for soe much as belonged to themselues they were Content to graunte) wee thought not fitt to finish the agremt vntill they had conferred with theire Corte aboute it, (whosoeŭ shall offer to testifie otherwise, shall comitt a greater eror then or Records can justly be charged with — and therefore wee desier that either, that Chardg vpon vs may bee put out of the Comission rs Records! or elce that this or difence may likewise bee recorded:

5 Reason o^r Last reason was from the vnexpected thrauldom ℮ð
℮ o^r ℘scription by ancient possession.

Answer   To this they answer, they Canot Consc̃aiue how it Can
bring any such thrauldom, or Inconveniencie sence the Comis-
sion^{r}s haue power to regulate ℮ð 2ndly that they had possesion
before Sprinkefield. 3^d. That Mr Pinchin himself (when hee ad-
heared to that Jurisdiction did aecknowled) the Justice of such an
Imposicion, and did incorag the Gent̃ men of Saybrooke forte ℮ð.

Reply

*141

To this wee reply 1 though the p^{r}sent Comissiõ^{r}s (whom wee know well
*And whose wisdom and Integcr̃ty wee doe Not Question) haue declared theire
tender care of an equall cource, betwene the twoe Colonyes according to theire
p^{r}sent aprehencioñ, of the case in quest̃ yet (for as Much as wee canot foresee
what comission^{r}s may folow in time sucseedeing) it canot bee expected that
wee should yealde vp any Lawefull Liberty god hath giuen vs to the will and
discresion of others, especialy such as wcc canot foresee whoe or what they may
bee, — 2^{ndly} the question of priority for possesion as well as priority of graunt
must needs bee determined for vs for the first possesion of Say brooke forte,
was tacken by Mr John Wintherope Nouemb^r 1635 and o^r possiõ was before
that, for those who went from Watertowne ℮ Camberidg and ℮ Roxebcry and
Dorchester the sumer before tooke possesion in o^r name ℮ Right and had a
Comission of Gou^{r}m^t from vs, and some ordinance for theire defence, and in
this state they remayned a good space — 3dly if Mr Pinchin were Now of
hartford Jurisdiction as hee then suposed himselfe to bee hee might say still
as hee did then ℮ ought to bee Subiect to theire Impossisions ℮ð —

Haueing thus Replyed to o^r breatherens answeres to o^r former Reasons
against the Impossision ℮ð. wee, desier the hon^{r}ed Comission^{r}s for theire beter
satisfaction, to consider what wee haue further to propound ℮ Obiect ags^t the
saide Imposition and the order for the Establishing thearof

First it is a Resãiued Maxem in Lawe — * Com aLiquide arteri dater
Conserdĩ Eatiam vydetur Elud sineco redita frui non Lotest, thearfore if a man
endoweth his wife of Land Lying in the midest of other Lands of his shee
shall haue a way to her Land in ioyntare though noe way were graunted —
Soe if a man hath fiue hundered Loads of wood sett vpon his Land, and hee
sells a hundered Loade of this to a strainger ₍ shall haue free egress ℮ Regress
℮ð to fetch of this woode, though it were Not expressed in the graunte ℮ð.

* [Cum aliquid ulteri datur concedi etiam videtur
illud, sine quo re data frui non potest.
Mass. Archives, vol. 2. 316.]

but if the owner of the Land will hier a man to watch his fower hunderd Load that it bee Not stoalen ℓℨ, though thearby the straingers wood is in more safety, yett hee canot bee Compelled to contribute to yᵉ charge of this watchman for the other was not bounde to tacke care of the Safety of his wood — Soe in oʳ Cace a maine end of the graunte was that the Land might bee Subdewed and planted wᶜh seing it could not bee, without the benifitt of pasage vp and downe Conectacut Riuer, it must bee intended that such Liberty of pasage was graunted with the Land though it were not expressed, and the rather because it is alsoe a ressaiued Ruile that all such grauntes for Comon good shallbee enterprited in the Lardgest sence: and as may bee most for the benifit, and advantage of the graunte ℓ if Saybrooke ℓℨ will erect a forte for theire owne Safety they canot compell vs to Contrebute towards it for they are not bounde to tacke Care of oʳ safety   2nd we ℥pound that if Sprinkefeild ought to Contribute to Say brooke forte because they may haue benifit by it, why then New hauen ℓ Stamford and all the townes one that side should Not contribute allsoe (and soe Sprinkefield Cardge will bee the more easey) for it is manifest they may haue benifit by it as well as Sprinkefeild for if ane enemy should posses the Riuers mouth hee may (by a smaule friget entersept the trade of those townes.

3dly vpon this it will follow that the Comission'ʳs of New hauen: Canot be judges Leagually equall in this Case in Regaurd of theire comon enterest, noe more then those of Conectacut, and this might bee a Leaguall obiection ag̊t the saide order ℓℨ:

Fourthly wee obiect against this order as being made without sight of the patent at Conectacut ℓℨ. (at Least by oʳ Comission'ʳs or by some of yᵉ Comission'ʳs whoe were ptyes to the saide order) and soe without just grounde for de Non Existentibus et non aperentibus Eiadem Rasiō, — and if the patent had beene ℥duced, ther might haue beene som Clause in it wᶜh might haue Cleared *The Cace on oʳ parte.

4

*142

Fifthly wee ℥pounde whither (Admiteing it were Lawfull) it bee expediente and whither the benifite is Licke to bee Tanti as may recompence the Inconveniencies wᶜh may arise hearevpon, wee Looke at it as a boane Cast in by Sathan to interupt oʳ happy peace ℓ brotherly vnion, and to raise discord amongst vs and soe put vs vpon temptacīs to helpe oʳ selues some other way, and the rather when we shall heare that som of oʳ breatheren, not contenteing themselues wᵗh what benifit oʳ Contriᵬ may afford, shall trivmph oᶠ vs as haueing gained a greate victory and enlardgeing theire conquests (inovissimum vs que Diem) to the furthest of oʳ Interest vpon that Riuer ℓℨ: wᶜh may indeede bee a j'st action of greife to vs whoe ernestly desier that Not onely the affaires of brotherly vnion, but the senceare afection also may bee p̃serued amongst o^r selues ⦃ deriued entire (w^thout any Monument of violaciō to the sucsed Gen^racion — wch wee humbly Comend to the Consideraciō of the honered Comission^{rs}

Lastly to bee ppounded to the Comision^{rs} in Consideracion that o^r Neighbo^{rs} the dutch, will not pmit any of o^{rs} to trade with the Indians within the Limits of theire Jurisdiction, and doe Imposse very greate Cvstoms vpō o^r people and force them to Ancho^r in places very inconvenient ⦃c̃. whither it be not Just ⦃ nessesary for the Colonyes, to barr the dutch from Trade with the Indians, within any of o^r Jurisdictions Either Narrogansct or Peaquod ⦃c̃.

JOHN WINTHEROPE Go^rn^r THOMAS DUDLY deputy Gou^rfl̃ ⦃
WILL HIBENS ROBERTE CAYNE HUMPHERY ATHERTON
JOHN JOHNSON

The Comissioners haueing p^rvsed and wth dew Respect Considered the former pposicions, wheaŕof som conscrne explicacion som ane Alteracion in the Articles of confideraciō betwixt the Colonyes: doe ioyntely and in Geñall concaiue that all and each of the articles from time to time as theire may bee occasion should bee soe vnderstoode, that noe such Interpretacion bee put vpon any one article as may Crosse the direct scope ⦃ Imporṭe of the rest or any of them, that the pvision made to maintaine a peculier and Intier Jurisdiction in each Colony w^thin itselfe, hinder not the atainem^t of the p̃blique ⦃ weighty ends of the Combinaṫ Namely the dew p^rservacion of the peace of the Colonyes, ioyntely by all Just meañs of a publike Concernem^t, according to the Articles, ⦃ the dew Manageing of warr in the pp^racions and other concern^ts of the same when the Colonyes are Nesesaryly called vnto it — This p̃mised,

first   The Comissioners conceiue that by the words (safety and wellfaire) in theire Second Article Noe power is graunted to thcm by wch they may make orders o^r Lawes to p̃vent or pvide in casses of famine, and pestolence, though yet in those and other caces of Like Consernem^t the Advice of Comission^{rs} Magistrats Elders, memb^{rs} of the Colonyes or any of them, should bee dewly ⦃ Respectiuly considered: According to the Nature ⦃ weight of it.

2   The Comission^{rs} consc̃aiue that the Eight Article in the trew scope of it extends only to Causes, whearein all the Colonyes are Conserned, or at Least more then any one Considered single and w^thout Reference ⦃ Influence into the safety ⦃ wellfaire of any of the rest, they conc̃aiue further that it is ⦃ may bee safe for any man to take an Indian Seruant, or for any plantacion to

admitt a ciuelized Indian to bee a planter, but by the third Article, (as they vnderstand it, ꝑvision is made that noe Jurisdiction Rescaiue any plantacion or Jurisdiction, whither English, French, Duch, or Indian, without Consent of the rest, wᶜh Consent is to be Interprited as in the sixth Article, wᶜh is a Cace of Genᵗall ⟨ weighty Consideration the Comissionʳs beleueing that seūrall plantacions of Indians will Redly Submitt to each of the Colonyes Respectiuely if they may haue guns, powther, shott ⟨c̃, sould vnto them, as the English, wᵗhin theire seuᵗall Jurisdictiõs but such a Cource Canot stand wᵗh the safety of the Colonyes, the ^ desier thearefor that all the Colonyes for the future will Consider how safe it may *Bee either to recaiue or to furnish any Indians wᵗh any prouision for warr.

3dly though the Comissonʳs Consider and order in the publique Consernemᵗs of the Colonyes within the Compasse of the trust ⟨ power contained in the articles (as in all treatyes Concerneing peace and warr, sending mesengers, opwoynteing Genᵗalls And other officers for warr when all the Colonyes are Interested opwoynteing Numbers of men ordering prouision, and Chardges Nesesary for the Seruice giueing Comissions tackeing accoumpts Sensureing offenders, and all things of Licke Nature wᶜh are the pʳper Concomitants or Consequents of such a Confideration yet the execucion to belong to the Jurisdiction wherein the Comissionʳs sitt or wheare the offender is or may bee founde, and to the Magistrates and other Inferioʳ oficers, but soe that if the Majestrates oʳ the officers doe deny or delay execuciõ in any Cace proper to the Comissionʳs Cognizenc̃ and whearein the other Colonyes are Interested, ⟨ may sufer such Jurisdictiõ to bee responcable for breach of Covenante, but what shall bee don in such Cace, or in cace any Colony should Change theire Religion ꝑfessed they Conscaiue Canot bee Now soe well Resolued, as when the Cace in the Compass and with all Sircomstances shall bee considered

In caces ꝑpʳ to the Comissioʳs whereas by the sixth article if sixe Agree not the ꝑposicions with the Reasons are to be Refered to the Fower Gen̄all Couʳts : the Comissionʳs aproueing the Mocion made by the Comity of the Masachusets doe recomend it to the Fower Gen̄all Courts that if any *of* three of the saide Courts agree or conclude of any such ꝑposicion it shall passe and bee accoumpted as the Conclusion of the vnited Colonyes as it should haue passed as ane act of the Comissioʳs if sixe of them had consented — For the 5th sixth ⟨ seuenth pʳposicions pʳsented from the Comissionʳs of the Masachusetts Importeing a reall Chang in the tearmes ⟨ Covenants of Confideration as noe alteracion Can bee made wᵗhout the Consent of all and each of the Gen̄all Courts soe the Comissioʳs Feare that any of the Alteraciõ mencioned would proue daingerous ⟨ Inconvenᵗ to all oʳ som of the Colonyes, the

4

tacken of the Number of malles they hope need not bee frequent Nor as it hath beene Caryed by the Comission's inconvenient, in pt of the seuenth pposicion they Conscaiue there is a mistack the Lardge trade of the Masachusets besid(, theire Nvmbers afford many advantages in Reference to estates wͨh the other Colonyes wante (but it is from the Free grace of god that all and each haue what they haue, they diser to bee thainkefull.

A dew Consideration of the Articles (what is allredy expressed in the p̃misses serue for answer to the pposicion in all caces wheare the Fower Gen'all Courts haue Not giuen the Comission's power to determine it will bee by mistacke if the ‸ ither make order o͐ Chardge breach of Coveñᵗ vpon any of the Colonyes for deseting, in other caces wheare they doe but advize (Recomend as the Articles giue warrante soe they doe Not yet ap͐hend, how such recomendaciõ may growe Interoductions to orders of power if they did, they should redyly Closse with the hon͐ed Courte of the Masachusets in p̃viding agsᵗ such ane Inconveniencie:

Lastly the Comission's haue seriously Considered what is p̃pounded from the Masachusets in reference to the dutch Imposicions and restraints by wͨh the english Marchants are burthened and much discouraged in theire trade (haue both wrighten to the dutch Gou͐ñ (his Covnscell and doe recomend to the seu'all Gen'all Courts, that answerable p̃p'acion may bee made that either vpon his Refuseing to answer or his not giueing Meete satisf' the Colonyes may seasonably p̃vid for theire safety (Conveniencie :

The Nynth pposicion in the wrighting p͐sented from the Masachusets Conserneing Conectacut (Sprinkefield in the Cace of the Imposicion at Seabrooke, the Comission's for Conectacut made answer to It in wrightiñ as Foloweth.

The Reply of Comity ‸ the Gen'all Courte of the Masachusets to what was answe͐d by the Comission's of Conectacut the Last yeare at Boston

to the Arguments *Then p͐sented against the Imposicion at sea brooke is soe Lardge yᵗ for the sooner dispāch of this meeteing (Dew consideracion, wee thought it Not ane vnreasonable mocion to p͐sent to y͏ᵉ Comission's of the other Colonyes that the question might for p͐snt remaine as it was determined the Last yeare (Liberty giuen to the Gen'all Courte at Conitacut to p̃pare a reioynder to the reply Now made agsᵗ the Next meeteing, which wee Concaiue is noe more then hath beene graunted to y͏ᵉ Masachusets, the heareing and determineing of this Cace haueing beene put of for a hole yeare vpon the bare aligacion of the Comission's, for that Colony that they were not p̃pared by any Instructions from the Gen'all Courte then to speake to it, and the disadvantg to Conitacut Seemes aparent (the Masachusets haueing had a full whole yeares Liber for ꝑpareing arguments to opose, ȼ the Licke for theire reply to the answer giuen in to theire argumᵗs) if a present returne to theire reply be required But seeing yᵉ Comissioners for the Colonyes judg it meete that answer bee made wee redyly Submit and adresse oʳ selues there-vnto, wᵗʰ as much breuity as wee can Reserueing oʳ selues for a fuller answer hereafter if acacion shall serue

to Theire ffirst Reply wee concaiue wee neede not say more for the Cleareng of that Coast then what is expressed in oʳ former answer ouely wee add this wᶜʰ wee hope Canot bee denyed, that the demaunds of the Imposicion being by vs it is in oʳ Liberty to state the question (and Not in those that oposse) wᶜʰ as formerly soe wee Now again do thus.

Whither for erecting and maintaineing a forte vsefull and seruiceable Quesᵗ to the *to the* whole Riuer it bee not Lawefull for the Jurisdiction of Conectacut to sett a moderate Imposision vpon some goods exported through the Mouth of the Riuer wheare the forte is, though it reach Sprinkefeild situat vpon that Riuer under the Consideracion of Lying wᵗʰin ane other Jurisdiction wᶜʰ yet is not soe cleared but yᵗ yᵉ Jurisdiction of Conectacut haue Liberty for theire Inquiry, and concaiue they haue Cause to macke Clayme therevnto, being reedy to atend all due means for the Isewing of this business allsoe ; this being the question ȼ Cace ꝑpounded by vs, wee Conceiue oʳ answer (to wᶜʰ wee Referre) is full, and it will bee no disadvantg to the Cace though Mʳ Phenwicke doe inioy what comes in from the same Imposicion, Notwithstanding what is in the second place theire reply that Sprinke-field is Not to recaiue oʳ Imposicion wᵗhout questioneing for wee still concaiue the argumᵐᵗˢ brought 	ₐ Must bee directed against the Imposicion as by vs Claymed either in the quantaty or quality of it or they reach Not the Cause : it Consernes them Not to question as wee saide before to what vse the meanes raised by the Imposicion is put.

Theire Reply to the seconde, Consisting of seuʳall ꝑticulers, wee answer thus and graunte the first that it is Noe good argumᵗ to say most Gouʳmᵗˢ in Europe doe thus Ergo such a pʳctice is Lawefull, but deny that any such thinge was afirmed by vs or can bee rightly Colected from what wee answered for the argumᵗ being that it is Iniurious to require a coostom to yᵉ maintainance of a forte to whome it is not vsefull ; wee answered that this as a posision in itselfe Nackedly considered *in it* seemed to lay most of the gouʳnmᵗs of Europe vnder the guilte of Injusᵗ (though it touched Not the pʳsent question *is* if there were Noe Lawfull grounde of requireing ℓ tackeing any Imposision or Costom to any wᵗhout retourneing a ꝓportionable aparent advantage ℓ good to those of whome it is rescaiued when as it is apʳently knowne Imposisions are Rescaiued, and that Lawfuly vpon other Consideracō wᶜh is soe obvious to eury mans apʳehencions, that wee neede Not instanc in ꝑticulers as is desiered ℓ therefore shall say Noe more to the Seconde

To the third ꝑticuler Conserneing the vsefullness of the foremencioned forte to Sprinkefeild wee Leaue that to Consideracion of such things as haue heene alredy pʳsented, in that respect onely shall add: that if ane Imposiciŏ may be tacken (wᶜh seemes to bee graunted) of such wᶜh onely come to trade in the Riuer: in Regaurd if they Licke Not to pay: they may avoyde it, wee concāu it much more Reasonable, for those whoe haue a more aparent ℓ Constante benifit theȓby, ℓ wee Might alsoe say there is Noe absolute Nesesity put vpon Sprinkefeild in this Imposicion if they will Cary theire Corne as mʳ Pinchin doth his beaū by Land they may avoyde it: ℓ wheareas it semes to bee intimated that all fords ℓ pasages Must be Lefte in the same freedom ˄ Liberty wᶜh Nature hath Lefte them, ℓ others at any time haue found them in, it oʳthrowes as wee concāu all ꝑticuler intrests and the p̄ctise

of all people even of the Masachusets Gouʳnmᵗ as may *Bee instanced.

Wee shall Not Much add in the third as being desierous to Contracte what may bee, ℓ there being soficient as wee concaiue in oʳ answer ℓ the expression in the Comissioʳs determinacion to satisfie, onely wee desier it may be Considered how Neere the p̄ctise of the Masachusets is heere to that they obiect agst: theire argumᵗ seemes to bee *to bee* thus it is Not right to demand that of breatheren wᶜh is Not of Strangers, but that the Masachusets, by vertew of the expressions in theire patent of goeing to the South Sea Clayme ane interest to Sprinkefeild (Warro Nocoe ℓŏ) after they were Setled vnder ane other Gouʳmᵗ yet they Clayme Not the Licke at forte Oramia that lyeth wᵗhout any Controuersy wᵗhin theire Limutes vpon that grounde: ℓ wee further concāiue if the Masachusets setle any plantacion vpon hudsons Riuer by vertew of theire graunte theire p̄sent plea for free egress ℓ regress in ℓ out of that Riuer would Not bee founde of a p̄vaileing power.

What was saide in the Fourth doth Not any way Contradict what was answered by vs : but the whole remaines vntouched, and wee could say alsoe that the adicion of the monosilable sence will Not helpe in the Cace vnless theire bee ane other Monosᵇˡ vizℐ: numbʳ 10: Converted into Eight, but wee are vnwilling to insist vpon all ꝑticulʳs Least wee should ꝓvoke, being content with any thing that may bee judged to bee of that Nature in oʳ Last wrighting oʳ this may bee expounged ℓ wheareas it hath beene afirmed, that though there were some Mistakes in the words, yet the strength of the argum^t is Euident, ˄ doe professe wee did Not at all aprehend in o^r first answer wheare that strength lay : ₵ Now after this interp^{r}ttaion made we diserne Not (phaps through o^r owne darkeness) were any apearance of p̃vaileing force of argum^t yet lyeth, all that Comes to o^r viewe is heere there was a ꝑposicion made by the Masachusets in 1638 at a treaty for Combinacion that they might haue the free Liberty of Conectacut Riuer for any plantacions that were o^r might bee vnder theire Goũm^t w^{t}hout Imposicion of Conectacut ₵ they not Consenting to that ꝑposicion hinderd the Combinacion Ergo it might seeme vnequall Now wee are combined to require any wee Need Not say any more to answer to this but that Conectacut was Not in a Capasaty then to graunte what was desiered ; Nor are they Now in the Condicion the˄ were in at that treaty : the Interest and Chardg of the forte being now theires, w^{c}h then was in other hands:

The very same w^{c}h is heere replyed to o^r answer, how the bondage ₵ inthrauldom of Sprinkefeild (w^{c}h was obiected) is p^{r}vented by the Confederation may bee obiected against that article, w^{c}h was ₵ is still soe good ₵ soe wholsom ₵ vsefull for p̃serueing peace w^{t}h Righteousness thearefore shall say Noe more vnto it

5

Secondly in the first argum^t Sprinkefields posesions ₵ Chardge is aledged Now the posesion of the Masachusets by all the townes, thence Isewed is ꝑdused, but Neither the one Nor the other Can as wee concaiue Cary this Cace the Comission of Go^{r}m^t Mencioned tacken from the Masachusets was taken Salua Jury of the enterest of the Gentlemen whoe had the patent of conectacut, that Comission takeinge rise from the desier of the *desier of the* people whoe Remoued whoe judged it in Conveniencie to goe away, w^{t}hout any frame of Gou^{r}m^t: not from any Clayme of the Masachusets Jurĩdictiõ o^r them by vertew of patent:

Thirdly the reply to o^r answer Conserneing Mr Pinchins proposicion to Mr Phenwix doth not satisfie, for that arose not from power of Jurisdiction the plantacions vpon the Riuer not being then vnder the Go^{r}m^t of the patentees nor vnder the authority of any order amongst themselues requireing such a Contrebucion but as wee concaiue from that prencipall of equity in his owne brest — qui sentet Comodum sentere Debet et onas.

To the fresh argum^{t}s Now ꝑduced wee breafely answer, that Maxem in Lawe hee sighted wee concaiue houlds not vniversally trew nor can bee aplyable to the p^{r}sent case, the instances giuen noe wayes suiteing, therew^{t}h, and wee concaiue all the Interest the patent doth or Cane in any way of reason giue vnto any in the Riuers hauens Creekes &c̃, can be extended but soe farr as the Lmeuts of *of* the patent extends

The second seemes to yeild the Cause by Confessing Sprinkefield to recaiue benifit by the forte wch was denyed, but wee add alsoe this the benifits Sprinkefeild recaiues is soe farr different from that of New hauen & the other townes mencioned &c̃: and this soe obvious to euery view as wee concaiue it Needs noe answer, the third wee Leaue to the Comission^rs to determ̃

Fourthly the Coppy of the patent was seene when the Confideracion was made the thing it selfe is well knowne to many, besids wee concaiue it canot bee vnknowne to the Masachusets that this patent hath beene Lately owned by the honorable Comity of Parlam^t & equall Respect & power giuen to it by *Them w^thin the bounds therein mencioned as to the Masachusets & Plymõh within theire Seu^rall Limit& Respectiuely

*146

Fifthly wee hope and much desier that in all the pseedings of this Confider truith & peace may soe kiss each oth^r that the pleadeings for truith may not ꝑiudice peace, but that wch seemes Rasionall & according to god may bee p^rsented w^thout offence, & wee hope the boasteing heerin Chardged vpon som of o^rs will either bee held forth in pticulers & Euidenced (that the guilty may com vnder dew sencure) or the Chardge recalled for as in our Judgm^t wee condemne such wayes soe it is o^r hope wee shall not bee founde to aproue in p^rctice

Wee haue breifely and sodenly retourned o^r answers to what hath beene presented from the Masachusets, & doe hope it will bee Satisfactory to those whoe imp^rscally Consider the Cace in hand, but if there shall appeare any defect in o^r answer, wee diser the same Liberty may bee graunted to vs ‸ was formerly to them, that Nothing bee concluded against vs vntill o^r Gen^rall Courte haue had consideracion of the reply and the more full reioynder bee from them retourned, vpon further argueing the cace in hand./ the Comissio^rs for the Masachusets p^rsented this ensewing wrightiñ

A addicion of som consideracions & ꝑ^rposicions Concerneing the Impost o^r Contrebucion required of Sprinkefeild, by the Comission^rs of conectacut to those *whoe* wee haue tendered from the Comity of o^r Gen^rall Courte wch wee desier may dewly be considered, wee desier that the comissio^rs of Conectacut may expressly declare w^ther theī desier the saide Ympost or Contribucion to the purchas of the forte at the riuers mouth or as cvstõ that soe wee may speake more distinctly to it.   Secondly wee haue Cause to suppose there is noe order of the Gen^rall Courte of coneçtacut that requires any thing of Sprinkfeild ˄ by way of Cvstom oᶜ Impost ℂ therfor if required at all it must be by way of contrebucion to yᵉ purchas as mʳ Hopkins Lettʳ to mʳ Pinchin Seemes to Intimate and a clause in the Comision's order the Last yeare doth the Licke, wheare it is sayde that from the first day that any of the plantacõns vpon the Riuᵗ haue payed, it hath vpon the same grounde beene demaunded and expected from Sprinkefeild wᶜh wee by purchas as appeares by Mʳ Hopkins his Lettʳ and yet the Comissio's of conectacut at least in oᵗ vnderstanding decline the same, yea deny the demaundeing of any thing at all of Sprinkefeilde: either as Impost oᵗ Contrebucion, to the purchas if therfore theare bee Noe order of Coᵗt for Custom or Imposicion and not required in way of contrebucion to the purchas there cane be nothing Justly dewe

Thirdly wee disier to se˄ order or orders of theire Genᵗall Courte for the requireing of this Impost or Contribucion of Sprinkefeild if they haue any that soe wee may haue opertunity to macke oᵗ obiections agsᵗ the same.

Fourthly wheareas the saide Impost or Contrebucion is pleaded to bee dew by the Comissio's order the last yeare, oᵗ answer is *is* wee concaine the Comisso's haue Noe power to macke ane order to Inioyne Custom or Impost to bee payed by any perticuler towne to its owne or any other Jurisdiction or forte therein, for that being an act of Goᶜmᵗ is ꝑserued Intire, by the third and sixth article of Confideracion, to each Jurisdiction Nor can they (as wee conscaiue) macke that dew in this kinde, wᶜh was Not dew by vertew of som order befor, they onely judg ℂ declare what is Just ℂ dew vpon other grounds then theire owne order, there being therefore Noe order of the Couᵗte of Conectacut formerly shewed ˄ can be Now produced (as wee concaiue) ˄ mackes Sprinckefeild *vn*iustly lyable to pay the foremenɞoned custom or Impost Nor any such order in being as wee supose nor patent produced now or formerly wee disier that the conclusions of the Comissio's yᵉ last yeare Soe farr as it concernes Sprinekfeild, in this cace may bee reuersed and that the pʳsent Comisio's wilbee pleased eaqually and indiferently to atend the Argumᵗs of oᵗ Comity agsᵗ yᵉ thing in Genᵗall for time to come ℂ wᵗhall to tacke Noatice that there hath beene Noe prõfe (soe farr as wee knowe) of any such forte, keept or maintained soe as may bee for the Safety of the Riuer but rather the indaingering of it *Being of noe force agsᵗ ane enemie of any considerable strength, in the Comissio's owne judgmᵗ expressed in theire last order touching this ꝑticuler and why Sprinkefield should pay to the maintainance of such a forte, wee must Needs profess wee want light to see

3

4

*147

1648.   Vnto wch the Comissio^{rs} of Conectacut returned as ffoloweth

September.   a short answer to the Adicionall proposicion p^rsented by the Comissio^{rs} of the Masachusets conserneing the formencioned Impost

I   To the first wee answer as before that what wee demaunde from Sprinkefeild is for the erecting and maintaineing a forte wch hath beene and is vsefull to them as the other townes vpon the Riuer, and according to the best of o^r aprehencions Nesesary for theire Gen^rall Safety, if others haue other & diferent ap^rhencions wee leaue them to the liberty of theire owne thoughts

2   Secondly wee afirme that there is a order of the Gefiall courte of Conectacut for what wee demānde and sefiall forfatures incured by som of Sprinkefield for goods put abord seu^rall vesells, lying in & pasing through Conectacut Jurisdictiō, contrary to the saide order the execucion wheareof hath onely been deferred for loue & peace Sacke vntill a full consideracion might bee had of the Imposition demānded by the comissio^{rs} & Isewed according to Righteousness:

3   To the Thirde wee answer that this being the thirde yeare that the ꝑsent Question hath beene one foote, and the ꝑdusing of the order from Conectacut not at any time heeretofore required, wee concaiue there wilbee founde noe Just ground to alter what hath beene allredy determined for the ꝑsent want of that especially considering the question & Diferance is Nakedly and clearely stated and wee concaiue it will not bee graunted that o^r order can macke the thing Just if in its owne *owne* Nature vnrighteous

    The Fourthe conserneing the Comissio^{rs} to answer and therein wee shalbe silent onely wee canot but Cleare o^r selues heerein, that wee noe waies judg what was done by them in the order mencioned is any incrocheing vpon the power of o^r or any other Jurisdiction, Nor can concaiue how others can soe looke vpon it

    The cace therfore haueing beene soe fuly argued, & the Copy of o^r patent haueing beene produced, as at the makeing of the Combinacion soe Now againe to all the Comisso^{rs} wee disier a finall end may Now bee put to this vncomfortable diferance, wch wee hartyly disier may bee according to truith & Righteousness.

    Vpon p^rvseall of the wrighting p^rsented from ye Comity of the Masachusets Gen^rall Courte the Comissio^{rs} for New hauen founde themselues conserned in one or twoe of the obiections, the Importe thereof seemeth to bee that they are ptyes w'h Conectacut in the Cause, and therfore Noe competent judges w'h the Comissio'rs both for Plym̄ and New Hauen would haue tacken into farther Consideraĉŏn, (in the meane time would haue respited the cause in Question betwēn the other twoe Colonyes, but the Comissio'rs for the Masachusets concured w'h the Comissio'rs for the other Colonyes that there was Noe force in the obiection, wherevpon the other ffower comissio'rs did ffully pvse and according to theire best light weighed the contents of the former wrighting delu'red in by the Comissio'rs for the Masachusets and Conectacut (doe concaiue that the Imposision in question is Not for purchas of Lands tenem's (đ but for erecting (maintaineing a forte at Seabrooke the better to Secure the pasage of the Riuer twoe and froe, for the benifit of the other townes soe of Sprinkefeild. 2. that the fort of Seabrooke as it was made or Raised and in former times maintained (though Not sufici' against ane armye or powerfull enemye nor could soe smaule a Chardge layd vpon the rest of the townes vpon that Riuer: in pporcion of what is Required of Sprinkefield either erect or maintaine a fort of such Strength yet) was Nessesary (vsefull ags' such atempts as were then considerable (tended to the Safety (benifit both of the other townes (of Sprinkefeild

That it is just for straingers in the same Condicion (Consideracion w'h Sprinkefeild to pay theire parte of the same Imposicion vpon the same grounds yet pbably vpon consideracion of the duch Clayme to all the whole tracte of Lands to Cape Cood and pticulerly to harteford it might Not bee convenient for *Conectacut to demānd it of them vntill things were cleared, or at least till the Comissio'rs were advized w'h

3

*148

Though that maxem in lawe ‸ aliquid alteri dater (đ; bee graunted (in som Respects admitted as suiteing the cace yet they concaiue if a pson by purchas or graunte haue Right to a peece of land Lying vncompased ‸ or so bordering vpon the lands of a towneshipp that his way must be through theire land(or falle into theire way they and hee beeing onely interessed in the way if Now the towne shipp vpon publique Respects finde just cause to expend a considerable Chardge either to secure or repaire the saide way, that pson in a dew pporcion ought to contrebute

4

The Copy of y' patent of Conectacut (đ hath formerly beene revewed by the Comissio'rs (lately owned in England but was not ether called for last yeare or not soe insisted one as to cause any demurr in the Comissio'rs p'sedings but vpon demānd the Copy of the said patent was Now pduced (read by w'h it clerly apeareth, that both the place (Jurisdiction is graunted to y' lords (Gentlemen (theire asosiates (asignes yett y' Comissio'rs ffor Plym̄ (New hauen (though ffor the psent they finde Not sufi-

5

1648.

September.

cient cause to reuerce what was done y⁰ last yeare) Considering that the Comissio⁰s for y⁰ Masachusets call for ℓ desier to see the order of the Gen⁰all Courte of Conectacut by wᶜʰ the foremencioned Imposision is required of Sprinkefield, suposeing they may thence haue further mater of consideracion ℓ argumᵗ conserneing the cace wⁿh the Comissio⁰s for Conectacut (though they afirme there is such ane order) canot pˢently produce haueing noe coppy of it heer not expecting it would bee called for nowe sence it was not demaûded in othᵣ of the twoe former meeteings at boston or New Hauen ℓ further Considering that the Comissio⁰s for conectacute haue formerly ℓ doe still lay Clayme to Sprinkefield as falling wᵗhin theire patent, and not wiᵗhin the Limutes of the Masachusets they thought it Not fitt to add to what was done the Last yeare or to macke further conclusion vpon what was Nowe one either parte ꝑsented or answered, but to settle (if it may bee) a right vnderstanding betwixt the other twoe Colonyes and to remove any occasion of offence or greife, y⁰ desier that a coppy of the order from the Gen⁰all Courte of Conectacut bee brought ℓ ꝑsented to the Comissio⁰s for furthᵣ Consideracion (if there bee cause the next yeare, and that in the meane time the twoe colonyes of the Masachusets ℓ Conectacut would agree vpon som equall and satisfiing way of rooneing the Masachusets line that it may wᵗhout further dispute appeare into wᶜʰ of the Jurisdictions Sprinkefield falls, wᶜʰ being don they supose that either the question betwixt the twoe Colonyes will sease or there may bee a dew consideracion of what shall further bee tendered, from the order of Conectacut ℓ in the meane time what was don the last yeare to stand as then concluded

[*Cambridge, Mass. Archives, 2, 326.]   Vpon the Mocion of **Mᵣ Dunster President of y⁰ Coledg** at⁎

Consideracion was had vpon paymᵗs made and Rescaiued iu peage wᵗher white or blacke, the Comisio⁰s were informed that the Indians abused the english wᵗh much false badd and vnfinished peage ℓ the English Trayders after it comes to theire hands chosse out what fitts theire markett ℓ occasions ℓ leaue theire Refuge to pass twoe and fro: in the Colonyes wᶜʰ the endians wᶜʰ best vnderstand the quality and defect of peage will not willingly take backe whearevpon (though they se not at ꝑsent how to propound a full reformacion in all ꝑticulers wᵗhout much difecalty ℓ inconveniency yett) they comend it to the seuᵣall Gen⁰all courtes and plantaciōs wᵗhin the vnited colonyes that noe peage neither whitte or blacke bee payed or Rescaiued but what is strung, ℓ in som measure strunge sutably Not smaule ℓ great vncomly ℓ disorderly mingled as formerly it hath been ℓ they further offer it to y⁰ Consideracion of the saide Gen⁰all Courtes wᵗher they thinke not fitt to provide, that if hereafter any of the endians in paym^t bee founde to offer peage vnto the English made of Stone or other vnalow *Mater or tender dyed peage for blacke that it bee forthw^{t}h broken or som other cource taken to convnce them of the descaipt and to supress it as the saide courtes shall thinke meete

And for the more speedy ℇ free pasage of Justice in each Jurisdictiō to all the Confiderates the Comissi^{r}s doe propounde ℇ Recomend to the Fower Gen^{r}all Cou^{r}t℞ for the vnited colonyes that if the last will and testamt of any man bee dewly proued in ℇ Dewly sertified from any one of the colonyes it be w^{t}ho^t delay expte^d ℇ alowed in ye rest of ye Colonyes exept som just exeption bee made ags^t such will or the pveing of it w^{c}h exeption to bee forthw^{t}h dewly sertified backe againe to the Colony wheare the saide will was proued that some Just covrse may bee tacken to gather in ℇ dispose of the estat w^{t}hout delay or damage they concaiue alsoe and desier it may bee considered, by ye Gen^{r}all Courts for the vnited colonyes that if any knowne planter or settled inhabitante dy intestat that Administracōn bee graunted by ye Colonye to w^{c}h the diseased belonged though he dyed in an other colonye and the Admincstracon being dewly sertified to bee of force for gathering in ye estate in ye rest of the Colonyes, as in the Cace of wills proued where Noe Just exeption is returned, but if any pson posest of ane estate whoe is Neither planter nor settled inhabitante in any of the Colonyes dy entestate the Admincstracion (if just cause bee found to giue Adminestracion) bee graunted by y^t Colony wheare the p^{r}son shall dye and departe this life at least that a care bee taken by ye Go^{r}n^t to gather in ℇ secure the Estate vntill it bee demānded and may bee deliu^{r}ed According to Rules of justice.

The Comissio^{r}s being informed and dewly considering Mr Eliotts Godly zeal ℇ great Care ℇ contineued paynes, in teaching the endians what may conserne theire Spirituall and Euerlasting good ℇ hoping that the god of Spirits ℇ of all grace hath ℇ will open ℇ prepare some of theire harts to Imbrace the truth in Loue and Sencerity vpon his mocion (notw^{t}hstanding all former Advice the strict obseruance whereof they still recomend to the Colonyes) they consent that twoe guns w^{t}h all suitable prouisions Not exeding twoe pounds of powther ℇ sixe pound℞ of shott for each gune p^r añum (each gune being first by his direction soe marked that he may knowe it from all others bee by him disposed either by guifte or leaue to such Indians as hee shall chose by y^m to bee vsed as hee shall opwoynte but not to be alianated for any

John Brow̄ Aproues not of this alowañ but thinks it inconvenent price or consideracion whatso^r, thus graunte to be onely for tryall ₹ to bee recalled when any enconveniencie shall apeare.

Not alowed

The Comissio^{rs} tackeing into their Consideracion that by ye intervening of extreordinary Occasions, theire meeteings haue beene somwhat deuerted from theire cource at first settled and concluded by ye articles doe concaiue fitt for the reduceing of the saide meeteings into order againe: that the Next meeteing bee at Boston the socond at Harteford, the third at New hauen, the Fourth at Plyñ: then Boston ₹ the other colonyes successiuely, as in the Articles, The Foregoing conclusions were agreed and subscribed by y^e Comission^{rs} the 19th of y^e seunth mõ 1648.

EDW. HOPKINS	WILLIAM BRADFORD
RO: LUDLOW	Presidente
THEOPh EATON	JOHN ENDICOTE
JOHN ASTWOOD	SIMON BRADSTREETE
	JOHN BROWNE

$\mathfrak{At}$ $\mathfrak{a}$ $\mathfrak{meeting}$ extraordinary of The Comissioners for
the vnited Colinies holden at Boston the 23th of the fift Month Called July
1649

The articles of Confederation being Read

An Order of the Generall Court of the Massachusets dated the 2^{cond} of the third Month 1649 was p^{r}sented and Read wherby it apeered y^t Tho : Dudley Esqr and Mr Symon Bradstreete were Chosen Comissioners for y^t Colinic for a full $\wr$ Compleate yeare $\wr$ were Invested with full power $\wr$ authority according to the tenor of the said articles Concluded at Boston 19th of the 3^d Month 1643

A like Order of the generall Court of New Plymouth dated the 6th of 4th month 1649 was p^{r}sented and Read wherby it apeered y^t William Brad-ford Esqr $\wr$ Mr John Browne were Chosen Comissioners for y^t Colenie for a full yeare $\wr$ Invested with full power $\wr$ authority according to the afor$\bar{s}$d articles

A like order of the Generall Court of Connecticot dated 17th of May 1649 was $\wp$duced $\wr$ Read wherby it apeered y^t Edward Hopkins Esqr $\wr$ Mr Tho : Wells were Chosen Comissioners for y^t Colony $\wr$ Invested with full power $\wr$ authority for one whole $\wr$ Compleat yeare according to the aforsaid articles of Confederation

A like order of the Generall Court of New hauen dated 30th of May 1649 was p^{r}sented $\wr$ Read wherby it apeered y^t Theophilus Eaton Esqr $\wr$ Mr John Astwood were Chosen Comissioners for y^t Colonie for a full $\wr$ Compleat yeare $\wr$ were Invested with full power $\wr$ authority according to the tenor of the articles of Confederation aforsaid

Tho: Dudley Esqr was Chosen President for this meeting of the Comissioners

*Wheras it is found by experience y^t the occations of the Colonies doe somtimes Require the meeting $\wr$ Consultations of theire Comissioners before the ordinary time appointed by the articles of Confederation in the 7th month

& so y^t meeting may Conueniently bee spared w^h thing was taken into Consideration by the Comissioners at theire meeting at Boston 26th of July.47. and an order theruppon made to ppound it to the seuerall generall Courts y^t it may bee left to the libberty of the Comissioners (for the time being) to order the time of theire meetings as the occasion of the Colonies may Require & so to forbeare the ordenary meetings in September as thay shall see Cause, prouided there bee one meeting euery yeare

To w^h propositions all the generall Courts (except the Massachusets) haue Returned their assent : it is therfore desired y^t the said Court of the Massachusets would declare theire mind heerin by theire Comissioners at theire next meeting. And it is ppounded as an addition to the former proposition y^t if there bee no occasionall meeting in the Summer before September y^t then the yearly meeting to bee held as in the articles of Confederation

The Comissioners of the Massachusetts acquainted the Rest of the Comissioners with a late order of theire Generall Court for the pcureing a further supply of powder & bullets & match ouer and aboue y^t w^h thay already haue or by order ought to haue desiring the same may bee Comended to the seuerall genenall Courts & y^t a due pportion bee observed & like provisions made of the foremensioned pticulars it being of so Generall a Concernment to all the Colonies

The sum of the said order is to this purpose first y^t two hundred pounds worth of powder shalbee forthwith bought & to bee and Remayne as an addition to theire publicke stocke. 2^{condly} y^t a barrell of powlder i50 pound of muskett bullets & a quarter of a hundred of match bee prouided for every fifty souldiers & this to bee done by the seuerall Townes before the 24th of June next vnder the penalty of five pound for every default. w^h said powlder bullets & match are to bee as theire Townes stocke

The Rest of the Comissioners approuing what the Court of the Massachusetts have done heerin did Redily assent to comend the premises *to theire seuerall generall Courts p^{r}mising at the next meeting of the Comissioners to acqvaint them with the issue & effect therof

From Newhauen generall Court it was ppounded to the Comissioners what Course might be taken for the speedy planting of Delaware bay The title som Marchants at Newhauen haue by purchase from the Indians to Conciderable tractes of land on both sides of the River was opened; ₵ the Comissioners did Read ₵ Concider what had pased at a former meeting of theires in Anñō 1643.

A writing delivered into New haven Court by Mr Leech Concerning the healthfulnes of the place the goodnes of the land Conveniency of the lesser Rivers with the advantage of a well ordered Trade there was also pused; The Comissioners with the premisses Concidering the p^rsent state of the Colonies, the English in most plantations alredy wanting hands to carry on theire nessesary ocations thought fitt not to send forth men to possese ₵ plant Delaware nor by any publick acte or Concent to Incurrage or allow the planting therof; And if any shall volentarily goe from any of the Colonies to Delaware ₵ shall without leaue ₵ Concent from the Marchants at Newhaven sitt down vppon any part or parts of theire land there or in any other Respects shalbee Iniurius to them in theire title ₵ Enterest there, the Colonies will nether protect nor owne them therin; The Newhaven Marchants being notwithstanding lefte to theire Just libbertie to dispose Improve or plant the land thay haue purchased in those parts or any part therof as thay shall see Cause

What was done about ye motion for dela-warr bay.

The Comissioners for Newhaven Informed the Rest of the Comissioners y^t in or about october last John Whitmore one of the Deputies of Stanford a peaceable Inoffensive man not apt to quarrell or provocke any of the Indians goeing forth to seeke his Cattell Returned not according to Expectation nor Could bee found by the English y^t sought for him; but quickly after the sonne of a Sagamore who liues neere Stanford Came into the Towne ₵ tould the English y^t John Whitmore was murthered by one Toquattoes an Indian ₵ to proue it tould them y^t Toquattoes had som of his Clothes ₵ pticularly his shirt made of Cotten linnin heeruppon the English ₵ som Indians went into the woods to seeke the murthered body for buriall but though thay bestowed much time ₵ labore Could not find it; diuers of the English at Stanford suspected the Sagamores sonne to bee *either the auther or the accessory to this murther but had not then satisfying grounds to seize ₵ Chardg him; about two or three months after Vncas Coming to Stanford Calling the Indians thether ₵ Inquiring after the murthered body the formensioned sagamores sonne ₵ one Rehoron another suspected Indian ledd som of the English ₵ som of Vncas his men derectly to the place wher the murthered body or the Relicts of it lay The Carkase was brought to stanford the Sagamores sonn ₵ Rehoron fell on trembling and therby Confermed the suspition of the English

*153

ℓ wrought suspition in som of the Mohegin Indians so yᵗ thay said those twoe Indians were nought meaning thay were guilty, but thay both tooke an opertunity ℓ fled away as for theire lives nothwithstanding which the Indians in those parts whether for feare or favor to the sagamore in Reference to his sonn or vpon som other Respects Charge Toquattoes alone with the murther excusing the sagamores sonne ; but to this day neither Toquattoes Can bee apprehended nor is the sagamores sonne brought to a due examination

John Whitmores Widdow both by messengers ℓ łres presses for Justice ℓ other Indians grow more Insolent ℓ sensure the English for want of due psecution in such a Case, it being either Conceved by the English or by som Indians Intimated yᵗ if the sagamores sonne should be seized ℓ kept in durance the Indians will forthwith size some English ℓ keepe them till hce bee freed ; The Comissioners for the vnited Colonies Considering the premisses thought it Just ℓ nessesary yᵗ the murtherer or murtherers in this ℓ other Cases Concerning the Confederated Euglish bee duly pursued ℓ prosecuted ℓ pticularly advised yᵗ either Tho: Stanton or som other able Interpreter bee sent to the Indians naighboring vppon Stanford Requiring them according to Justice ℓ theire Couenants ℓ Ingagements to the Euglish to make knowne ℓ deliver vp the murtherers to Examination ℓ tryall wᵇ if thay Refuse to doe or doe not duely attend ℓ yᵗ Toquattoes (accused by them Cannot bee found out ℓ apprehended yᵗ then the sagamoie bee Required to bring and deliver vp his sonn to examination ; if yᵗ bee denied or delayed yᵗ then himselfe or his sonn bee seized ℓ kept in durance till the murtherers be brought forth ℓ Justice haue its due Course according to euidence.

The Comissioners being minded that Asqnash a murtherer of an Englishman som yeares since in or neare the bounds of Fairefeild lives yet (according to a general Report) among Indians neare to som of the English plantations in those parts, ℓ yᵗ the non psuite of so notorius a malefacter is like to proue *preiudiciall to the English by giveing Incurragment to the Indians in other malicius and murtherus attempts. It is therfore thought fitt yᵗ the two Western Colonies vse the best meanes thay Can to take him ℓ then pceed with him according to Righteusnes. An Information being also given of som Indians at long Iland that (by the accusation of a native yᵗ suffered lately at hartford for a murther) are guilty of the death of som English who suffered boatwracke some years past in a vessell belonging to one Cope at or neare long Iland. It was desired ℓ thought expedient yᵗ all oppertunities p'senting bee Improved for making Inquiry ℓ searching after the truth ℓ (if euidence appeere) the murtherers be prosecuted to Justice.

*154

The Comissioners taking into Concideration the great danger y^t is like to beffall the Colonies by ye mischievous Trad that is yet Carried on by selling amunition to the Indians. Wherin as som English are Conceved to bee deeply guilty who are deservedly Liable to seveere sensure if at any time thay may bee discovered, so vppon more then probable grounds it is apprehended y^t many of the Dutch haue been long acquainted with the secretts of y^t Trad ; and in pticulare thay were Informed y^t Govert Lockman (of whose Iregular proceedings in y^t kind the Dutch Governor formerly Informed the English) was Represented to the Goverrer of Conecticot as deeply Enterested therin ₵ had vppon his being Called Into question for the same at hartford Entered into a bond of two hundred pounds with sureties for his appeerance att the Court to answare ; but fayled therin The seuerall Euidences allso both of English ₵ Indians from long Iland of his guilt were Read ₵ the Judgments of the Comissioners desired therin. Which being duely weighed both in the great Iniurie to all the Colonies by y^t dangerus ₵ vnlawfull Trad ₵ the many Testimonies against him The Comissioners Conceve y^t if the Court of Conecticot have evidence y^t hee was not hindered by the hand of God for attending the said Court according to his bond but y^t it Cam to pase through want of due Care or pvidence of his owne y^t then the said Court may lawfully take all or so much of his bond as thay shall Judge meete: Espetially Concidering hee the said Govert when hee came to Conecticot Refused to attend a Court the Governor would haue Called on purpose for his triall vnles hee might haue it at his owne time

A Declaration being p^{r}sented to the Comissioners by Mr Hopkins vnder the hands of Mr John Gosmer ₵ Tho: holsey of Southhamtom touching the danger thay were in ₵ difficulties Exposed vnto vppon the late murther in y^t towne wherby thay were nessesitated to arme themselves ₵ stand vppon theire defence for many dayes. The Indians being gathered together in an hostile posture ₵ therfore desired the Charge therof might bee borne by the whole Combynation w^h being Concidered *₵ former proceedings in Anno 1644 att Fairfeild ₵ Stanford Reviewed it was Conceved ₵ Concluded y^t as no such Charge was then allowed so it doth not fall within the articles to bee attended

*155

The Comissioners were minded of the Continewed Complaint of Vncas against the Narragansett ₵ Nianticke Indians y^t notwithstanding all former Ingagments thay are still vnderminding his peace and seeking his Ruine ₵ in pticular y^t their late Endeavor to bring in the Mowhaukes vppon him ₵ when y^t fayled by witchcraft to take away his life; A Narragansett Indian in an English vessell in Mohegen Riuer Rann a Sword into his brest wherby hee Receved to all apeerance a mortall wound w^h murtherus acte the assalent then Confessed hee was for a Conciderable sum of wampam by the Narragansett (Niantike Sachems hired to attempt

The Comissioners then vnderstood y^t Nenagrett of his owne accord was Com to boston to Cleare himselfe, hee was Called to attend (in the p^{r}sence of Mr John Winthorp by Tho: Stanton as Interpreter vppon oath hee was minded of his breach of former Covenants made at Boston in Anno 1645 Subscribed by the Narragansett Sachems (his deputie (Confermed by himselfe in Anno 1647 y^t hee with the Rest of his Confederates haue fayled in all the branches therof. the hostages were not duely sent the wampam agreed vppon was not payed nor p^t of the tribute dew for pequots Satisfyed Indian fugetives belonging to the English were not Returned nor Captives (Canowes taken from Vncas Restored but aboue all hee was put in mind of the desturbance made by him (his Confederats in the publicke peace by hyering the Mowhakes to Com vppon Vncas the last yeare and the aforemensioned attempt to take away his life by Cuttaquin a Narrahigansett Indian Ninagrett vtterly denied the Last afferming y^t Cuttaquin who accused himselfe (the other Sachems was drawen therevnto by torture from the Mohcges and Indeavoured to clear himselfe of the former. but he was tould y^t the assalent before hee Cam into the hands of the Mohcges p^{r}sently after the fact was Comited Layed the Charg vpon him with the Rest w^h hee Confermed the day folowing to Captaine Mason in the p^{r}sence of the English y^t were in the barkque with him (often Reitterated it at hartford though sence hee hath denied it; y^t hee was p^{r}sented to Vncas vnder the notion of one appertaining to Vssamequin wherby hee was acknowlidged as his frend (no provocation giuen him; vnto all the Rest was added y^t Cuttaquin affermed hee was

nessesetated to attempt y^t murtherus "acte by the desparateness of his owne condition through his great Ingagment to the said Sachems haveing Receued a Conciderable quantity of wampam w^h hee had spent who otherwise would haue taken away his life. by all w^h the guilt Charged vppon them apeered very probable to all the Comissioners; theire Indeavours to disturbe the peace by theire Confederasy with the Mowhawkes was so euedent by Mr John Winthorpe (Mr Williams Relation the last yeare together with the Confossion of the Mowhawks themselves to Tho: Stanton who now again Confermed the same in the p^{r}sence of the Comissioners

Ninegrett (a western Indian brought by Ninegrett to wittnes for him (tendered if Convenient time might bee allowed him to bring the pocomtuke

Sachems face to face to Euedence the same y^t in the Judgment of all p^{r}sent it was beyond all Rationall Deniall

The accoumpt of wampam Receved vppon agreement being also taken into Concideration, Ninegrett affermed y^t ther was litle more then 2 hundred fathom vnpayed. But the Auditers accoumpt of the Massachusetts being Called for ₰ examened it apeered y^t no more then 1529½ fathom hath been brought to the accoumpt of the Colonies nor Could Ninegrett by any euedenc make any more to apeer ; only hee alledged y^t about 600 fathom was payed by measure w^h hee accoumpted by tale wherin ther was a Concidrable difference The Comissioners not willing to adhear to any strict tearmes in y^t pticular (₰ though by agreement it was to bee payed by measure ₰ not by tale) were willing to allow 62 fathom ₰ halfe in y^t Respect so y^t there Remaynes due 408 fathom But Ninegrett psisting in his former affermation ₰ not Endeavored to giue any Reasonable satisfaction to the Comissioners in the premisses, a smale Inconciderable pcell of beaver being all y^t was tendered to them though thay vnderstood hee was better pvided. The Comissioners Expressed themselves as alltogether vnsatisfyed in the whole frame of his pceedings ₰ haveing tendered vnto him as formerly was appointed at the meeting att Newhaven (w^h was neglected by him) an Imptiall hearing ₰ determination of all his Complaints against Vncas att theire next session if thay found in him a Complyance with theire p^{r}sent Reasonable expectations ₰ not Receauing a Returne from him Answarable to theire desires thay left him to his owne wayes ₰ pfessed thay must pvide for the peace of the Cuntrey ₰ preservation of Vncas according to theire Covenants by such meanes as in theire owne Judgments may best Conduce therunto ₰ therfore doe Refer it to the serious Concideration of all the Colonies to bee in such Constant Redines either for deffence or offence as the state of occasions may Call for ₰ Require w^h is like to bee turbulent ₰ difficult w^h thay the Rather p^{r}sent to Consideration from an Information thay Receved sence *theire siting; of a marriage shortly Intended betwixt Ninegrets Daughter ₰ a brother or brothers soone of Sassaquas the mallignant furius Pequot wherby pbably theire aimes are to gather together ₰ Reunite the scattered Conquered Pequates into one body ₰ sett them vpp againe as a distinct nation w^h hath alwayes been wittnesed against by the English ₰ may hassard the peace of the Colonies.

Mr John Winthorpe being p^{r}sent with som of the Indians y^t lately Resided near Nameok. The busines was taken into Concideration both in Refference to the English ₰ Indians And the Comissiones leaveing the things pp to Conectacot to bee desided by that Goverment according to Justice Could not but dislicke ₰ ptest against the Pequots Resolute withdrawing

*157

from theire subiection to Vncas ₰ if thay persisted therin ₰fessed theire Continued Resolution of haueing them Compeled by force But these present ₰fessing a Redy willingness to herken to the Comissioners advise it was Concluded y^t som fit place by the Concent of Conectacot no wayes Preiuditiall to the Towne allredy begune at Nameoke may bee found out wher thay may haue libbertie for the p^{r}sent to settle ₰ plant thay owneing Vncas as theire Sachem ₰ in all things Carring themselves as his other subiects, ₰ the Comissioners Required foxon who wayted all this meeting on the behalfe of Vncas to Inform Vncas y^t it is the mind of the English y^t hee Carry himself towards them in a loveing way ₰ doe not Tiranise over them hee was allso Informed y^t Cuttaquin who wounded Vncas shallbee deliuered vpp to him to ₰ceed with him according to Justice ₰ vppon the Pequots due Subiection the things taken from them last winter are to bee Restored

Mr. Willam Westerhowse Marchant and now A Planter at Newhauen as formerly at Plymouth did now againe deliuer in a petition to the Comissioners Informing ₰ Complaining against the dutch Goue^r of the Monhatowes y^t Contrary to the tenor ₰ Import of his owne Cornission sent to the said Westerhowse at New hauen ₰ vppon pretence y^t Newhauen is within the Pattent ₰ Jurisdiction of the Dutch hee did Iniuriusly seize within Newhauen harbore a shipe ₰ goods belonging to him the said Willam Westerhouse to the vallew of 2000^t as it Cost in holland ₰ though for Satisfaction hee hath made seuerall adresses vnto the said Duch Gover^r yet hetherto hee Can obtaine nothing from him ; hee therfore desired healpe ₰ Releife from the Vnited English Colonies ₰ as att Newhauen hee had formery moued y^t som duch Vessels then within the harbore might bee attached or arested to bring his Cause to a further ₰ due triall the w^h the Gove^r of Newhauen thought not fitt to graunt till hee had first aduised with the rest of the Comissioners so now hee ₰pounded ₰ desired *that hee might haue Comission from the Vnited Colonies to Recover his lose and damnage as hee should find opertunity by way of Reprissall

All w^h bing duely weighed ₰ Concidered the Comissioners as formerly so still found Just Cause to wittnes against the vnjust seisure to the great lose ₰ damnag of Mr Westerhouse ₰ Iniurius to the English Colonies the shipe beinge taken out of New haven harbor vppon pretence of the Dutch title ₰ Enterest to ₰ in all the lands, harbors Riuers ₰ê from Cape henlopen to Cape Cod or point Judeth yet thay thought it not Conuenient to graunt Mr Westerhouse (A Stranger ₰ no planter in Newhauen when the shipe was seised) a Comission of Mart or Reprissall and though they haue not denied Justice to strangers by way of atachment or arrest to bring the Cause to hearing ʠ Just tryall yet thay thought fitt first to signify the offence to the Duch Goveʳ ʠ accordingly to bring seuerall other questians and differences depending ; They wrot to him as foloweth

Honered Ser

from Plymouth September i648 wee wrot vnto you largly ʠ in sundry pticulars what might Trouble or settle a Comfortable ʠ safe peace betwixt vs ; youer answare wee Receued long sence from Newhauen but found it in sundry Respects deffective and vnsatisfying you are alltogether sylent Concerning the dangerous Trad of of guns Powlther shot ʠ driuen with the Indians at Aurania foɪt wʰ is allso by som of youers (to our great Preieduce Carried on ʠ Continewed within the English Jurisdictions Gouert Lockorman hath giuen much offence therin presuming posably yᵗ no Indian Testimony how full soeuer will pase ʠ bee taken against him ; how fare our marchants are freed from Customs Recognitions ʠ Inward ʠ outward ʠ whether those burthens bee vtterly abolished or onely suspended for the pʳsent you Informe not ; what Restraints are Continewed vppon Trad ʠ in what Casses our marchants Lyable to Confiscation of goods you are not pleased to answare ; though it bee just ʠ nessesary our marchants should know both theire duty ʠ danger ; ʠ the Goveʳ of Newhauen did latly desire it from you ; Wee aquainted you with Mʳ Wiltam Westerhouse his grevance ʠ Complaint with his offer to Cleare himselfe from being either Rebell or fugetive too or from his native Cuntry ; in youer answare you Refer him to the Justice of holland. Time doth not yet abate his sence *of yᵗ lose. hee now againe   *159
attends ʠ petitions the Comissioners for som way of satisfaction ʠ Redrese ʠ desires libertie to atach or arrest such vessell or vessels of youers as Com into any of the harbors belonging vnto the Vnited Colonies yᵗ hee may bring his Cawse to a fayre ʠ Just hearing ʠ Tryall in these pticulars wher hee is a planter and where his Occasions lye ; wee denye not Justice to Strangers of any nation yet wee thought it suttable to the amytie ʠ Corespondenc wee desier to hould with youer selfe ʠ the Jurisdiction not to graunt it tell wee had acquainted you with his request ʠ the equitie therof.   Wee Cannot but assert the English Title ʠ Just Right both to Newhauen Lands ʠ harbor ʠ to all the English plantations ʠ theire apurtenanses from Cape Cod ~to~ or point Judeth both on the mayne ʠ the Ilands wʰ are possesed by the English at pʳsent vnder theire Gouerment as anciently graunted by the Kings of England to theire Subiects ʠ sence duly Purchased from the Indians ʠ peacably planted ʠ Imployed by the Inhabitants of the Vnited Colonies Respectively: ʠ accordingly Cannot but wittnes against the Iniurius ʠ hostile seisure of a shipe

made by you in Newhauen harbor vppon an vniust pretence of title ℰ Enterest in the place; Wee haue pused the łres you sent both to the honered Gover of the Massachusetts ℰ of Plymouth with what by way of answare you wrote to the Gover of Newhauen Concerning Delaware bay wee haue formerly heard ℰ Concidered the Right ℰ title our Confederats of Newhauen haue to sundry tracts or pcells of land within Delaware bay by you Called the south Riuer with the Iniuries thay Receued from youer predesseser Monsier Kift in anno 1643 M Winthorpe Gouer of the Massachusets ℰ Pesedent of the Comissioners wrot the aprehension ℰ sence the Comissioners had of his pceedings ℰ Receved his answare but without satisfaction; our frinds of Newhauen will neither Encroch vppon youer Limmits nor any way desturbe youer peace but they may not let fale the English Right and Enterest there.

These with other differences might haue been Concidered and other issewed or prepared for Europe had you been pleased to haue giuen vs a meeting att Boston as was ppounded ℰ desired but y not suting youer Conueniency wee shalbee constreyned to pvid for our owne safty ℰ first finding the Trad of guns powlder ℰ shot with the Indians soe mischeueous to vs all ℰ yet so hard to bee descouered ℰ proued wee must nessesarily ℰ speedely wright after youer Coppy ℰ forthwith forbid all Trad direct or indirect with

*160   any of the Indians within the *limits of any of the vnited Colonies vnder the penalty of Confiscation of vessels ℰ goods if thay bee there found so Trading or after proued to have Transgresed ℰ offended therin, to all psons but such as are Inhabitants within the said English Jurisdictions ℰ subiect to theire lawes ℰ Gouerment; Wee shall ad no more at present. But againe desire youer answare may bee Returned to the Gouer of Newhauen y from him the Rest of the Comissioners may vnderstand youer mind in the premisses so wee Take leaue ℰ Rest youer Loueing frinds

Boston August the sixt 1649 Stilo anglia

The Comissioners Taking into Concideration the dangerus ℰ vnlawfull Course of Trading guns poulther shot ℰč to the Indians by the French Duch ℰ other foraine nations Residing in these parts of america tending greatly to the preiedise of the English heere; and to the strengthening ℰ animating the Indians against them as by dayly Experience they find As also y the said French Duch ℰč doe prohibitt all Trad with Indians within theire Jurisdictions vnder penalty of Confiscation of goods and vessel. ℰ y wampam being kept amongst the English (it being generally made within theire Limits may bee of good benefitt ℰ advantage to them many wayes vppon the Conciderations

aforsaid the Comissioners thought meete in this case of soe generall Concernment to Comend it to the seuerall generall Courts to Restraine all p^rsons
of or vnder the aforsaid forraine nations for Trading with the Indians within
any of theire Jurisdictions vnder the like penalty they Impose vpon others
℮ to the end y^t in Case this ꝑposition bee accepted there may bee one ℮ the
same Law in this pticulare in the seuerall Jurisdictions ; The Comissioners
thought meet to propound this Insuing Draught

Wheras the French Duch ℮ other forraine nations doe ordenarily Trad
guns powlther shot ℮c with the Indians to our great preiedise ℮ strengthening
℮ animating the Indians against vs as by dayly experience wee find ℮ wheras
the aforsaid French Duch ℮c doe ꝓhibbite all Trad with Indians within
theire Respectiue Jurisdictions vnder penalty of Confiscations ℮c It is Therfore Ordered y^t after due Publication heerof it shall not bee lawfull for any
French man Duch man or any p^rson *of an other forraine nation whatsoeuer
or any English liueing amongst them or vnder the gouerment of them or
any of them to Trade with any Indian or Indians within the limits of our
Jurisdiction either directly or Indirectly by themselues or others ; vnder
penalty of Confescation of all such goods ℮ vessels as shalbee found so
Trading or the deue vallew therof vppon Just proufe of any goods or vessels
so Trading or Traded ; ℮ it shalbee lawfull for any p^rson or persons Inhabiting within this Jurisdiction to make seisure of any such goods or vessels
Trading with the Indians as by this lawe ꝓhibbited ; one halfe wherof
shalbee to the ꝑper vse ℮ benefit of the ptie seising and the other halfe to the
publick

*161

Wheras att the last meeting of the Comissioners att Plym there were
seueuerall ꝑpositions Comended to the Concideration of the generall Courts
of the vnited Colonies videlecet : the Conclusiue power of theire generall
Courts in Case of non agreement of six Comissioners Concerning the Reg-
ulateing of peag Concerning the Duch Imposition Concerning the probation
of wills Concerning adminestrations

Now vppon Examination wee find by the Returne of the Comissioners
y^t all the said generall Courts haue assented onely to the last videlecet y^t
Concering wills ℮ adminestrations which thay haue agreed to in the words
of the ꝑposition ; and wheras att the said meeting at Plym̄ there was a ꝑpossi-
tion made for the giueing or lending of two guns to the Indians by Mr Elliott
the meaning of the Comissioners was ℮ is y^t two guns should bee given or
lent at this time onely ℮ not yearly

A letter being p'sented to the Comissioners from the Towne of War-
wecke the Enseuing answare was Returned by the same Messenger.

Wee Receued a letter from you on the twenty sixt of this p'sent wherin
you ppound seuerall Iniuries offered to you by the Indians ℓ desire to bee
Informed whether wee haue not receued an Iniunction from the Parlement in
England to acte in youer deffence.   To wᵇ wee breiffly answare yᵗ no such
thing hath hetherto bene Comended thence to the Comissioners of the Colonies
on youer behalfc nor by you Can Rationally bee Expected from vs in the state

*162   wherin you now stand ; but wee shalbee Redy to attend theire *late direction
as any opertunitie is p'sented to find vnder what Colonie youer Plantation
doth fall ℓ then in all future pceediugs both with the English ℓ Indians
endeavor to acte according to Rules of truth ℓ Righteusncs

Boston July 3i i649

To the Comissioners declaration or aduise at Plym in the difference
wherin Springfeild is Concerned ; The Generall Court for the Massachusets
answared yᵗ in the booke of the actes of the Comissioners folio 20 it appeer-
eth yᵗ Mʳ Fenweke was to Joyne with vs in Runing the south linne to deside
the question about Warranoco ℓℓ   But Mʳ Fenweke fayled to send in any to
Joyne with vs wheruppon wee did it ╷ our owne Charg ; ℓ Warranoco was
theruppon ordered by the Comissioners to the Massachusets But wee shalbee
Redy to Joyne with our bretheren of Conectticot in another Soruey so as they
wilbee at the whole Charge in this as wee were in the other ; ℓ withall pduce
theire pattent as wee haue done ;

Vppon Reading of wᵇ answare from the Massachusits the Comissioners
for Conecttacott expressed themselves altogether vnsatisfied the foundation
therof being a great mistake And what is p'sented not Conduceing in theire
apprehensions to the desired End ; for wheras it is affermed yᵗ vppon som
former agreement Mr. Fenweke fayling to send any to Joyne with the Massachusits in Runing the westeren linne they did it at theire owne Charg ℓ therfore Conclude yᵗ what is further to bee attended therin ought to bee at the
Sole Charg of Conecttacott ; it was offered to Concideration ℓ an vndeniable
truth yᵗ what ever promise Mr. Fenweke might make of Endeavoring to Clear
Sprinkfeild from being within the Massachusets pattent (wherin yet hee dif-
fered from what the order of the Massachusets holdeth forth wᵇ Could not
bind him without his Concent) yet nothing is expressed in the order; of any
agreement for Runing the linne nor did the Massachusits after the making of
yᵗ order Run the linne menssioned or vppon any agreement with Mʳ Fenweke
as is Implyed in theire Answare But what was done in that kind was effected

att least the yeare before y^t agitation betwixt the Massachusets ($\wp$ Mr Fenwike
and therfore it is p^{r}sented by the Comissioners of Conecttacott as the most
Redy way to issew the difference according to truth and Right *that the most
Southwardly Extent of the Massachusets pattent bee first agreed vppon ($\wp$
Settleed ($\wp$ then at a mutuall Charg the line bee Run by som skilfull man
Chosen by eich Colonie ; wherunto they pfesse themselves for love ($\wp$ peace
sake willing to Submite Though they doe Conceve the Massachusits ought in
Reason both to Cleare theire Euterest by pattent to Sprinkfeild and to beare
the whole Charg therin the towne of Sprinkfeild being by vollentary agreement settleed in Combination with the Gouerment of Conecttacott at that time
when Challenged by the Massachusets ; ($\wp$ therfore y^t Colony ought not to bee
depriued of theire Just Possession vppon a bare Challeng without proufe if
the southeren Extent of the pattent cannot to mutuall Satisfaction bee
isseued ; the Comissioners for Conecttacott desiring to promote all wayes of
loveing accord ppound to the Massachusets y^t they willbee willing to
attend the determination formerly made betwixt themselves ($\wp$ the Colonie of
Plymouth in the like Case if it bee p^{r}sently accepted though it is like to bee
to theire disadvantage, but if the Massachusits thinke it not fit to Joyne with
vs heerin wee Referr the Concideration of what wee p^{r}sent to the other
Comissioners ($\wp$ shall Submite to what in theire better Judgments shalbee
ppounded But if they thinke it not fitt out of Experimentall or other Conciderations to Enterpose or y^t the Massachusets Rest not in their determination
wee shall desist from further prosecuting this matter at p^{r}sent and attend such
other wayes of providence as may bee p^{r}sented for Isseuing the difference
according to god

A Reply to the answare of the Comissioners of
Conecttacott by the Comissioners of the Massachusits

Wheras the Comissioners for Conecttacott are plessed to say the foundation of the order of our generall Court Concerning the Runing of our south-
ernly linne is vppon a great mistake ($\wp$ therfore Rest wholy vnsatisfied therin
wee Reply the sum of the answare of our Court Consists of two pticulars,
first y^t wee haue run the said linne allredy at our owne Charg 2^{condly} it is
Implyed in the order y^t Conectacott hath not pdussed any pattent or authen-
ticall Coppy therof to make good theire Challeng to sprinkfeild or the land
aiacent ($\wp$ in all this there is no mistake ; It is therfore desired by our Court
y^t the pattent of Conectacott may bee produssed before wee bee put vppon
the Runing of our linne againe ($\wp$ y^t wee suppose will seeme but Reasonable

to Rationall men ; besides the want of their pattent *was obiected the last
yeare at Plymouth in Sprinkfeilds Case ₵ therfore in Reason ought to haue
been produssed now ; But to this part of our Courts Order the Comissioners
of Conectacott in theire answare are silent ; if ther be any mistake in the said
order in any surcomstance of time or the ocation alleged of Runing our linne
in Reference to Mʳ Fenwekes promise of Joyning with vs therin wee shall
not owne the same but for the pᵗsent Can nether afferme nor deney tell wee
haue made further Inquiry, however it little or nothing weakens the answare
of our Court much les makes the foundation therof to bee vppon a great
mistake as before is expressed for yᵗ wee Ran it att our owne Charg is
Certaine but yᵗ wʰ Cheefly obstructs the Issew of the difference is the want of
the aforsaid pattent, wee have done sufficient allredy for the determining our
bounds to our owne Satisfaction and the wʰ should bee to the Satisfaction
of all others yᵗ Can make no legall ₵ due Claime to the lands aiacent wʰ
Canetacott Cannot without a pattent; And wheras it is alledged yᵗ the
Towne of Sprinkfeild was formerly in Combination with Conectacott ₵
therfore yᵗ Colony ought not to bee dispossessed therof vppon a bare
Challeng ; wee answare yᵗ to the Combination wee can say little but leaue
Sprinkfeild to answare for themselves which wee doubt not but they are
suffissiently able to doe not knowing for what time or vppon what tearmes it
was made or how or by whom broken nor doe wee well Remember (it being
long sence) whether there were euer any or no ; but this is Certaine without
question yᵗ both Mʳ Pinchon ₵ those yᵗ went from hence to Inhabite at
Sprinkfeild were of this Jurisdiction ₵ went hence with a promise so to
Continew as did the rest of the Townes vpon the River 2condly they tooke a
Comission for Goverment from the Jurisdiction of the Massachusets thirdly
at the meeting at Cambridge about tenn or twelve yeares sence Mʳ Pinchon
in the behalfe of Sprinkfcild declared his desire to bee ₵ Remayne vnder
our Goverment ₵ so haue Contineued ever sence without question or word
speaking against it yᵗ wee Remember tell somthing was moved to that purpose the last yeare at Plymouth, wee proffes ourselues vnfaynedly desirus of a

Just ₵ Righteus *end to bee put ₵ yᵗ with all Conuenient speed to this or any
other difference with our bretheren of Conectacott or any other of the Jurisdictions ; and in order therunto ₵ as yᵗ in our apprehenssions conduseth
much to promote the same ; wee desire the Rest of the Comissioners would
bee pleassed to Reuerse the order or orders yᵗ aiudges sprinkfeild to pay
Custom or Contribution to the Erecting or mayntaineing a fort at the Rivers
mouth ₵ for yᵗ end seriusly to attend these Inseuing Reasons amongst many
others yᵗ hath been formerly alleged

first there hath bene no pattent or exemplifycation yet ꝑdused by Conectacott to prove Sprinkfeild within theire Jurisdiction nor order of theire Court
for Imposing Custom vppon them but only a part of an order to y^t purpose
now ꝑdused w^h is very darke and ambigius to vs so fare as concernes
Sprinkfeild; our desire therin ₵ the Comissioners thervppon at Plym being in no sort (as wee Conceaue obserued as by Comparing our ꝑpositions
₵ the Comissioners order with what is now ꝑdused together will appeer the
whole order not being brought but y^t left out which wee suppose would make
most for our advantage in the Case

secondly there hath bene no Evidence (so fare as wee know) of any fort
at all in being worthy the name of a fort and therfore according to a clause
in the Comissioners order page the 3^d no Custom or Imposition is to bee
payed; the words are these; ꝑvided y^t the said Impossition bee contineued
no longer then the fort in question is mayntained ₵ the passage therby secured
as at p^{r}sent; which in Rationall Construction supposeth y^t the said fort was
then mayntained ₵ the passage therby secured or at least y^t the Comissioners
Conceued it so to bee but the contrary is now apparent.

Thirdly suppose the fort in question were or heerafter might bee of vse
to secure that passage yet wee propound it to Concideration whether ever it
hath been known or any Instance Can bee given of any Goue^{r}ment in the
world y^t hath Compelled the people of an other Jurisdiction to Contribute to
the Erecting of a fort or place of strength by w^h they may Rule ouer them
₵ order them at pleasure as well as bee a protextion to them; (if y^t were the
case) vnles it were in way of Terany ₵ oppression; our Request therfore is
as before y^t the said orders may be Reuersed and sprinkfeild left in point of
paying Custome or Contribution in statue coprius till it bee made apeer y^t by
pattent or other Just Right it fales within the Jurisdiction of Conectacott;
Our motion heerin being attended ₵ graunted wee shalbee *shalbee Redly *166
willing to Imbrace ₵ dillegently to comend to our Court any equall ₵ Just
motion y^t shalbee made or aduise y^t shalbee given by the Rest of the
Comissioners for the finall ending of this difference betwixt vs in Refference
to the bounds of our pattent ₵ y^t w^h depends theruppon

The Comissioners of Conectacott doe Conceaue it is esily apparent to all
who duly Concider the foregoing Reply of the Comissioners of the Massachusits how short it fales of Clearing the Order of theire generall Court or
taking of what is Justly ₵ treuly obiected by our selues ₵ therfore shalnot
need to say much in way of Returne onely desire it may bee attended with
due Respect to truth in Simplissity; That the foremenssioned order saith y^t

Mr Fenwike agreed to Run the linne with them which is one mistake secondly it sayth Mr Fenwike fayled therin ; and y^t is a 2^{cond} of the same nature : and thirdly the order affermes y^t hceruppon thc Massachusits Ran the linne at theire ownc Charg which also is a great Error ℘ was tendered to bee proved so vppon oath by the Comissioners of Conectacott if it were desired. And if this bee not a fundamentall Mistake ℘ not sercomstanciall only as is pretended (it beeing almost all y^t is said if the words bee attended in theire due conection) Wee must confesse our selues to bee in a great mistake and shall so owne it when its made to appeere ; But for the p^{r}sent wee must take leaue to Judgo wher premisses are not treue The conclussion or Inference Cannot bee strong   In our answare wee touched not vppon theire Calling for a sight of our pattent because wee desired according to the propossition of the Comissioners att Plym: to propound y^t w^h wee conceue might tend to a present Isseu of the difference if it might bee accepted and the standing vppon a sight of the pattent shuts vpp the way it being well known to them as to our selues y^t the pattent is in England And though the last yeare att Plym: it was stood vppon yet it was verily apprehended by vs the Returne then made by the tendering of a true Coppy therof to veiw and the equall Respect given vnto y^t pattent as to the pattent of thc Massachusits ℘ Plymouth by the Right honorable Comitty of Parlement knowne well to our honered frinds of the Massachusets had satisfied y^t particular

      That sprinkfeild was in Combination with Conectacott ℘ so owned by the Gouerment of the Massachusets is more Cleare then to bee left vnder any doubt ; propossitions being sent in Anno *1637 by the honered Goue^r latly desseased to all the plantations vppon that River Concerning a Combination with the Massachusits ℘ Mr Pinchon in procecution therof Chosen ℘ sent as Comissioner from that Colonie to acte in the treaty for them in Anno 1638, att which time ℘ not before hee declared his apprehenssions y^t sprinkfeild would fall within the Massachusets linne ; and was so accepted without any proufe of what was aledged, ℘ that motion by Mr Pinchon arose (as is verily Conceved) from a present pange of discontent vppon a sensure hee then lay vnder by the Gou^{r}ment of Conectacott

      Wee shall not Insist for breuity sake vppon a pticular answare to all y^t p^{r}sents in Refference to the Imposition vppon sprinkfeild, most if not all of y^t which is alledged haveing Com vnder Concideration in former agitations about this business ; The order of the generall Court of Conectacott so fare as Concerns and may bee satisfactory in the p^{r}sent Case is brought ℘ p^{r}sented. A fort vsefull to the whole Riuer hath been maintained at Seabrooke at a great Charg nyc 14 yeares past; the p^{r}sent decayes therin are Indeavored to bee Releived by the building of a new worke of stone wherby the Entrance into the Riuer may bee secured ℓ wee doubt not when Instance is given of a place for Scittuation parralele to sprinkfeild vnder a distinct Goue^{r}ment from other Townes aiacent but it wilbee found in Comon Concernment it hath been Liable to bear a part in the Comon Charg

To Conclude wee desire it may bee Concidered y^t both the Court of the Massachusits ℓ theire Comissiouers fall not in with the desire of the other Comissioners for a speeddy Issewing of p^{r}sent differences but Retard the same by Requireing y^t which they know att p^{r}sent cannot bee attained.

Secondly That theire Comissioners mannifest au Eresolucdnes and vnwillingnes to Refer differences of this nature to the determination and Judgment of the Comisioners of the other Collonies which wee had Rather our much honered brethern of the Massachusits would duely Concider how agreeable it is to the fundamentall articles of the Confederation wherunto wee all ought to haue a Consiencius Regard then to make any Coment ourselues:

Among the orders or Wrightings from the generall Court of the Massachusits a Lawe Imposing a Custom or Imposition vppon the other three Confederate Collonies was by the Comissioners Read *Red ℓ concidered the Tenure wherof is as followeth:

*168 -

Wheras the Comissioners for the Vnited Collonies haue thought it but Just ℓ equall y^t sprinkfeild a member of this Jurisdiction should pay Custom or Contribution to the Erecting ℓ mayntaining of Seabrooke fort being of no force against an Enimy of any concidcrable strength (before it was burnt) In the Comissioners owne Judgment expressed in theire owne order page 109 which determination against sprinkfeild they haue also continued by an order att the last meeting att Plym: (though the said fort was then demollished by fyer ℓ the passage not secured) Contrary to a Clause in their Order pvided on springfeilds behalfe page 111 and forasmuch as this Jurisdiction hath Expended many Thousand Pounds in Erecting ℓ mayntaining seuerall forts which others as well as ourselues haue receued the benefit of And haue at p^{r}sent one prinsipall fort or Castel of good force against an Enemy of Conciderable strength ℓ well Garisoned ℓ otherwise furnished with suffisient amunition, besids several other forts ℓ batteries wherby vessells ℓ goods of all sorts are secured

It is Therefore Ordered by this Court and the Authority therof That all goods belonging or any way appertaining to any Inhabitants of the Jurisdictions of Plym: Conectacott or Newhauen y^t shalbee Imported within the Castle or exported from any part of the Bay shall pay such Custom as heerafter is expressed:

Videlecet all skins of beaver Otter Moose & baare twopence a skine And all other goods packed vpp in hogsheads or otherwayes tenn shillings a tunn; meal & Corn of all sorts 2 pence a bushell, bisket six pence per hundred; And It is further Ordered y^t all such skins & other goods as shalbee Imported or Exported as aforsaid shabee duly Entered with the Auditor Generall & the Custom therof payed or depossited before any part of the said goods bee either sould shipte landed or otherwise disposed of; vnder the penalty of forfeiting the said goods not so Entered or the due valleu therof; And if any Inhabitant of this Jurisdiction or stranger shall buy any of the aformensioned goods belonging or any wayes appertaining to any of the Inhabitants of Plymouth Conectacott, or New hauen aforsaid Imported to any other part of our Jurisdiction or shall sell or deliver to any Inhabitant any other goods in any part of the Bay without the Castle hee shall Enter the said goods with the Auditor Gen-

*169   erall and *And pay or deposett for the same after the same mannor & pportion and vnder the same penalty as is provided for the goods &c brought within the Castell; This Order to take place the first day of the next month And the Auditor Generall is heerby appointed & authorised to take Care for the execution of this Order in all the pticulars heerof either by himselfe or by his Deputie or Deputies

per The Generall Court

ENCREASE NOWELL Secretary

The Coppy of a Wrighting or Order produssed by the Comissioners for Connectacott Concerning the Impossition layed vpon Sprinkfeild

Att a Generall Court held att hartford for the Jurisdiction of Conectacott Sxto Junii 1649

Conecticott

Vppon Reading the acts of the Comissioners for the vnited Collonies att the meeting held att Plym: the last seaventh month; It was observed y^t in the agitation of the difference betwixt the Massachusits Colonie & this in Refference to the Imposition Required from sprinkfeild vppon som goods passing out at the mouth of this Riuer towards the Charge expended att Sebrooke tending to the good & benifit of all the plantations vppon the River; It was questioned by the Comissioners of The Massachusits whether there were any Order of this Court extant for the payment of any Impossition by goods appertaining to the Inhabitants of Sprinkfeild brought from them and passing downe this River

This Court doth declare That by Exprese Order of the fift of Febreuary 1645 all Corn laden on board of any Vessell vppon this Riuer ƪ passing out to Sea att the Riuers mouth was to pay 2ᵈ per bushell in the foremensioned Respects; and beauer twenty shilling per hogshead, wherin as sprinkfeild was Intentionally Included soe this Court had due respect therunto as then Concidered vnder the Massachusits Gouerment; That no greater burthen might fall vppon those Inhabitants then according to Cleare grounds of equity ƪ Righteussnes in theire best apprehensions they ought Redily to submit vnto, and was equall for them to beare ƪ no more then they should haue Expected to bee Imposed vppon themselues in the like Case *Case which order hath been sence confermed ƪ a penalty of Confiscation of such goods anexed in Case of non payment; the Execution wherof in Refference to our brethern of sprinkfeild hath onely been defered vntell the Judgment of the Comissioners of the other Collonies might bee vnderstood in the premisses according to the articles of Conffederation wherin provission is made for desiding of any differences yᵗ might fall in betwixt any of the Collonies wherunto they Reffered themselues in this Case although they are yet altogether vnsatisfied yᵗ sprinkfeild doth pperly fall in within the true limmitts of the Massachusets pattent which they much desire may with all Convenient speed bee Cleared ƪ Issewed in a way of loue ƪ peace according to truth

*170

JOHN CULLIK Secretary

The former passages betwixt the Massachusets Generall Court ƪ theire Comissioners on the one part ƪ the Comissioners for Conectacott on the other part Concerning sprinkfeild together with the Order or lawe Imposing Customes vpon the three Collonies being duly Concidered six of the Comissioners did declare ƪ Remonstrate to the generall Court for the Massachusits as followeth

A Difference betwixt the Massachusits ƪ Conectacott Concerning an Imposition att sebrook Required of sprinkfeild haueing long depended; The Comissioners hoped (according to advise at Plymouth might at this meeting haue been satisfyingly Issewed; But vppon pussall of som late Orders made by the Generall Court for the Massachusets they find yᵗ the linne on the south side of the Massachusits Jurisdiction is neither Run nor the place from whence it should be Run agreed; That the originall pattent for Conectacott or an authentick Exemplyfication therof (though Mr Hopkins hath offered vppon Oath to assert the truth of the Coppy by him p^{r}sented) is now Required ; And that a burthensom Custom is by the Massachusits latly Imposed not onely vppon Conectacott Intressed in the Imposition at Sebrooke but vppon Plym: ℓ New hauen Collonies whose Comissioners as arbitrators according to an article in the Confederation haue been onely exercised in the question ℓ y^t vppon the Request of the Massachusits, and have Imparsially (acording to theire best light) declared theire apprehenssions therin which Custom ℓ burthen (grevius in it selfe) seemes the more vnsatisfiing, and y^t because diuers of the Massachusits deputyes (who had

*171   a hand in making *making the said lawe acknowledg ℓ the preface Imports it y^t it is a Returne or Retalliation vppon the three Collonies for sebrook ℓ the law Requires it of no other English nor of any stranger of what nation soever ; how fare the premisses agree with the lawe of love ℓ with the tenure ℓ Import of the articles of Confederation The Comissioners tender ℓ Recomend to the serius Concideration of the Generall Court of the Massachusits ℓ In the mean time desire to bee spared in all further agitations Concerning sprinkfeild

A question being propounded whether notwithstanding the p^{r}sent meeting of the Comissioners begun in July ℓ not ended tell august there should not bee another meeting in September ; The Comissioners Concidering y^t in anno 1645 and in Anno 1647 when extreordinary meetings were Called either by the Generall Court or by the Gou^r of the Massachusitts they did serue ℓ satisfy for the ordinary yearly meetings ℓ y^t in 1647 The Comissioners did propound it to the fower Generall Courts y^t in Case of an extreordinary meeting in any yeare no other meeting without an apparent Cause should bee expected ; And three of the generall Courts did Concent therunto ; and the Massachusets generall Court haue not in the least declared any dissent ; theire Comissioners possibly not advising with them therin ; And lastly the ocations of the Collonies being Concidered ℓ debated according vnto what hath been now p^{r}sented the Comissioners see no Cause to meet againe a month hence They agreed therfore y^t no other meeting bee expected or attended this yeare vnles som vrgent ocations of the Colonies Call for new Concederations ℓ Counsels

Vppon a question betwixt the two Collonies of the Massachusits and Plymouth formerly propounded and now againe Renewed by the Comissioners of the Massachusits concerning a Tract of land now or latly belonging to

Pamham and Soconoco two Indian Sagamores who had submited themselves
⟨ theire people to the Massachusits Gouerment vppon part of which land
som English (besides the said Indians) in Anno 1643 were planted ⟨
setteled ; The Comissioners for Conectacott ⟨ New hauen Remembring ⟨ duly
Concidering what had passed in Anno 1643 and in anno 1646 did ⟨ doe
still Conceaue y^t the Comissioners for Plymouth did Concent ⟨ agree y^t the
aforsaid Tract of land though it fall within Plymouth bounds should bee And
from thence forward acknowlidged as a part ⟨ vnder the Massachusits Jurisdiction ; nor doth it yet apeere y^t Plymouth when those Conclusions of the
Comissioners Anno 1643 were Red in the generall Court did protest or doth
declare against it That the *the Massachusits might haue Concidered theire
way before they expended so much Charge in Samuell Gortons bussines ;
But what direction Counsell and Order Plymouth Comissioners had from
theire generall Court so to doe, wee vnderstand not ; and what power any of
the Comissioners haue to Resigne or pase over any Tracte of lande within
theire pattent to another Jurisdiction without Concent ⟨ exprese lycence from
the Generall Court Intressed ⟨ Concerned therin is of waighty Conciliation
to all the Collonies ; They therfore advise ⟨ desire y^t by a Naighborly ⟨
friindly Treaty a due Concideration may bee had ⟨ a Course settleed both about
the Charges Expended and how Pomham and Sokanoco with theire people
may bee Gouerned and protected

*172

Mr Dudly one of the Comissioners for the Massachusits and Presedent
for this meeting being latly fallen sicke ⟨ vnable to attend the present ocation
in hand ; the other Comissioner for the Massachusits declared himselfe vnsatisfied with this Returne of the Comissioners of Conectacott ⟨ New hauen as
seeming to detract from the Conclussions of the Comissioners in this case in
Anno 1643 ⟨ in Anno 1646 where the Lands in question seem to bee
graunted ⟨ aiudged to the Gouerment of the Massachusits ⟨ the way propounded not lickly to Issew the p^{r}sent difference there haueing beene Tryall
formerly made therof but without any effecte ; The like vnsatisfiednes hee
expressed in the last answare or Reply of the Comissioners for Conectacott
but for the Reason before mensioned ⟨ p^{r}sent straights of time deffers
Replying to som other opertunity

The Comissioners for Conectacott ⟨ New hauen who were p^{r}sent in the
former agitations Conceue they haue Retracted nothing in any Respect from
what they did in Anno 1643 ⟨ in Anno 1646 And therin Refer to an Indifferent ⟨ due Concideration of those passages ⟨ what is now declared But they

1 6 4 9. proffes they never thought themselues Interessed in the question betwixt the
Massachusits ⟨ Plymouth vnles as Wittnesses *Wittnesses in both those yeares
July.
*173 they being neither Concerned in Samuell Gortons busines or in the Tract of
land in question But concured in what was Just ⟨ warrantable y⁺ a due peace
might be setteled for the Comfort of all the Colonies ;

These foregoing conclussions were Subscribed by the Comissioners
The 8ᵗʰ of august 1649

The Presedent being sicke as
aforsaid Could not Subscribe

EDWARD HOPKINS
THO: WELLES

SIMON RRADSTREET
WILLAM BRADFORD
JOHN BROWNE
THEOPH: EATON
JOHN ASTWOOD

At a meeting of the Comissioners for the Vnited

Colonies in New England at hartford the 5th of September **1650**

The Articles of Confederation being Read an order of the generall Court of the Massachusetts dated the 22^{cond} of May 1650 was ƥsented and Read Wherby It apeered that Mr Symon Bradstreete and Captaine Wilłam Hawthorne were Chosen Comissioners for one full and Compleat yeare being invested with full power and authoritie according to the tennor of the said Articles

Mr Tho: Prence and Mr John Browne were Chosen Comissioners for the Colonie of New Plym: as apeered by an order of theire generall Court dated the 4th of June 1650 which was ƥsented and Read

Mr Edward Hopkins and John Haynes Esqr were Chosen and apointed Comissioners for the Colonie of Conectacot as appeered by an order of theires generall Court dated at hartford the 16th of May 1650

Theophilus Eaton Esqu^r and Mr Stephen Goodyeare were likwise Chosen Comissioners for the Jurisdiction of Newhauen for this p^rsent yeare to treat and Conclude of all things according to the tenor of the articles of Confideration as appeered by an order of theire generall Court dated at Newhauen the 30th of May 1650

Mr Edward Hopkins was chosen President for this meeting

The Comissioners for the Massachusetts ƥsented a letter from Mr Steele President of the Corporation in England directed to the Comissioners for the Vnited Colonies ; and withall Informed that Mr Winslow hath for som yeares past spent and Improved most of his time about the busines of the Indians seteling the Corporation in England and procuring other priuileges of Comon Concernment to all the Colonies as well as That of the Massachusets and therfore moved the Comissioners to Concider that som honerable and equall *Recompence may bee allowed him for his past paines and Charges either out of the Collections for the Indians or out of the three Jurisdictions of

Plym: Conecticot and Newhauen   That of the-Massachusets haueing disbursed allreddy vpon that acount betwixt three and foure hundred pounds; and allso to Consider whether the Comissioners Judge it meet to Continew the said Mr Winslow still in England to atend vpon the aforsaid Implayment; and if soe what may bee a meet allowance for time to Com ; Informing likwise that theire Court had giuen order the last yeare for his Returne   Mr Steels letter being Read and Considered the Comissioners Joyntly Returned answare as by the Coppy will appeere   But to the pposition Concerning Mr Winslow the Comissioners for the three Colonies expressed theire owne thoughts and apprehensions that had the Massachusetts at first or at any meeting sence ppounded any publick service wherin the other Colonies might haue been Concerned they would haue found a Reddy Concurrance both in sending an agent and in Contributing to a meet allowance ;   But Mr Winslow was sent forth anno 1646 vpon pticular oeasions and Concernments of the Massachusets and though the Comissioners for the Colonies haue mett seuerall times sence ; yet they neuer were aduised with either about his goeing stay Returne or how to Improue him there ; soe that they know not vpon what grounds or by what arguments to ppound or perswade theire Respective Courts to Contribute to the Charg past ; though they hope theire seuerall Colonies will thankfully acknowlidg his loue in any Concernments of theires ;   But being Informed by Mr Steele That his ꝑsence hath a speciall Influence in that great worke in Raising meanes in England for the publishing of the Gospell among the Indians, a seruice they judg very acceptable to God and of great Import to the natives they are afrayde to hazzard or hinder it by his over hasty Returne but rather thought fitt to Comend it to the ꝑsedent and assistants of that Corporation *That 100^ł may bee paied to Mr Winslow out of those Collections towards his expence and Incurragement with ꝑmise that if they shall soe advise the Colonies in their seuerall ꝑportions shall heere Returne the same without lose to the worke Intended.

*177

The tenor of the foremencioned letter from the Presedend of the Corporation is as followeth

Worthy Gentlemen

This day the Corporation appointed by act of Parlement for Carriing on and ꝑmoteing the Gospell of Christ in New England being Informed by Mr Edw: Winslow (youer agent and one of the assistants nominated in the said acte) of his letter to you sent (wherin he desireth for Reasons to himselfe best knowne that you would bee pleassed to send ouer som other in his place which allthoug it be Contrary to the mind and Judgment of the said Corporation to part with soe worthy a member yet wee Cannot ꝑvayle with him to Revocke his said letter ; And wheras in all ages it hath been the designe of vngodly men to hinder and oppose the spreding and ꝑpagating of the Gospell of the lord Jesus of which wee are truly sensable ; In Refference to those discorragements we haue mett withall sence wee had soe great trust vpon vs yet through the blessing of god the busines of the said Corporation is in a good forwardnes and the Integritie abilities and dilligence of the said Mr Winslow being well knowne both to you and vs as allso his great Enterest and aquaintance with the members of Parlement and other Gentlemen of quallitie in the respectiue Counties of this Commonwealth ; Wee Cannot but Conceaue his ꝑsence and Residence heere to bee of absolute nessesitie for the Carrying on the work for wee Cannot Conceaue you Can send ouer any that hath the like Influence and enterest in the affections of such as may bee most healpfull heerin ; Wee Confes and must acknowlidg it is vncomfortable to him to bee soe long from his famyly and psonall occasions ; But as *'To that you and wee must see hee bee no sufferer but if hee leaue vs the work in all likelyhood willbee hazzarded (if not fall) which is at pᴦsent in an hopefull way notwithstanding all the oppositions wee haue mett withall ; Wee therfore thought good to Informe you of the nessesitie of his Contineuance with vs, haueing found him very instrumentall in the Carrying on this work ; And therfore wee once more Intreat youer Concurrance with our desires That soe with Cheerfullnes wee may Carry on the work wee haue begun which wee hope will Center in the Glory of god the good of many and our mutuall Comfort which is our earnest desire and prayer

*178

London these 24th   Signed in the name
of March 1649   and att the desire
     of the said Corporation

WILⱢAM STEELE

Presedent

The Answare Returned by the Comissioners to the forgoeing letter was as followeth

Hono^{rble} Sir

youers of March 24th 1649 wee have Receaued and in the name of these Vnited Colonies wee doe thankfully acknowlidge youer great labore of loue to Raise and settle due meanes and Incurragement that the Gospell of peace may bee further published to these miserable Indians which haue long layne in grose darknes and haue worshiped the prince of darknes not Considering that theire way and euery stepp of it tends to death and euerlasting destruction Wce are sory that a work soe acceptable to God and of such Concernment to these poore men should meet with opposition ; But the Almighty whom you serue heerin Can easily Remoue Impediments and make euery mountaine becom a playne, and wee are assured youer eye is towards *him whoe obscrues to the kindleing of a fier vpon his aulter and a Cuppe of water giuen with sperittuall aymes all the loue and labour of his people and in no seruice will suffer the Intervening difficulties and exersices to pas without a waight of Recompence ; Vpon a serivs Consideration of a state of affayers Comitted vnto the Care and Trust of Mʳ Winslow and with tender Respect to his family and occasions in these parts his Returne was expected this last Spring (yet if the Comfort of his Relasions may be ꝑvided for wee Concent to his ꝑsent stay That the worke in hand be neither hazzarded nor hindered ; What money is allreddy Collected vpon that accoumpt wee Cannot Coniecture but if youer selfe and those worthy Gentlemen youer assistants Concure wee desire that one hundred pounds may bee thence allowed and payed towards his expence and Incuragement And if vpon any Respectes you haue other thoughts vpon a word of aduise wee shall Reddyly heer supply the same without lose to the work entended. Mʳ Elliott hath allreddy spent much time and labore in fitting himselfe and preaching to the Indians Mʳ Mahew hath made a good entrance into the same way and work ; if you please for theire Incurragement and som nessesary healpes for the Indians to pay the assignes of Mʳ Elliott the som of one hundred pounds more wee hope it will proue a Reall furtherance to the seruice ; Lastly Wee humbly desire that one thousand pounds or any lesser sum according to the stock in hand may bee payed to Harbert Pelham Esqʳ and the said Mʳ Winslow whose Care and paynes wee shall intreate to send it hither in such Comodities as may suit the end ꝑpounded ; Thus in our *our measure and according to our oppertunities wee desire to put our hands to this pius work leauing the whole successe to him whose the harvest is and who by weak meanes and instruments can work wonders, even of such stones Raise vp Children vnto Abraham And with our due Respects wee comend you and the waighty occasions vnder youer hand to the guidance and blessing of our good God Resting

It was allso Thought fitt that letters should bee directed one to Mʳ Winslow and another to Mʳ Pelham and Mʳ Winslow Joyntly ; The tenoʳ wherof was as followeth

Honored Sir By a letter from Mr Steele the Hono^{rble} Presedent of youer Corporation wee are satisfyingly Informed of youer Care and paynes for the ppagacion of the Gospell among the Indians in these parts (a work of high Concernment as wee Conceaue for the Glory of God and for the sperituall good of these poore Creatures Wee are sory but Cannot think it strange that you should meet with difficulties in such a way the prince of darknes whose throne hath been long highly advanced in the harts of these barbarus heathen will sertainely by himselfe and his Instruments oppose the Kingdom of our Lord to the vtmost tell hee find himselfe Rebuked by him whose power hee hath felt and trembleth att; Wee heare that the Massachusetts both with Respect to theire owne occasions and the Comfort of youer Relations expected youer Returne this last spring; But vpon the aduise Receaved wee all Concure and Consent to youer p^rsent stay Wee hope the foundations are well layed and the busines allreddy *in a good forwardnes that a little more time may settle and establish it as a work the Lord ownes and prospers Wee hope that some that are yet bakward may yet see theire error and that others willbee free and Cheerfull in so pious a seruice how larg a sume or to what vallew you haue allreddy Collected wee Cannot forsee but desire our advise may bee Considered with due Respect to the stock in hand Wee haue written to the Honord President that if the Treasury will afford it they would out of the Collection pay an hundred pounds to youer selfe towards your expence and Incurragment yet with promise that if himselfe and the worthy assistants Concure not in that way vpon the least word of aduise or Information It shalbee heer Repayed and Imployed to the best aduantage of the seruice Intended Mr Elliott hath spent much time and paynes and continews zealous in the seruice of Christ and loue to the soules of the Indians Mr Mahew hath made allso good entrance into the same worke and goeth on to fitt himselfe to open and display to these poore Natiues in theire owne language the vnconceaueable exelency of that Prince of peace if therfore one hundred pounds may bee payed to Mr Elliotts assignes partly for their Incurragement and partly to provid som Conveniencies for the Indians wee hope it may much further the worke in hand; Lastly wee ppound and desire that a Thousand pounds or any lesse sume accordinge to the pgresse you haue made in these Collections may bee made to our honored frind Harbert Pelham esq^r and youer selfe which wee desire may bee Imployed and sent ouer in Comodities according to the Inclosed note; Wee are assured of youer Care and faithfullnes and the great Master whom wee serue will Certainly and abundantly Recompence youer labor of loue into youer bosoms.

*181

*The formencioned note was as followeth

		£
In shoos plain and strong of all sorts ———————————	100
In stockings that are strong and most Irish ————————	100
In good strong Canvas for shifts summer Clothing and beds	200
In light axes broad and narrow howes sawes &c —————	100
In nayles, hookes hinges and spades ———————————	150
In strong Carsies of a low prise ———————————————	200
In blankets for beds ———————————————————	100
In haberdasheey ware especially thred ———————————	50

The Joynt letter to Mr Pelham and Mr Winslow Was as followeth

Honorrd Syrs

Wee haue Receaued Informacion of the acte that passed the Parlement of England for the ꝓmoting and ꝓpagating the Gospell amongꝭ the poore natiues which though wee look vpon as a gracius effect of their loue and zeale to the name of the lord Jesus yet wee Cannot without Incuring a iust Imputation of to much Ingratitude but owne and acknowlidge youer selues or in an especiall manor instrumentall to the furtherance of the work which wee humbly and hartily desire may throug the Rich blessing of God answare all the holy ends of such as ꝓmote the same ; wee find ourselues by the Acte put in som trust for the Carrying on this great busines and desire to Improue our vtmost Care and dilligence therin that no time may bee let slippe but the

*183 meanes advanced for the worke may bee Imployed in it to the *first and best advantage which hath drawne from vs a letter to the much Honorrd President of youer Corporation that about 1200^t may be payed vnto youer selues if so much bee Com in vpon that Collection Wee presume of youer willing Reddynes to Improue youer selues in bringing the work to a greater perfection and are abundantly Confident of youer abillty and faithfullnes in laying out what Coms to youer hands in the best and most suttable way which Induceth vs to leaue the Care and trust with you though it may seem to great addition to the waight of youer other Important affayres ; Wee haue in our pticular letter to Mr Winslow giuen more especiall directions about disposing the moneys you may Receaue from the Treasury ; and because there may such advise Com out of England by shippes not yet Com in as may Call for more Consideration and direction about the ꝓmises then Can Conveniently in such seasons and straights of time as may fall in bee attended by the Comissioners at the distance they wilbee in after the desolution of the ꝓsent meeting ; Wee

desire you would bee pleassed to obserue such aduise as you may Receaue by
the last shipping this p̃sent yeare from the much honered Govr of the Massachusetts and the Comissioners of that Colonie whom wee haue entreated and
Intrusted in the former Respects to acte according to the Emergency of occasions Wee shall add no more & /

The Comissioners for the Colonies in further p̃secution of the trust
Comitted to them in Regard som things may entervene and fall in nessesarily
to bee attended before the next sitting within the ordinary Course ‸ will not
bee vntell the next Returne of this month doe think fitt and desire that for
this p̃sent yeare the Honord Gou^r of the Massachusits and the Comissioners
for that Colonie bee pleassed to take such things into due consideration and to
acte therin as in theire Wisdoms may best p̃mote the work in hand; And in
p̃ticular that in Case Intellegence bee giuen from England that any Considerable sume more then is allreddy wrote for bee there in Reddynes and that
That order is expected from hence for the disposall therof they giue aduise
and direction for the sending ouer of soe much as they Judge meet in such
Comodities as may best Conduce to the furtherance of the worke; and to
Receaue such goods as are sent; make p̃vision for theire p̃servacion from damage; and if need bee dispose of the vallue of one hundred pounds to or for
such Indians as are Inclineable to attend waies of Civellity and the things of
the Gospell; But it is p̃vided notwithstanding and desired that as opportuni-
ties are p̃sented aduise may bee giuen to the Comissioners of the other Colonies of such occorrents as happen with the p̃sent state of these occasions that
wherin a joynt Consideration ̸ Concurrance may bee had without preiudice
to the worke it may not bee Neglected.

*184

Vncus Sachem of the Mohegins Informed the Comissioners and complained that the Mohansick Sachem in long Iland had killed som of the said
Vncus his men, bewitched diuers others and himselfe allso and desired the
Comission^{rs} that hee might be Righted therin But because the said Sachem of
long Iland was not p̃sent to answare for himselfe It was thought meet and
accordingly advised that Comission bee graunted by the Gouerment of Canec-
tacot to Captaine John Mason Mr Howell Mr Gosmer and Tho : Benedict of
Southhold or any three of them to examine the matters Charged by Vncus
and if pro^{rs} bee Cleare to labor to Convince y^{em} therof Require satisfaction
and in Case of reasonable Complyance to endeauor a Composure therof; but
if no satisfaction willbee giuen for Iniuries p^rved then to lett y^{em} to know they
give the English Just Cause of offence and will bring trouble vpon themselues

1650.

*The Comissioners taking into Consideration the seuerall offensiue prac-
tisses of the Narragansetts wherby they haue broken their Couenants and
endeavored to disturbe the peace betwene tho English and themselues ; And
how yet they delay to pay the Wampam which hath been soe long due notwithstanding the many demaunds that hath been made both formerly and
Renewed at the last meeting att Boston sence which time they haue sent onely
i00 fathome ; It was therfore thought meet and agreed to keepe tho Colonies
from falling into Contempt amongst the Indians and to preuent their Improueing the said Wampam to hire other Indians to Joyne with themselues against
vs or Vncus, as formerly they haue done that 20 men well armed bee sent out
of the Jurisdiction of the Massachusetts to Pessicus to demaund the said
Wampam which is 308 fathom and vpon Reufusall or Delay to take the same
or the vallue therof in the best and most suitable goods they Can finde : Together with so much as will satisfy for theire Charges following in all pticulars
the Comission and Instructions following ; and if opposition bee made by the
Indians to the taking away the life or rescuing the said Wampam or other
goods taken in lue therof; That then a meeting of the Comissioners to bee
held att Boston ; forthwith Sumoned by the Gouer or Comissioners of the
Massachusetts, if they see Cause and in the meane time that such pparations
and pvisions for warr bee made by all the Jurisdictions as the Case shall
Require

A draught for the heads or Substance of a Comission or Instructions to
bee given by the Gouerment of the Massachusetts to such Comanders and
Souldiers as they shall think meet to send to the Narragansett Sachems

*Comission and Instructions for   sent
from the Massachusetts in the name of the Comissioner for the vinited English
Colonies to Pessacus and Ninnigret two of the Narragansett Sachems

You shall with all convenient speed and with as little Noyse as may bee
Repayer to the Narragancetts and aquaint Pessacus That the Comissioners
desirus by all due meanes to preserve peace between the English and them
have both delivered bake theire hostages and for seuerall yeares have with
much patience waited for a due observation and pformance of Couenants ; But
have found nothing but offenciue excuses and delayes ; besides the breach of
seuerall other engagements 308 fathom of Wampam is yet behind which
should have been payed in long sence ; The Comissioners are therfore nessesitated to send men to fetch the said Wampam or the full vallew ; which if
vpon a peacable demaund they forthwith pay together with Just allowance

for the ꝑsent service It shall yet satisfy And the Comissioners will hope the Rest of the Covenants may speedyly bee atended But if vpon what ꝑtence soeuer they deny or delay payments you are to seize and bring backe with you soe much wampam, beauer or other suitable Comodities as may answare both the debt and the aformencioned Charges or if other meanes bee wanting you are to scize ⌃ (with as little hurt as may bee) bring away either Pessacus or his Children or such other Considerable Sachem or psons as they prize and may probably bow them to Reason ; But if you meet with any hostile opposition to the hazard of youer lives you are in a prudent way to secure youer selues and make an honorable Retreate you are allso to obserue their speaches actions and whatsoeuer else may giue light to our future ꝑceedings that if Called therunto you may giue account vpon youer oathes This done som of you are to repayer to Ninigret And *aquaint him That the Comissioners are Informed that hee had giuen his daughter in marriage to Sasecos his brother who gathers Pequats vnder him as if either hee would become theire Sachem or againe Possese the Pequat country both which are expressly Contrary to former engagements and by no means may bee suffered ; You shall therfore Inquire where Sasacus brother Resides what number of men Pequates or others are with him, whence hee hath them ; and what his purpose and aime may bee and require Ninegrets answare and Resolution about him that some further Course may bee taken as the Case may Require ; You shall acquaint Ninnegret that Weekwash Cooke Complaines of sundry wronges ; that the Comissioners as they would deale Righteusly with all men soe they with the Indians would not disturbe the publicke peace by oppressing one another (they are allso Informed that Ninnegret ꝑtends some graunt or libirtie to hunt within the Pequat country the Right and title to the place and allso the Royalties therunto appertaining they must assert as due onely vnto the English and onely at theire dispose ; nor may Ninnigret as things stand betwixt the English and him Challeng or vse any such libertie there) lastly you shall Informe him that about 12 yeares sence a Mare belonging to Elty Pomary of Winsor in Conectacott was killed willfully by Poquiam a Niantick Indian brother to Ninnegrett which Mare Cost 29ˢ for which satisfaction hath been often Required by the English and promised by the Indians but not yet pformed ; The Comissioners therfore without further delay expect due payment that there bee no further Cause of Complaint or proceeding

*187

Wheras the Mohauks haue by the pocomptuck Sachem as we are Informed made theire Request to the Gouerment of Conectacott that Sequascon might haue libertie without offence to Returne to his former habitation alledging how Reddy and willing they have been to gratify the English in what they have Requested, *It is therfore thought meet that an answare bee Returned to this purpose, That the English neither formerly haue nor yet doe pʳhibite his Returne soe that hee Carry himselfe inoffenciuely for the future hee may Come at his pleasure and that they are now the more free for it being Requested by them:

The Comissioners for the Massachusets Informed the Comissioners for Canecticutt and Newhaven how fare they had ꝑseeded according to advise giuen at theire last meeting at Boston to issue the difference betwixt them-selues ꝑ Plym: Conserning a tract of land lately belonging to Pomham and Socononoco two Indian Sachems; That the generall Court for the Massa-chusetts had by theire Comissioners first offered to Resigne theire Interest in the aforsaid lands ꝑ appurtenances to Plym: if they would engage to ꝑtect and to adminester Justice equally both to Indians and English within those limmits; But that Plym: Collonie had Rather Chosen to pase over theire Right by pattent and had Resigned the said tract of Land ꝑð And left them for euer to bee vnder the Gouerment of the Massachusetts

They Informed allso with what tendernesse and forbearance they had sence dealt with Samuell Gorton and his Companie though sundry and great Complaints had been made and Renued against them not onely by the Indi-ans but by the Naighboring English vnder the Massachusetts Gouerment; They shewed allso a letter from Mʳ Easton President of Road Iland Wherin in the name of the Counsell there hee declareth that Road Iland and War-wicke (where the said Gorton liveth) are Combined and bound mutually to support one another They desired therfore advise from the Rest of the Com-issioners how they might further ꝑseed sence vpon tryall they find that without at least a leagall force they Can neither Redresse Iniuries nor bring the Inhabitants of Warwicke to acknowlidg and Submite to theire Gouerment

The Comissioners Remembring what advise had been given by the Honʳᵇˡᵉ Comitte of Parlement in this and like Cases that the bounds of Pattents should bee first sett out by a Jury of vnenteressed ꝑsons and That

*That all Inhabiting within the limmits so set forth should fall vnder the Gouerment established by pattent and vnderstanding that the formensioned Resignation made by Plym: was not with full Consent and satisfaction to all the Freemen of that Jurisdiction and without any agreement or Consent of the Inhabitants of Warwick who pretend an enterest in Mʳ Williams his pattent but will by no peacable means bee brought vnder the Massachusetts

Gouerment; and being desirus as much as may bee to prevent Inconvenience and by all due meanes to preserue and settle peace within and betwixt the Collonies and with all Naighbors according to Rules of Righteusnesse and Prudence ; Thought fitt to Recomend it both to the Massachusetts and Plym: as theire Most serius advise ; that the Massachusets vpon the afformensioned Respects) doe aquite and for ever Relinquish the Right and title they have to the lands of Pomham and SoconONOCO aforsaid and the Jurisdiction therunto belonging and that Plym: doe forthwith Reassume the Right they formerly had by pattent to the place ; That they Ingage and promise a due ptection and equall adminestration of Justice to all the Inhabatants English and Indians according to the Massachusets engagement ; And that all faire meanes bee with the first Conveniency vsed to reduce Warwick (c̃ to a due Submission to the Gouerment of Plym: that Justice may have a free Course and all greivances betwixt them and theire Naighbors may bee satisfyed and Remoued ; But If they Refuse that then the Just and wholsom aduise of the honorable Comittee of Parlement Conserning a Jury & ⌄ bee forthwith duly attended that the Inhabytants of Warwick may know where they fall and to what Gouerment they ought to Submit ; But if Plym: accept not this advise or if the said Inhabitants proue obstinate and will neither Submit to Gouerment nor by other meanes make due Satisfaction for trespasses or wronges done to Neighbors Justice must haue its Course The Massachusets *Massachusets or Plym: whom it may Conserne Cannot but ptect and puide for the Conveniences of those within theire Jurisdiction ; in such Case wee thinke it nessesary and advise that Reall Damages Duely proved bee levied by leagall force though with as much moderation and tendernesse as the Case will pmitt

*190

The 13th p̃sent the Duch Gouer being arived two daies before vpon a desire (as hee expressed to treat with the Comissioners, p̃sented the following writinge

Honed Sirs

Six Considerations Conserning the publick wellfare haue moued to vndertake (this to mee) troublesom Journey to meete youer Worsps hcere and allsoe two pticulares the one Conserning my selfe the other one of the Inhabitants, which I haue thought convenient to ppose in Writing that all Inconveniencies by verball speaking either out of hastinesse or otherwise may bee p̃vented ; but principally that I may giue account to my Souraignes the high and Mighty States generall of the vnited Belgick Provences and the Honble Lords Bewinthibbers of the West India Companie

I

The first is the wrong and Iniury done to the H. M. and the Right Hon^rble West Indian Companie by sertaine of youer Nation by their vnjust vsurpacon and possesing the land lying vpon the River Commonly Called Conecticott or the fresh River, being the lands of the said Companie bought and paid for to the then Right ppriotors the Natiue americans before any other Nation either bought or p^rtended Right therunto for the which wee desire a full Surrender and Satisfaction according to the quallitie of the Cause.

2^cond

*191

Wee Cannot but Conceaue youer Wors^pps Cannot but bee sensable of the advansing and Incroaching of som of youer Cuntrymen *vpon the p̃tended lymits betwixt vs and youer Nacion in these parts and the pretended Rights of H. M. and the Right honorable Westindia Companie Wheras in our native Countryes a long and happy peace hath been observed and faire naighborly Comerse and Correspondency before and sence my arrivall and Gouerment which haue occaconed Certaine Contestations and troubles the which for our parts I should very gladly see Removed and taken away and for the Remocon therof I Conceaue either a generall or p̃visionall lymett may bee settled betwixt vs for the accomplishment wherof I Conceaue it will Conduce much therunto if wee shall either by a Joynt writing to our Superiors at hom or sending our agents request it may be by them decided

3

The detaining of sertaine fugitiues by the Right Worthy Goue^r and Maiestraits of New hauen vpon my first arrivall gaue to my great greife cause of some Discontent on either side for the p̃vention wherof for the future I desire that som Course may bee Resolved vpon that all ocacions of Distast that way may bee p̃vented

4

Whereas by ̃lers from the Right Wor^sh Governor Eaton by order of the Honor^ed Comissioners and likwise by Comon fame wee vnderstand the honered Comissioners the last yeare passed an act of p̃hebition of trade for our Nacion with the Natiue americans in these p̃tes vpon Confiscacon of Shipp and Goods I Cannot but for the wellfare and p̃perity of our Nacion in these p̃tes but desire the said act may bee Repealled or that the honorrede Comissioners willbee pleassed to give mee vnder theire hands theire Reasons and grounds for the forbiding the said trade within the pretended lymitts H. M. and West India Companie

5

*192

And for that likwise by Relacion of divers Credable psons of youer Nacion and ours one Mr Pinchon vseing trade and Comerce with the Native americans hath soe fare advanced vpon the trade of that the trade and Comerce in these p̃tes of these ioynt Nacions is much damnified and vndervallued *not onely to the Inriching the said Native barbarians but the overthrow of the trade haveing likwise by pticular Testimony from two psons of quallity vnderstood that the said Mr Pinchon gaue eleuen gilders to the said Natives for a beauer skine the detriment y^t may therby arise I shall Refere to the wise Consideration of the honored Comissioners that som Course as they in theire wisdoms shall best Conceaue may best bee agreed vpon that the said Inconveniencies may bee Removed

6

Wheras likwise there was a sertaine shipp detained and the goods vnladen by them of Road Iland the said shipp being taken from the spaniard somtimes our enemies but now our frinds by vertue of a Comission from vs the which said shipp being by them of Road Iland detained sold and desposed of to Severall Seamen vpon pretences of shares due vnto them Contrary to the mind and will of the owners haveing the greatest enterest therin; the said owners making many Complaints vnto mee for Satisfaction either by way of arestment of any of theire Barques or Reprisall the which I was vnwilling to graunt tell I had aquainted the honered Comissioners therwith that the said honered Comissioners will please either to Cause them of Road Iland to make Restitusion according to equity or els that it may not bee in any measure offencive to the honered and Naighbor Collonies to seek our Right by way of Reprisall

The two pticulars the one is that I may receue Right for the scandall Raised vpon mee by Tho: Stanton the which I sppose is knowne to som of you by what my Ensigne did speake and desire at New haven from the Gouer^r there : ad calumnias tacendum non est non avt Contra dicendo Nos vllsis camus sed ne mendatio in offensum pgressum pmetamus.

*193

*The second is that Govert Lockman making Complaint to mee of wrong Receued by him from the Gouer^r and Court of Hartford about a sume of Money paid by him of the which in my letter to youer honored Comissioners of the last yeare I made Complaint and desired satisfaction in that point being still by him vrged with the vnRighteusnesse of the pseeding ; I can doe no lesse in Relacon of my Duety but Request the honered Comissioners will take a Review of the pseedings that in Case you shall find a Mistake in the sentance Restitusion may bee made to the plaintife or els so much light showen that the plaintife may bee Convinced

PETER STUYVESANT

New Netherland

September the 23^d sti Nouo i650.

This Writing being Receued and Read the Comissioners Returned in writing the answare following

Hon^rd Sir

Youer selfe hath often ppounded a Meeting to Compose differences and the Comissioners haue euer Reddyly imbraced it by youer agents wee haue now vnder youer hand Receved som ppositions and might Returne severall waighty greivences wherin wee Cannot but expect Just Satisfaction but youer selfe have now Cast a barr in youer way of youer treaty expected youer ppositions written this day in Hartford bear date in New Netherland September 23 Stila Novo what Comission you have for it youer selfe best knowes but sertainely wee shall encurre blame from our Superiors to admit such ptence of title to this place vnlesse therfore you bee pleassed to explaine or Retract wee may not pseed

EDW : HOPKINS Presi͵

Hartford in New England
the 13th of September
i650 St Angliæ.

in the name of the Comissioners
of the English vnited Collonies

*194

*The Duch Governor Returned in Writting as followeth

Honered Sirs,

It was love of peace and Naighborly Complyance that brought me hether and am Redy to attend all occasions that may therunto Conduce and 23^d this Instant new stile I sent my ppositions to that end but as I vnderstand by youer Missive I put a barr in the way by dating my ppositions as in New Netherland I thought my first pposition would have Removed that barr but to shew I would not willingly put any obstract to the treaty expected the honered Comissioners may please to know the substance of what was pposed was agreed vpon by my selfe and Counsell at the Monhatoes and there dated and Subscribed but the papers being left aboard for the gaining of time I Caused them to bee Coppied out and translated soe nigh as I Could Remember from the originall ; And therfore Conceaued it most pper to stile it New Netherland but for the prevension of any misapprehension for the future if the honered Comissioners shall please to forbeare the Calling of this place Hartford in New England I shall forbeare the stiling of it New Neatherland but if you shall Conceaue it most expedient to stile it soe I conceave it is but Reason I should haue the same liberty to date my writting as in Conectacut in New Netherland the which may not bee any obstrucsion to the treaty soe I Rest

Youers in loue

Conecticott September 24
new stile i650

PETER STUijUESANT

To the forgoeing that which followeth was Returned by the Comissioners

*Hon^rd Sir

Wee haue perused youers of the 24th wherin you leave out what was offensive and date onely from Conecticott which for the present doth soe fare satisfy that the treaty if you please may goe on though the English title by Purchase pattent and possession wee are assured wilbee found good & firme both in Europe and america youer Comission wee shall expect to see when youer vessel Comes vp but to Redeeme time wee shall Consider your ppositions and shall allsoe with ouer first Conveniencies acquaint you with our greivances but if you accept it wee Rather desire to treat by a frindly conference then by writting which will draw out the businesse to a greater length thē pbably will suite either youer or our Conveniency soe wee Rest

	Youers in all wayes
Hartford the 14th	of love and Righteusnesse
of September 1650	EDW: HOPKINS
Stil Angl:	President

The answare to the ppositions formerly expressed was as followeth

Hone^rd Sir   Wee have Received youer ppositions and breifly Returne the answare following

first the Right the English haue to Conecticott River with the plantations and lands vpon or about the same hath been often asserted and as wee Conceaue is either fully knowne or Sufficiently Cleared to the English Duch and Indians in these p^ts wee have not heard yet any thing of waight obiected against it but how much land the Duch heere Claime where it lyeth from whom Purchased wee have onely heard allegcions without proofe which Cannot Satisfy

*It needs both explycacion and euidence where and which of ours haue made any encroachments vpon the ptended Rights of the states of the vnited Provences Wee hope to prove our Right to what wee enioy by pattent Purchase and possession ; and that if the happy peace soe long Continewed betwixt our Superiors in Europe haue mett with any disturbance it is by seuerall Iniuries wee haue Receved by youer pdessors and youer selfe in these p^ts of which wee haue Complained heere and should willingly Refer the examinacion and Issue to Europe if wee might see any Comission or Instructions from thence directing and warranting you therin.

Wee are assured New hauen Maiestraits were free for all offices both of

Justice and amity but youer selfe Cast in Impediments by Claiming both the place and Jurisdiction and som of you vsed offencive and threatening language ill arguments as the state of affaires then stood ; But if in other pticulars this treaty may bee brought to a Comfortable Issue a due Consideration may bee had of fugitives and how to settle a Right vnderstanding and Naighborly Corespondency betwixt vs

4^{ly} The Comissioners never Intended to direct or Regulate the duch trad within theire owne pper lymits ; they onely desired that the mischevious trade of pouder (& which soe directly tends to the damage and hurt of both nations might bee Restrained at aurania ffort, the phebition vnder the penaltie you mension extended onely to the English pper bounds as by the Comissioners ters from Boston the last yeare may apeere

5^{ly}
*197   *by what Rules the Traders whether at Aurania ffort or Springfeild walke the Comissioners enquire not ; Trad is free and Marchants attend theire owne Conveniencies and will hardly Continew a Trad driven to lose but lawes to lymite if not well Considered will soone bee Repealled

6^{ly} The Comissioners vnderstand not how or vpon what ground the Inhabitants of Road Iland have proseeded about the shipp menčoned nor where the Right is though they bee not Combined with the other Collonies yet as naighbors and as our Cuntrymen wee Cannot but desire theire welfare soe farr as wee may advise they should doe you Right and you them no wrong but wee Can neither examine nor Judge in the Case

To the two last pticulars wee answare as followeth

I   Tho: Staunton as wee are Informed hath ever pffessed that what hee spake was both truth as hee Related it and to discharge his engagement by oath to the Jurisdiction hee delivered it but as an Indian Report it was no otherwise entertained ; som of the longe Iland Indians haue sence attested the same before the Maiestraits of Conecticott and som other Indians vpon the mayne concure with them ; which may thus fare satisfy that Tho: Stanton Raised not the Report nor Intended any hurt to youer selfe but the Indians are subtile and might have theire owne ends in Reference to which wee then did and shall doe Suspend beleife

2^{condly} The Report of Govert Lockmans large but mischevivs Trade with the Indians filled these p^{tes} as wee are Informed was brought to the Monhatoes the evidence against him to the Court of Conectticot was as Clear and full as may bee expected in such a Case hee might once and againe haue had his Case tried but hee Rather Chose to issue in a Composition ; But sence as

wee heard hee hath expressed a Resolution to pseed in the same Trad ; wherin
hee will giue new offence and bring himselfe into further Trouble.

EDWARD HOPKINS,

President

Hartford vpon Conectticutt
the 14th September 1650

*To the foregoing answare there was Receued from the Duch governor
that which followeth

    Honered Sirs

    Youer paper of the 14th September Stil: vet I receaved in answare to
my ppositions

    Youer answare to my first pposition is as I expected for wher there is
an affermetive of Right due the negative must needs follow from them that
detaine that Right from the true pprictors ; and allthough happily I Can
pduce Testimony by Duch English and Indians to a Certaine quantity of
land Purchased paid for and in p^t posessed by vs, and other p^t vsurped by
them of Hartford yet I shall forbeare the further psecucion our said title wher
my p^{ties} are both President Judge and p^{ties} in the cause

    My first explained the second and for the euidence in time Convenient
may bee produced and wheras you are pleassed to Charge my pdessors and
selfe with severall generall Iniuries you haue Receued by vs ; for what my
predessesor hath done as I am ignorant soe I Can not be Responsable but for
my selfe I Can not but take speciall notice you are pleassed to Condemne
mee of Iniuries done to you before it bee duely proved and my answare
heard which giues mee Cause to suspect the Cause is likly to bee vnequally
ballenced allthouge as yet I neuer had question with the honered Collonies of
Massachusets and Boston

    youer assurance that the Maiestrates of New haven were free for all
Naighborly offices and so forth ; but that my selfe Cast in Impediments in the
way (and that som of our people vsed offencive and threatening language
vpon a due examinacon I suppose it wilbe found otherwise ; and for offencive
and threatening language vsed by any of ours there it was Contrary to my mind
and order ; and when I know the pties accusation and profe against them (if
vnder our Gouerment) wee shall take Course that Reparacion shallbee made

    *To my fourth you give no positive answare for my pposition was not
Conserning the directing or Regulating the Trad but the phebition of the
Trad in these parts with the native americans to all that are vnder our Gouerment of New Netherland my desirs then being and still are that you will
either Repeall the said acte or give mee a Cattagoricall answare the grounds of

*198

*199

youer act being for the ꝑvension of the sale of guns powder &c̄ to the Indians I know no Reason that the Innocent should suffer for the guilty in case any of ours shalbee found to Trad in that nature it is but Reason hee should bee punished for our parts as wee haue an order for the pᵗhebition of the said Trad soe wee put it in execution vpon due proofe

Conserning my pposition about Mᵗ Pincheon I onely proposed it as what I Conceaved might bee to the detriment of the publick Trad in these pᵗᵉˢ Refering it to the wisdom of the Comissioners to Consider of it but for my owne pᵗ shall herafter bee silent

for them of Road Iland I pᵗposed for advise and the taking away of offence that might be given to my Naighbor Collonies

for that of Tho: Stanton I am vnsatisfyed as being a Publike pson vntell such time as I may face to face answare to my accusers

for what may bee duely prooved by good Testimony against Govert Lockman in his Trading with the Indians in these ptes for guns powder &c̄ if fairly prooved I shall very well approve of the proseedings of the Court at hartford therin ; but vntell it bee made euident to mee by good Testimony of any Transgression by him Comitted against the publick lawes of this Cuntry I Can not but require satisfaction in that behalfe ;

ffor the furthering the treaty the Right honorable Comissioners haue often ꝑpounded a verbal Confference with them in theire Court ; for my part I Cannot see any Conveniency in it being the Causers of any difference are both Judge and pties ; but to shew to my principalls and to all others whom it may Conserne that I am free and Inclined to peace *and to naighborly Corespondency and to give and Receue due satisfaction sence my arrivall by equall pties as wee Call it a Chamber of my ptie ; If it shall please the Right Worshipfull Comissioners to deligate two Indifferent psons out of the Collonies of Boston and Plym: with full power I am willingly reddy to depute two others with the like power and Refering to each others theire Rights and titles and soe refer the Issue of Iniuries Receued and given to theire award ; otherwise if the pties aggreived will please to bury all former passages betwixt vs I shalbee free and willing therunto and to Joyne and fall vpon Considerations of what may bee thought may Conduce to the publick good of both nations in these ptes ; if neither of these bee not graunted, I cannot see any light to ꝑseed fvrther on in this Treaty but with all thankfullnes to accknowlidge the Respective Intertainement I haue Reseaued from you sence my arrivall among you and shall Rest yoᵗs in all offeces of loue

    Conecticott the 26ᵗ of September   PETER STUijVESANT.
    i650 Stila Nov:

The Comissioners Replyed

Honered Sir

To youers of the 26ᵗ Present newly Receved wee shall breifly make Reply onely wee shall first mind you that you Came to treat with the Comissioners have directed your writtings to them and therfore Could expect noe answare but from them.

The English Colonies when they first entered this vnion and Confederation Inquired and by all due meanes serched into the Claime the then Duch Goverᵣ made to som part of Conecticott; they pused the letters Monsʳ Kieft had written Considered his allegacons and proofes and Compared them with the Defence the English at Conecticott made for themselves and Cause which they thought a Cleare and satisfactory way to find out where the Right lay; and vpon a full Ɛ Serivs Consideration *The Comissioners together with the generall Court of the Massachusetts tell further light were by the Duch ₽duced thought Conecticotts title and prosseedings faire and Just; and accordingly sertifyed theire apprehensions to the then Duch Governor; But if yet wee may vnderstand what and vpon what Grounds you Challenge wee shall Indifferently Consider and aduise; but hetherto youer Claime hath been various and vnsertaine somtimes to all the lands vpon that Riuer somtimes to a part somtimes vpon one ground and otherwhiles vpon an other which leaves vs in the dark and vnsatisfyed

I

*201

Wee vnderstand not how the first of youer ppositions explaines the 2ᶜᵒⁿᵈ wee Conceued them as two of youer destinct greivances which Caused our answare to Run in that frame wee hope wee shall see and bee satisfyed with youer Comission though you exprese nothing of youer mind therin; youer selfe Charge Iniury Wrong Incroachment vsurpacon Ɛ̃ vpon som of the Collonies before any shaddow of proofe; and yet take it ill that you find any such expressions in our papers wherin yet wee determine nothing but sertify how things yet stand in our apprehensions tell further light and proofe bee held forth

2 ᶜᵒⁿᵈˡʸ

The Comissioners for Newhaven are free and willing that the Case of the fugitives and all that depends theron bee duly Considered and Judged by Indifferent men.

3 ˡʸ

Wee Conceaue our former answare was full and satisfying yet at youer desire wee shall add that as both ffrench and Duch ₽hibite Trad with the Indians in thire seuerall Respective Jurisdictions; Soe the Comissioners Conseaue the English Collonies may doe within theire ₽per lymits, yet if this

4 ˡʸ

1650.

September.

5^{ly}

6^{ly}

*202

7^{ly}

8^{ly}

*203

treaty in other Respects issue to Content and Satisfaction that acte may bee further Considered and ꝑbably Repealled

Wee rest in what you are pleassed to Conclude Conserninge orderinge or lymiting Trade.

Wee Cannot but take well what you ꝑpounded Conserning *Roade Iland wee Can advise no further but are satisfied with youer aymes and desires that peace and Righteusnesse may *may* duly bee ꝑserved betwixt you

Tho: Stanton is expected heere to day or tomorrow but ꝑbably hee will thinke himselfe discharged by bringing the Sachem and other Indians to Justify what hee Reported as from them, however wee shall neither in him nor any other Countenance any thing which may appeare Iniurivs to any much lesse to youer selfe.

Conserning Gouert Lockman you wholy waue the substance of our answare ; himselfe being Consius of his guilt in that mischeuivs Trad as was Conceaved by the Maiestraits of Conecticott) Chose Rather to issue all by a Composition then to Run the hazard of a legall tryall. and you well know in such Cases; volenti non fit iniuria.

To the Conclusion in youer last paper wee haue and still doe ꝑffesse that in all passages of the treaty ppounded wee look not at ourselues as a Court or Judges or that any thing should be carried by vote ; but ppounded a free Conference betwixt p^{ty} and p^{ty} that a Right vnderstanding may bee gained and differences by mutuall Consent Composed ; youer desire of peace and naighborly Corespondency wee fully approve ; and shall not differ with you in the way of arbetracon mencioned onely wee desire to see youer Comission and what you will Refer and what not that wee may the better see and Consider our way ; not doubting but if our meeting issue without fruite wee shall Cleare our Intencions by our Carriage and offers to all Indifferent Judges wether heere or in Europe.

In another paper these ensueing greiuances and Complaints were at the same time ꝑsented to the Duch Governer

Honered Sir,

Our Joynt ayme (wee hope is) that this meeting may be Improved as an Audit seriusly to Consider and duly to issue all acounts betwixt vs ; youer ꝑpositions or pcells *Wee haue ꝑused and answared wee shall now aquaint you with severall pticulars which stand Charged in the English bookes which wee desire you wilbee pleased duely soe to weigh that all Reconings may bee Justly Cleared and a naighborly Corespondency setled:

The English at Canecticott haue formerly Complained of many

vnworthy passages and Iniuries Receued from som of those who have been Imployed by the Duch as agents from them there to which noee satisfing answare was euer yet Returned as the entertainement of English fugitives and helping them to file of theire Irons pswadeing servants to Run away from theire Masters Retaining and buying stolen Goods and refusing to Returne them vpon equall satisfaction vpon demaund marrying som English Couples Refused at the plantations with seuerall other of a like Nature.

Som of them allso further Complaine for the non payment of debts due for goods taken vp by theire publ Agents who haue left the Place without giveing due Satisfaction and payment denyed by theire Successors as not appertaining to them

lasty The Maiestraits for Conecticott Complaine of an Insufferable Iniury latly Comitted by the Neger belonging to the Duch house ; that wheras a notorius delingquent vpon a Capitall offence was heere Imprisoned the said Neger did assist him to breake prison and to make escape for which they have not yet Called him to accoumpt

The Comissioners for Canecticott and New haven doe Joyntly Complayne that wheras Captaine how and som other English purchased of the Indians the true ppriators all that tract of land from the easteren part of the Oyster bay to the westeren part of a bay by them now Called How or Holmes bay to the middle of the great playne being halfe the breadth of long Iland to the Norward ; Monsr Kieft the then Duch Governer Caused the English to bee seized Carried thence by force and imprisoned them

*the Comissioners for New haven Inform and Complayne first that wheras by theire agents they had duly purchased of the Indians Sachems and theire Companies seuerall tracts or pcells of land on both sids of Delaware bay or River to which neither the Duch nor Swedes had any Just title yet without any leagall ptest or warning Monseire Keift the then Duch Governer sent armed men i642. and by force in a hostile way burnt theire trading house seized and for som time detained the goods in it not suffering theire seruants soe much as to take a Just Inventory of them ; hee there allsoe seized theire boate and for a while kept theire men prisoners for which to this day they Can get no satisfaction

I
*204

That the said Duch Governor i642 Compeled Mr Lamberton theire agent by force or threatenings to give in at the Monhattoes an accoumpt of what beauers hee had Traded within Newhauen lymits at Delaware and to pay Recognicon for the same

2^condly

John Johnson the Duch agent with the Swedes Governer at Delaware Charged Mr Lamberton as if hee had ploted with the Indians to

3^ly

1650.   Cutt them of a Capitall Crime for which they Imprisoned and tryed him
September.   but Could bring no proofe to satisfy themselves who both accused and
satt Judges yet they sett a fine vpon him for Trading within Newhauen
lymits there

4^{ly}   youer selfe soone after youer entrance vpon the trust and Charge at the
Monhattoes Came and seized a shipp with the goods in her by force in theire
harbor pretending title to the place ; and after you Complaine of a purpose
and Resolucion in them to vindicate theire owne Right in a lawfull way ; you
Required them to send theire Duch Marchants and theire goods with Recognicon to the Monhattoes and if directions were not attended you threatened
hostilytie to Newhauen pretending to keepe peace with the other Collonies

5^{ly}   In youer letter dated october 12th 1647 you Required *sertaine fugitives
*205   in an offenciue manor as if the place and Jurisdiction had been vnquestion-
ably youers though by ancient pattent from the Kings of England all this
part of america called New England in hreadth from 40 to 48 Degrees of
Northerly latitude is graunted to the English ; And the Inhabitants of New
haven had Right therby to Improve a smale portion therof and accordingly purchased land of the Indians and have built fenced and settled themselves there ;
and in many yeares after not hearing soe much as any the least p^rtence of
title the Duch did or Could make to any of the lands or appurtenances

6^{ly}   In behalfe of Wiltam Westerhouse a Duch Marchant but an Inhabytant
and planter in Newhauen they desire and expect Restitucion and satisfaction
for the aforsaid shippe and goods seized and Carried out of theire harbor to the
great damage of the said Westerhouse and his principalls for which hee still
Calles both vpon the Comissioners and the Maiestats of Newhauen for Justice
and expects that by an arrest vpon youer vessells the Cause may bee brought
to a due tryall within the English Collonies where the shippe was seized

The p^rmeses being duly Considered and Issued whether by Conferance
or arbytracion as youer selfe ppound if yet there Remayne any question about
title or lymits of lands or about Jurisdiction which Can not bee heere Cleared
and ended to mutuall satisfaction wee shall Reddyly agree that such difference
may bee by Consent truly stated and soe Refered into Europe for finall determinacion and that in the meane time such bounds and lymits bee agreed
betwixt the English of the vnited Collonies and the Duch Jurisdiction that
eich may know what to expect and Inioy without disturbance till a Resolucion and determinacion may be procured and settled

Hartford on Conecticott   EDWARD HOPKINS
September 16th   President &c
1650

*The next Writting Receved from the
Duch Governer was as followeth

Honored Sirs

In youer Reply of the 26th proof is Required haply the pretendant Collonies Hartford and New hauen seeing noe sufficient authoritie in theire anticipacon of vs from the enioyment of our p^rtended Rights; had Recourse to the Indesputable pattents of the Massachusets and Plym: to shrowd themselues vnder theire winges and therfore pduced such evidence and letters as might serue theire owne ends but that all our allegacions and proofe were duly and truly weighed and Considered in a right way ℄ manor before Indifferent Judges in the p^rsence of the pties defendant; I Conceaue Can never bee prooued for the verity of my Claime as it is true I haue layed Claime to all the lands betwixt Cape henlopen westward and Cape Cableyou eastward for matter of title; and to this about hartford as the pper demeane of the West India Companie as being purchased paid for and Surrendred by the then Right ppriators the Natiues vnto vs

My Comission you may please to see when you shall desire it allwaies pvided on the other side I may see the Comission of my pties; I Could doe no lesse then Charge Iniury and vserpation upon some of you vpon our lands and still must vntell the question bee lawfully decided

To the third I fully agree with the Comissioners of New hauen.

I question not the power of the Comissioners for making any orders in theire pper lymits but desire those vnder our Gouerment and Jurisdiction may enioy the freedom of trade with the Indians in our ptended lymits according to what they had formerly allwaies enioyed

for the fift and sixt I am fully Satisfyed withe the answare of the Comissioners

for Tho: Stanton I freely pase it by being well satisfied with the good opinnion of the Comissioners in that point

In the Case of Gouert Lockman being I am Informed it was his owne volentary acte I am satisfyed I shall *onely desire a Coppy of the agreement from the Secretary of the Court at hartford ; And for that I vnderstand the said Lockman vsed some threatening words after his agreement I onely Require the Testimony of what they were and I hope the Comissioner shall Receaue satisfaction.

In my former paper I expressed what I would putt to an agitacion and am Reddy to performe it when I shall know youer deligates ; I hope my desire and Indeavor will Cleare mee before any Indifferent Judges of my Reddynes to bringe matters to a Comfortable Issue betwixt vs and that there rest noe blame on mee if otherwise it fall out

The points to bee agreed vpon by the deputies I Conceaue may bee Comprehended vnder these 4 heades

    1 the Composing of differences

    2 a prouicionall lymite of land betwixt vs

    3 a Course to bee agreed vpon conserning fugitives

    4 A neaighborly vnion betwixt vs so nigh as may bee agreed

Conecticott the 27th   youers in all offices of loue

September 1650 Sti no: PETER STUijVESANT.

The Returne from the Comissioners to the present Writting ensueth

    Honered Sir

    Though wee desire to put the most favorablest Interpretation vpon all yor expressions whether by word of mouth or writting yett wee Conceaue you still Cast new Impediments in the way of any faire accord when you would mittigate the greivance att Newhauen for seizing a shippe in theire harbore vpon a Claime to the place you plead a mistake Comitted by youer Secretary *leaving out a word which you say was in the originall coppy; it should haue Run pretended Claime or title wherin wee see you put a difference betwixt a Reall and a pretended title yet in youer last Writting bearing date this p^rsent day you Call Conecticott and Newhauen p^rtendant Collonies Imply against them an Iniuryous anticipacon of som Right you p^rtend to that they shroud themselues vnder the wings of pattents not Including them; that the Duch euedence was not fairly produced to giue light to youer Claime; all which if not Retracted Cannot but offend; you againe proffese a Claime from Cape henlopen to Cape Cod; Somtimes you say but to Cape Judith somtimes you doe but p^rtend a title but hitherto you haue not been pleassed to shew either pattent or purchase to Justify any pretence of youers to what is in question; soe that if you Charg Iniury and vserpacion vpon any of the Collonies without better grounds you Cannot but expect a Just defence and Returne.

    The pmises being satisfyingly cleared wee Can freely treat p deligates according to youer desires to Compose all differences agree vpon prouitionall lymites where there is any question about title or bounds to Returne fugitives and settle a Naighborly Correspondency betwixt vs

                               youers in all seruice of loue

Hartford vpon Conecticott   EDWARD HOPKINS

September the 17th i658   President &c

              Sti: Angl.

*208

vpon the Receipt of this a writting of the following Contents was sent by the Duch Gouerner to the Comissioners

Honered Sirs,

youer last paper being Receued I answare It was loue of peace as I formerly write vnto you brought mee- hither and not to make alteracion by writting; I thank you for youer fauorable Interpertacion; I would not willingly Cast any Impediment in the way of the treaty if my thoughts had been soe I might better haue stayed at home and not trouble my selfe or others; I suppose you all know I Cannot deliuer my selfe so promt in youer language as mine owne and as I would willingly and therfore Conceaue noe advantage should bee taken against mee for the two Mayne things now obiected for the hinderance the treaty. I shall explayne my selfe that my words being the pretendant Collonies of hartford and Newhauen : I look vpon them as my pties in Case any dispute should arise for matter of Right and title of lands

To the 2^{cond} the difference betwixt a ꝑtended Right and a Reall Right I shall state the Cause as I apprehend a man may ꝑtend a Right to that which hee doth not possesse and yet haue a Reall Right and a man may ꝑtend and possesse where hee hath noe Right vnto but to take of disputes that way if the Comissioners please wee will leaue it to our Superiors to Judge where the Reall or ꝑtended Right is ; and in the Interim for the furtherance the treaty to our Common wellfare I am free and willing to treat with you all· as with the vnited English Collonies expecting youer Wor^{shipps} speedy answare I rest

*209

youers in all loue

Conecticott ₴₮th September
i650.

PETER STUijVESANT

The Returne of the Comissioners was as followeth

Honered Sire

In youer last writtinge you giue noe answare nor doe soe much as mencion som things Justly offenciue in youer former paper yet accepting youer explycacion soe fare as it goeth ; youer ꝑffession not to Incroach vpon our Rights ; and freenes to treat with vs as the vnited English Collonies wee shall pase by som vnsatisfying expressions hoping wee shall find the Reallity of youer Intencions of peace in a Reddy yeilding to satisfy Just greiuances in the treaty wee haue therfore according to youer desire Intreated or deligated two Comissioners out of the Massachusetts and Plym: Collonies to whom wee giue full power for the Composing of all differences in Case of Iniury and damage to set provitionall bounds in all places where there is difference betwixt vs Conserning title and lymites to Consider what may bee done in the Case of fugitiues and to settle a Just Corespondency and desire you wilbee pleassed forthwith to name youer two deligates and to Invest them with like power that the treaty may begine and proceede without further vnnessesarie lose of time; Wee haue Chosen and Intrusted our worthy frinds Mr Symon Bradstreet and Mr Tho: Prence to the seruice wee Rest

youers in the truth and for

peace according to it

EDWARD HOPKINS Presedent &c.

Hartford on Conecticott

the ⅒th September i650.

*The next writting from Mon^r Stuijvesant ensueth

Honored Sirs   youers of the ⅒ i650 being Receued in answare to mine of the ½ this Instant month giues mee great hopes that matters wilbee Comfortably issued betwixt vs and in each Respect Comply with you in that way of deligacon and doe make Choise of my worthy frinds Mr Tho: Willett and Ensigne Gorge Baxter to whom I shall and doe giue as much power in each Respect as you haue or shall to youer worthy deligates and Rest

youers in loue of Peace

Conecticott ⅒ i650   PETER STUijVESANT

The Reference being agreed vpon the Duch Gouerner gaue Power to his delegates by a Writting Containing as followeth

Bee it Knowne vnto all men whom these p^{r}sents may any way Conserne That We Peter Stuijvesent Gou^r generall of the New Netherland Curasoe Aruba &c. by vertue of a Comission from the high and Mighty Lords the States Generall of the Vnited Belgick Prouences directed vnto vs for the Generall Rule and Gouerment of the Prouence called New Netherland ; and likwise for the entering into a Couenant of peace legue and amitie with any prince people or state as by the said Comission more at large doth and may appeere and being desirus that the said loueing Vnion and Correspondence betwixt the two Nations in these Northeren parts of america may bee observed preserued and mayntained as in our Natiue Cuntries of the vnited Belgick Prouences and England ; Doe by vertue heerof Confiding in the Wisdom

integrety and Sufficiency of Captaine Tho: Willett and Ensigne Gorg Baxter
depute the said Captaine Tho: Willett and Ensigne Gorge Baxter to treat and
agitate with the Comissioners of the vnited english Collonies giueing and
graunting and by vertue of these p^rsents I doe giue and graunte full power
and authoritie vnto my said deputies to Joyne with other two deputed *by the   *211
Comissioners of the vnited English Collonies and with them to treat agitate
examine all or any difference betwixt the two nations in these parts and absolutely by the Joynt Concurrence of the other two deputies to end and determine them according as they in theire Wisdoms and entegryty shall think
Just and Right ; with power likwise to my said Deputies to enter into such
tearmes of accord for provisionall lymits and league of loue and vnion betwixt
the two nations in these parts as to them shall seeme expedient   Ratifying
and Conferming and by vertue of these p^rsents will stand bound to Ratify and
Conferme whatsoever my said Deputies shall agree vnto on my behalfe according to such directions and Instructions for the Comon good as wee haue giuen
them ; In Wittnes and Confermacon wherof I haue heervnto sett my hand
and Seale this 28th September i650 Stil: N̅o̅

PETER STUijVESANT

The House the Hope on Conecticott Comonly Called the fresh Riuer

A like Comission with full power was graunted to Mr Symon Bradstreete
and Mr Tho: Prence in the following words

   Know all whom it may Conserne the Wee the Comissioners for the
Vnited English Collonies by vertue of the letters pattents graunted by the
Kings of great Brittayne vnder the great Seale of England for all New England lying in that part of america from the Northeren latitude of fourty to
fourty eight and according to the Conffederacon formerly made and a full
power this yeare giuen by the fower Generall Courts of the Massachusitts
Plymouth Conecticott and New hauen to the p^rsent Comissioners by which
they are enabled to treat and Conclude in matters of publick Consernment
that former and late greivances betwixt the honered Gouernors or agents for -
the high and mighty States of the vnited Belgick Prouences in such parts of
america as are possessed *or Justly belonging to the said H ꝑ M ꝑo and the   *212
English Collonies may bee duly Composed and a Just and naighborly
Correspondency settled; Confiding in the entegrity and sufficiency of our
worty frinds Mr Symon Bradstreet and Mr Tho: Prence haue and heerby doe
intreat and deligate them to agitate treat and Conclude with the deputies
appointed and authorised by Peter Stuijuesant Esqr the p^rsent honered Gou^r

of the Prouence of New Netherland to Consider and Compose all differences to agree and Conclude prouisional lymits in all places wher there is question of title or bounds a Course for ordering or Returning fugitiues and settleing a Just Correspondency Ratifiing and by these prsents Confeirming what our said deputies according to directions and Instructions giuen shall agree and Conclude in the prmises or any part therof in Wittnes Wherof the President for the Comissioners hath heerunto sett his hand and seale

EDWARD HOPKINS

President

Dated in Hartford vpon
Conecticott $\frac{18}{8}$th of
September i650

Vpon a serius examinacon and Consideracon of the pticulars Comitted to Reference the Arbetrators delivered in the following award

Articles of agreement made and Concluded at Hartford vpon Conecticott September 19th 1650 betwixt the deligates of the honered Comissioners of the Vnited English Collonies and the Deligates of Peeter Stuijvesant Governor Generall of New Netherland

I

Vpon serivs Consideracon of the differences and greivances ppounded by the two English Collonies of Conecticot and New haven and the answare made by the honered Duch *Duch Governor Peeter Stuijvesant Esqr according to the trust and power Comitted vnto vs as Arbetrators or Deligatts betwixt the said pties ; Wee find that most of the offences or greivances were things done in the time and by the order and Comaund of Monsr Wilłam Keift the former Governer and that the prsent honered Gouer is not duly ppared to make answare to them ; Wee therfore think meete to Respet the full Consideration and Judgment Conserning them tell the prsent Gouernor may aquaint the H. M. States and Westindia Companie with the pticulars that soe due Reparacon may accordingly bee made

*213

2

The Comissioners for New haven Complained of seuerall high and hostile Iniuries which they and others of that Jurisdicon haue Receued from and by order of the aforsaid Monsr Keift in Delaware bay and River and in theire Returne thence as by theire former ppositions and Complaints may more fully appeere ; and besids the English Right Claimed by pattent prsented and shewed seuerall Purchases they have made on both sids the River and bay of Delaware of seuerall large tracts of land vnto and somwhat aboue the Duch house or ffort there with the Consideracon given to the said Sachems and theire Companies for the same acknowlidged and Cleared by the

hands of the Indians whom they affeirme were the true ppriators testifyed by
many Wittnesses ; they allso affeirmed that according to theire apprehensions
they have sustained 1000^t damage p^{tly} by the Swedish Gouerner but Cheifly
by order from Monsr Keift and therfore Required due satisfaction and a
peacable possession of the aforsaid lands to Inioy and Improve according to
theire Just Right ; The Duch Gove^r by way of answare affeirmed and asserted
the Right and title to Delaware or the south River as they Call it and to the
lands there as belonging to the H. M. States Westindia Companie and pfessed
hee must ptest against any other Claime ; but is not pvided to make any such
profer as in such a treaty might bee expected ; nor had hee Comission to treat
or Conclude any thinge therin vpon consideracon wherof *Wee the said Arbitrators or Deligates wanting sufficient light to Issue and determine any
thinge in the p^{r}mises are nessesitated to leave both parties in State quo privs
to plead and Improve theire Just enterests at Delaware for planting or Trading as they shall see Cause ; onely wee desire that all pseedings there as in
other places may bee Carried on in love and peace tell the Right may bee further Considered and Justly Issued either in Europe or heere by the two States
of England and Holland.

1650.

September.

*214

Conserning the seyzing of Mr Westerhouse shipp and goods about 3
yeares sence in New haven harbor vpon a Claime to the place ; the honered
Gou^r Peeter Stuijvesant Esqr pfessing that which pased in Writing that way
was through the error of his Secretary his Intent not beeing to lay any Claime
to the place and withall affeirming that hee had order to seize any Duch shipp
or vessell in any of the English Collonies or harbors which should trade there
without exprese lycence or Comission ; Wee therefore thinke it meet that the
Comissioners of Newhaven accept and acquiesse in this answare

3

Conserning the bounds and lymitts betwixt the English vnited Collonies and the Duch provence of New
Netherland Wee agree and determine as followeth

That vpon long Iland a lyne Runne from the Westermost part of the
oyster bay soc and in a straight and directe lyne to the Sea shalbee the bounds
betwixt the English and Duch there, the Easterly p^t to belong to the English
the Westermost pt to the Duch

1

The bounds vpon the mayne to begine at the West side of Greenwidge
bay being about 4 miles from Stanford and soe to Runne a Northerley lyne
twenty miles vp into the Cuntry and after as it shalbee agreed by the two
gouerments of the Duch and of Newhaven pvided the said lyne Com not
within 10 miles of hudsons River.

2

1650.

September.

*215

And it is agreed that the Duch shall not at any time heerafter build any house or habitacon within six miles of the said lyne *The Inhabitants of Greenwidge to remayne tell further Consideracon therof bee had vnder the Gouerment of the Duch

3

That the Duch shall hold and enioy all the lands in Hartford that they are actually possessed of knowne or sett out by sertayne marks ₵ bounds and all the Remaynder of the said land on both sids Conecticott River to bee and Remayne to the English there

And it is agreed that the aforsaid bounds and lymites both vpon the Iland and mayne shalbee observed and kept Inviolate both by the English of the vnited Collonies and all the Nacion without any Incroachment or molestacon vntell a full and finall determinacon bee agreed vpon in Europe by the mutuall Consent of the two states of England and holland.

Conserning fugitives

It is agreed that the same way and Course shalbee observed betwixt the English of the vnited Collonies and the Duch within the prouence of New Netherlands as according to the 8th article of Confederacon betwixt the English Collonies is in that Case pvided

Conserning the pposition of a nearer vnion of frendshipp and amity betwixt the English and Duch Nacon in these parts especially against a Common enimie Wee Judg worty of due and serius Consideracon by the seuerall Jurisdictions of the vnited Collonies and accordingly desire it may bee Comended to them that soe a Resolucon may bee had therin at the next yearly Meeting of the Comissioners

And in Testimony of our Joynt Consent to the seuerall forgoeing Conclusions wee haue heervnto sett our hands this 19th Day of September Anno Domi. i650

SYMON BRADSTREET
THO : PRENCE
THO : WILLET
GORG BAXTER./

*216

*The Comissoners for the Massachusets ppounded that a Course might bee taken for the Recovering of such tribute as is due from the Indians to the Collonies ; and it was Concluded that Captaine Mason bee desired at his goeing to long Iland to Require payment there. and to Indeavor to settle it in such a way that it may bee punctually heerafter discharged according to Couenants ; And for the pequats that are with the Narriganssets Nianticks Mohe-

gens or any others; Tho: Stanton is desired and appointed to demaund and Receue the same and to giue an account at the meeting of the Comisioners what hee hath Recouered and who they are that Refuse and vpon what grounds hee is also to attend the Constant yearly meetings of the Comissioners or any other extreordinary meeting vpon Convenient notice to interpret and pforme such other service as may ⌃ in Reference to the Indians for which the Collonies promise to allow him thirty pounds p Annum

Wheras an order forbiding trade with the Indians within the lymits of the vnited Collonies to all foraine Nacions vpon the waighty Consideracion therin expressed the lyberty for seizing such vessells as transgresse is lymited to the members of that Jurisdicion wher the offence is Comited It is thought fitt that it bee Recomended to the seuerall Generall Courts that for the more effectuall execucion of the said order it may bee lawfull for any pson or psons Inhabiting within any of the vnited Collonies to make Seazure of any goods or vessells trading with the Indians within any of the Jurisdicions Contrary to the tenure of that order.

The Jurisdiction of Canecticott hath lyberty to take East hamton vpon long Iland vnder theire Gouerment if they submite

The Comissioners of the Massachusets ppounded that for the pventing of all future differences betwix the *Collonies of the Massachusetts and Conecticut ther might bee som speedy Course agreed vpon to settle the bounds and lymits betwixt them, but the Comissioners for Conecticott not haveing at psent any other Coppy of theire pattent then what was formerly psented and the Comissioners for the Massachusets standing vpon the original Pattent or a Coppy vnder seale or sufficiently Wittnessed to theire satisfaction, there Could bee noe agreement for the psent.

*217

The foregoing Conclusions
    were agreed and Subscribed
    by the Comissioners for the vnited english
    Collonies at Hartford this
        23ᵈ of September 1650.

                EDWARD HOPKINS Presedent
JOHN HAYNES   SIMON BRADSTREET
THEOPH: EATON.   WILŁAM HATHORNE
STEPHEN GOODYEARE THO: PRENCE
                JOHN BROWNE

At a meeting of the Comissioners for the vnited Collonies in New England att New haven the 4th of September 1651

The articles of Confederation being read ; an order of the generall Court of the Massachusetts dated the 7th of May i65i was prsented and Read wherby it appeared that Mr Simon Bradstreet and Captaine Wiltam Hathorne were chosen Comissioners for one full and compleat yeare and envested with full power ₹ Authoritie according to the tennure of the said articles ;

Mr John Browne and Mr Timothy Hatherley were Chosen Comissioners for the Collonie of New Plymouth as appeered by an order of the generall Court dated the 4th of June i65i which was prsented and Read

Mr Edward Hopkins and Mr Roger Ludley Esqr wer chosen and appointed Comissioners for the Collonie of Conictticott as appeered by an order of theirer Generall court dated at Hartford the 15th of May i65i

Theophilus Eaton Esqr and Mr Steven Goodyeer were likwise chosen Comissioners for the Jurisdiction of Newhauen for this prsent yeare to treat and conclude of all things according to the tennure of the articles of Confederation as appeered by an order of theire generall court dated at Newhauen the 29 of May i65i

Theophilus Eaton Esqr was chosen prsident for this meeting

Letters from Mr Wiltam Steele President of the corporation for propagating the Gospell in New England and from Mr Winslow dated aprell i7 165i were Receued and Read the tennure wherof is as followeth

Gentlemen

by a letter to Mr Wiltam Steele our Presedent *dated at hartford 28th of September i650 and another to Mr Winslow wee pceaued ours came to youer hands and withall wee are glad to take notice of ye Redines that is in you to put youer shoulders to the worke in the management of yt ; therby contributing what is meet to bee done and giueing a due pportion of encuragement to every deserueing pson as well English as shalbee Imployed in it as Indian that is or shalbee wrought vpon ; for truely Gentlemen as ye care of providing lyeth vpon vs y⁰ corportion heer soe the care of Distribution and Improuement will Rest vpon youer selues the Comissioners for y⁰ vnited Collonies there of whose faithfullnesse wee haue not the lest cause to doubt;

Wee are sorry soe much time hath been lost and yet wee hope wee haue gained by our stay in som Respects for many minnesters in London haue promoted the ·act that were Resolued against yt and wee beleeue the like in the Countrey because they are constreined either by light within them or example without them beyond theire late Resolucions but wee conclude it is of God and trust wee shall find a blessing vpon our joynt endeavors

Tis strang to see what ₵ how many obiecttions arise against the work som from the ill management of former Gifts bestowed on y⁰ Countrey of New England of which no account hath been given to y⁰ doners and som psonally Reflecting vpon Mʳ Wells and Mʳ Peters som vpon our selues the corporation as if wee had so much p pound of what is collected or might feast our selues liberally therwith wheras through mercy wee never yet eat or drank of the fruit or charge of yt; and neither haue had or expect a penney or pennyworth for all the paines wee shall take therin but contrary wise account it a mercy; God giuing vs an oppertunity to bee exercised in a work wherin his Glory and the salvacion of soe many is soe *so neerly Conserned as for Mʳ Peters and Mʳ Wells they haue sufficiently satisfyed vs with what hath been formerly answared as by the Coppy of Mʳ Wells letters heere enclosed yet wee could desire y⁰ Gouerment of y⁰ Massachusets or theire speciall Comissioners would give vs from thence a word or two what account hath been giuen by Mʳ Wells and what satisfaction theire court Receued by his account thither sent; and send it in such tearmes as wee may publish it to the world if wee see cause this will Conduce much to the furtherance of y⁰ work but wee leaue it to your descreion

*223

Wee are glad to see youer Care in giueing direction in Mʳ Winslows letter for such things as you see Nessesarie to be sent ouer this pʳsent yeare, and howeuer we are not in a capacitie to send soe much at pʳsent haveing newly begunne the Collection and very little moneys Com in as yet; wee haue sent you for the pʳsent som few hoes and Iron tooles to carry on the work of y⁰ summer and hope that by the next shipp wee shalbee able to send you som woolen shoes and stockens according to youer direction or at least according to our abillitie for wee find the proceeds of the Collection goes slowly on both in Citty and Cuntry and that it wilbee long worke

And because wee must Receue our Instructions from youer selues wee Intreat you to confer with Mʳ Eliot ₵ Mʳ Mayhew by your selues or som such as you shall depute what willbee nessesarie for the next yeare what publick meeting houses and what other buildings will be Nessesary what Mayn-

*224

tenance to Minesters and Scoolmasters and Mistrises shalbee Imployed in teaching of Children and wee pray you consider whether it will not bee Nessesarie to treine vp English and Indian together for the better obteining each others language what the charge of all this will amount vnto att first and what to maintaine p annum from time to time that *That* soe wee may heere Improve what the lord shall send in to the best advantage; that if money com in together which wee much feare wee may bee enabled to purchase som lands to raise som yearly profits to Carry on the same

As for youer desire that one hundred pounds may bee paid to Mr Winslow either out of the Treasury heer or to bee Charged vpon you there to bee by you made good in the Country to the service of the work wee haue not as yet any monyes in stock to doe it but incline to the latter and in due time you shall heare further of vs in that kind for howeuer hee now actes as freely as our selues yet wee know hee could not but bee much out of purse in psuing things to pfection and those other services of youer cuntrye before hee accepted the publick service of the state and therfore had Rather it should be done by youer selues then by vs; And wheras you desire the monneys to bee layed out should bee put into the hands of Mr Pellam and Mr Winslow and they to make the provision; Mr Pellam hee is seldom in towne and Mr Winslow will by no means be pswaded to meddle with the Receipts of Money But wee shall put it into such a way as wee trust shalbee satisfactory to all; and to that end wee entreat you as wee shall now and heerafter send you any Invoyce of what wee send; and so doe you Returne a pticulare account of all you Receue from vs that soe one account may answare the other and the mouthes of all adversaries may bee stoped; And that it may bee soe wee suppose as wee onely haue a Clark and Messenger in pay soe you will haue some Steward there whom you will betrust with the accoumpts of the whole and once a yeare at least transmitt a Coppy over to vs that may bee extant and in Reddines to giue satisfacon to euery Doner that shall Require it then which nothing willbee more Satisfactory

It shalbee our greatest care and vtmost endeavor to Carry on the work with all convenient speed in all parts at once or as fast as wee can; that soe

*225

soe the Prinsipall bee not eat vp as it comes but som Money bee layed out to purchase a standing Revenew but it is the lord must Crowne our endeavors with his blessing to which end that our joynt Requests may meet at the throne of grace is the earnest desire of   Gentlemen

youer loueing frinds and
fellow laborers of the
Corportion and signed by
WILŁAM STEELL Prsdent

Postscript

Gentlemen

Wee haue sent you heer enclosed an account of such provisions as wee haue shiped which goods wee haue Consigned to Mʳ John Cotten and Mʳ John Willson who are onely to take vp yᵉ said goods and lodge them vntell they can send to the Comissioners you may vnderstand by the bill what pticulars are in euery Cask as allsoe the Number and Mark vpon the same

To the aforsaid letter the following answare was returned by the Comissioners

Honoᵗable Sʳ

By a second letter of youers lately Receued wee take notice of youer continewed love and unwearied paines in this service of the Gospell that the countenance and Authoritie of Parliament and the Christian liberallitie of well affected psons may bee duly Improved for the honor of Christ in the sperittuall good of the Indians ; wee are sorry that any obiecṭions or Imped- *226 iments should lye in youer way and would gladly answare *answare and Remoue them but those ancient Gifts and summs of Money Raised for New England were most (as wee conceiue) expended in foundation worke not onely before the Collonies did Combine but before two of them had any being ; and though the Gentlemen Intrusted might in those times haue giuen a satisfying answare to soe Just a demaund yet som of them being sence dead and others Removed wee feare it wilbee now difficult if not Imposible onely wee shall the more seriusly consider and endeavor that yᵉ money which by the favor of yᵉ state and the pius care of yᵉ corporacon shalbee collected and sent ouer may bee not onely duly Improved but that a Just account bee kept (and as occasion may Require bee duly Rendered and for that purpose wee haue thought on Mʳ Edward Rawson a man well approved in the Massachu- sets who lives at Boston as a Steward or agent to Receiue what shalbee sent over and to disperse and distribute as the Comissioners for the Collonies shall see cause to order What Moneys Mʳ Wells and Mʳ Peters haue Receiued and how Imployed wee haue desired and hope you will Receiue satisfaction from the Massachusets though wee found no letter of his enclosed according to youer Intimation ; The hoes and other Iron ware now sent over Mʳ Cotten ɵ Mʳ Wilson or som by theire appointment haue lately Receiued which wee shall order for the healp and Incurragement of the Indians in theire buildings and plantings and with the like care and to the like ends wee shall Imploy and distribute the linnin woolen shooes and Stockens when they come

1651.   to hand ; And our friends and bretheren Mr Bradstreet and Captain hathorne

September.   Comissioners for the Massachusets vpon Conference with Mr Elliot will

forthwith sertifye what may bee most Convenient for the next yeare ; And

heerafter as wee shall see more of the Counsell of God in carrying on this

great worke wee shall Impart our apprehensions conserning Minesters Scool

Masters for the education of ye Indian Children Mr Elliot and Mr Mayhew

continew their Pius labours in sowing sperituall seed amongst them and M^r

Leueridge Mr Blinman Mr Person &c are Studying the language that they

may the better treat with them Conserning the thinges of theire peace And

for our selves as oppertunity serueth wee shall account it an honer to bee

Intrusted and Imployed in the consernments of our Master with assurance

that hee that is lord of ye harvest will accept and prosper our endeavors ;

with our due and humble Respects we rest

Sir

youer servants

Newhaven the 10 September 1651

*227   *Contents of the letter from Mr Winslow

Were to this purpose

Gent :

Receving a letter from you ; notwithstanding the large letter sent by the

Corporacon to youer selves, I can doe no less then give you thankes for youer

Respect therin vnto my selfe and care of mee least I might sinck vnder the

p^rsure of following publick busines at my private charge the time is not yet

come for mee to expect any Releife there being very little of ye Collecttions

come into the Treasury more then what hath been expended in printing &c

and paying Mr. Gennors librarye which I desire may bee looked after

according to the Catalogue sent over for his Nessesities pressed vs to a

p^rsent disbursment of 30^lt and to Recover it againe would bee an hard mat-

ter yee to hard for vs hee liveing in Norfolke but a word is sufficient and it is

better to lose som then all, I shall speedily write to Mr Weld and aquaint

him alsoe with the Reddines that is in the Corporacion to pay the 34^lt to

him alsoe (haueing order soe to doe) for his library left with Mr Elliot soe

that I trust that Gapp wilbee soone stopped

The Collection is hopfully begun in London and I beleiue will Rise to

a considerable summe but you would wonder to heare the severall sorts of

obiections that are made against it by men that after all are ashamed to

neglect it ; as what haue wee to doe to Raise great summs to promote y^e

Gospell amongst naked people the Gospell is goeinge away from vs and wee

healp it forward wee had more need to support learning at home then abroad; **1651.**
And then our leuelers they will haue nothing to doe to promote humaine
learning there is to much of it allreddy and yet notwithstanding it goes
hopfully on (ᵈ

September.

Yesterday as I was informed Mʳ Cottington had somthing done for him
at the Counsell of State which I beleive was his pattent Confeirmed for the
truth is sence I pceive by letters from Plymouth that after another yeares
warning nothing is like to bee done in Reference to the old order of lords
and Commons sent ouer in 47 (as I take it) I looked vpon it as a vayne thing
to *to striue against the streame when as endeed that was the mayne matteriall　*228
obiection aboue a twelvemonth sence which I could not answare That wee
had such an order but did not looke after the pformance therof nor made any
Returne vpon it and if I could not then answare it how much lesse now after
another yeare if not 18 months expiracion but the will of the lord must bee
done in it however I suffer in my Reputation heere; to make soe great a
bustle and forced to let all fall at last; had I not had pticulare Instructions
from Plymouth therin I had never stired in it but I shalbee more warye
heerafter how I engage in busines of that nature yet when I have said It I
shall not dare to neglect the least service wherin any or all of the vnited
Collonies are Conserned

Heere is a great murmuring at the great provisions of powder and shott
the seuerall shipps get licence for yeare after yeare 40 barrell of powder and
50 is an ordinary pportion to a shippe nay somtimes an 100; and lead and
Armes pportionable tis layed to our charge that being Custome free wee
enrich ourselues by furnishing Barbathoes Verginnia though ennimies (ᵈ
with that and other comodities and there hath been vpon that very account a
serivs debate about Revoking our free Custome and excise I haue labored in
it and satisfyed many of the Parliament and Counsel of State shewed youer
Care not to suffer any powder more then ships store to bee Transported away
that wee are faine to land all wee bringe hether for feare of fiering the ships
in the Riuer and must get lycence for that allsoe vpon Returne that the Master is forced to get lycence for more then hee bringes that soe hee may beare
out his passengers pticular stores I haue shewed them how many shipps and
theire lading wee had lost by the kings ptie tould them what profitts they had
by the Returnes of New England for whether they went for Spaine Streites
Barbathoes (ᵈ they all paied Custome and excise home; that wee onely had
suffered with and for them and for theire sakes were hated of all the English
abroad; This hath made a pʳsent stopp But I assure you it conserne the
Cuntry to take *take notice of it and bee carfull that our Marchants and such　*229

as trade thither abuse not the freedome wee enioy nor know I better to whome to Impart it then to you the Comissioners that are the Rep^{r}senttatiues of the vnited Collonies I pray God to direct you heerin amongst other the waighty affayers of the Countrey, &c &c &c

Genś

Youer most humble

London Aprill i7. 5i   servant E. W

The answare to the foregoing Letter followeth

Hono^{r}d S^r

Wee haue Receiued youers of the 17 Aprill past and therin take notice of youer continewed Respects to this Cuntrey and ensesent endeavors for the promoting the wellfar of the poore Natiues wee haue alsoe seen the envoyce of ye goods sent which as wee vnderstand are taken vp at Boston according to the tennure of the bills of lading and secured by those to whose care you comitted them; it is some disadvantage that the prises of ye seueralls are not mencioned which for future you may please to Rectify wee shall endeavore throug ye grace of Christ that what comes to our hands may bee Improued to the best advantage of the worke as it comes vnder our view and that such accounts bee kept of the desposalls therof and returned to you as may (if not fully answare the expectation of all who are conserned; yet evidence our faithfulnes in the trust comited to vs; In order wherunto wee haue deputed Mr Edward Rawson of Boston as our Steward or agent to Receiue what is sent despose and keepe accounts of ye same according to such order as hee Receiueth from vs and notice shalbee taken according to youer desire what difference there is in the proffe of ye tooles now sent; Wee shall enquire after the Catalogue of Mr. Genners librarye and endeavore that neither youer nor our ends therein may bee frusterated It is apprehended by som that according to the entent of ye Act of Parliament an eye may bee had in the *230   *The destrebutions to the enlargment of the Colledge at Cambridge wherof there is great need and furtherance of learning not soe Imeadiately Respecting the Indian Designe though wee fully Concure not yet desire to know what the apprehensions of the honered Corporacion are heerin; If the one might Reseaue som encurragment without p^{r}judice to the other wee hope the kingdome of our Lord Jesus the Generally proffessed end of all enteresed in ye work may bee advanced therby It hath been and is the great care of the Gouerments in the severall Collonies that the Imunities graunted vs by the hono^{r}able Parliament may not bee abused by any of ours and therin haue had a speciall Respect to the Trad of powder which wee can not but feare hath been to exorbitantly managed by somm though the wellfare of the Collonies in many Respects is deeply conserned and hazarded wee shall add what strength wee may to the sensers allreddy made That if no other consideracions will p̃vaile selfe consernments may deterre Though wee haue not vnderstood that any from vs hath been transported to Barbadoes or Verginia the great enconuenience wee lye vnder is from that mischevius trad of Guns powder and shott (c̃ Carried on by ffrench Duch and .Sweads with Indians and Temtations arising to som of ours therby which hath occasioned many to vrge to a setting open that trade amongst our selues Conseiuing that as the case stands the best way to put a Checke to y⁰ Currant it now Runs soe strongly in but wee haue been slow heerin nor dare wee yet set open such a dore yet could bee willing to vnderstand from you what Interpretacion you conceiue would bee made by y⁰ State there if Restreints vpon the aformencioned Considerations should for a time bee taken of

Wee vnderstand Mr Eaton hath at larg written vnto you about theire just title to Considerable parts of land on both sides Delaware bay and Riuer how they were formerly desturbed in theire trade and planting by force and other vnlawfull practises both of Duch and Sweads youer selfe may Remember *and hee hath aquainted you with a late vnneighborly and iniurius Carriage of the Duch Goue^r when at least 50 of Newhauen Jurisdiction were on theire way to plant there but were stayed Imprisoned and forced to Returne with great lose to those enteresed in that designe ; and hath desired youer healpe in procureing a pattent ; These things by a peticion from those conserned in y⁰ late lose and disapointment haue been Recomended to our Consideracon Wee are Justly sensable of the dishoner put vpon the English Nation by this vniust afront of our duty to p^rserue y⁰ English title to soe Considerable place as Delaware and that a Just Repaire and satisfaction bee made to those soe wronged both in their psons and estates and from you desire enformacon what esteeme the old Pattents for that place haue with the Parliament or Counsell of State where there hath been no Improvement hethcrto made by the Pattentees whether the Parliament hath graunted any late Pattents or whether in graunting they Reserue not libertie and encurragement for such as haue or shall plant vppon theire formerly duly Purchased lands as allsoe how any engagement by the Collonies against the Duch vpon the formencioned occasion willbee Resented by the Parliament of which wee desire enformacion by the first

*231

Vpon occasion of som former letters written by Mr Winthorpe somtimes Gou^r of the Massachusets and som other Majestrates of that Jurisdiction

September.

*232

*233

to procure and settle free trade between the English and French in these parts of America Monsieur Dalliboust Goun^r of New France sent Mr Gabriell Derwellets as his agent about october i650 to treat with the Massachusetts and Plym: Collonies about a league offenciue and deffenciue but being enformed that the 4 English Collonies are confederate and that all treaties and leagues conserning warr or peace with others naighboring Nations or Collonies are now *now Referred to the Consideracon and conclusion of ye Comissioners who meet yearely in September and the next yeare in course in New haven, hee then Returned but himselfe ℓ Monsr Godfrey were after sent to Boston with Comissions from ye said Governer and Counsell of New France and with letters from them to ye Comissioners of the vnited Collonies, dated June 20. i65i wherin they complayne of ye Iniurius Treacherus dealing of ye Mohaukes in making hostile assaults vpon them and theire Naighbor Indians without cause and contrary to agreement and leagues of peace ; from Boston Mr Derwelletes as Agent both from the French Collonie and from the Freuch and Kenebeck Indians ; of which som of them are (as hee afeirmeth) baptised Christians and other Chatechumeni or learners in that way wrote to the Comissioners of Conecticot and Newhaven desiring that the Comissioners would meet at Boston (but that was Inconvenient) hee alsoe gaue severall arguments to pswade the English Collonies to joyne with them in a warr against the Mohaukes as that ye warr is just they breaking solomme leagues made for peace ; and managing theire warrs with much Crueltye It is a holy warr for defence of converted Indians and encurragement of Chatechuminis who are psecuted and Cruelly handled when taken by the Mohaukes as proffessers and frinds to the Christian Religion It is of common Consernment the Inroades of the Mohaukes tending to the destruction at least to the great desturbance of the Trade wherin both French and som of the English both of Massachusets and Plym: are Intersed and that themselues haue no Convenient Passage to carry on a warre against ye Mohaukes the way being long and full of difficulties by land and no passage by water not soe much as for a loaden Cannooe Wherfore in the name both of the French Governor ℓ Counsell of the Indians aforsaid hee desireth the Collonies to joyne in warr and in theire names promiseth a due Consideracon and allowance for charge ; or that the French may have libertie to take vp Volenteers in the English Jurisdiction ; and bee furnished with victailes for that service at least that they may pase through the *the Collonies by water and land as occation may require To these letters such answare was Returned by all the Collonies as might haue stopt all further proceedings but It seems by theire Comissions or Instructions they were jnioyned to treat with the

Comissioners and from them Joyntly to Receive theire answare soe that they came allong with the Massachusets Comissioners to Newhaven and p^rsented three Comissions one from the French Governor a 2^cond from the Counsell of New France and a 3^d by which Mr Gabriell Drwellets was sent to publish the doctrine of ye Christian faith amongst the Indians ; hee againe allsoe opened the case betwixt the French ʢc and the Mohaukes and Improved his abillities to the vtmost to pswade the Comissioners that the English Collonies might Joyne in the warr against the Mohaukes ; at least that they would pmitt volenteers and afford passage through theire Jurisdictions or take the Converted Indians and Chatachumini vnder theire protection which being graunted hee offered Treatye about settleing a free trad betwixt the English and French in these parts of america ; The matters ppounded being of weighty Consernment were seriusly considered and answare was Returned to the French agents by word of mouth and to the Governer and Counsell of New France in writting according to the tennure of the ensueing letter and Conclusions enclosed being Translated into Latine

    Most Illustrious Sir
    and much Hono^red Gentlemen

    Wee have received youer seuerall letters pused youer Comissions p^rsented by youer honered agents and seriusly Considered what hath been by them either in writing or by Conference propounded Conserning those Iniurius and hostele attempts made by som of the Mohaukes vpon som of youer Naighboring easteren Indians of which (as wee are enformed) som are Converted to the Christian faith and others are willing to bee taught and may in time prove Desiples to our saveing lord and Master as such wee pittey them but see not how wee can protect or afford the healp desired without exposing the *The smaler English plantations and our owne Naighboring Indians of which some allsoe professe Christianitie) to danger Wee giue due Credite to youer Deputies and can conceive you may have Just grounds for a warr but wee haue yet noe cause of Just quarrell with the Mohaukes nor is it safe for vs to engage in a controversy which wee neither doe nor haue means satisfyingly to vnderstand, the Mohaukes neither being in subiection to nor in any Confeaderacon with vs ; Wee are free to hold a naighborly corespondency with you and would have settled a free Comerce betwixt ye English and French Collonies but youer agents thought it either vnseasonable tell mater were Composed betwixt the Mohaukes and youer Indians or els propounded such Restrictions as would haue taken away all conveniency and freedom from the trade what hath hindered our p^rsent Closure (the

    *234

enclosed writing will shew, but if a fitter oppertunitie bee offered wee shall not bee wanting to contribute to a more satisfying Issue, in the meane time wee Rest

September 6 i65i

New hauen Sti: Angli:

An answare to the ppositions p^rsented by the honered French agents to the President and Comissioners for the English vnited Collonies

I   Vpon due consideraĉon and Respecte to what the honered Deputies from the Illustrivs Gou^r of New France haue enformed and vpon experience our selves haue had of the Insolency and treachery of som of the Barbarians wee can conseaue and graunt that the French and those Easteren Indians may have Just grounds to theire owne satisfaction for a warr against the Mohaukes

2·   The English looke vpon all such Indians as Receive the yoake of Christ with another eye then vpon others that Worship the Diuell

3   The English desire by all Just meanes to keep peace If it may bee) with all men even with these Barbarians

4   *The Mohaukes liveing att a distance from the Sea haue littel entercourse
'235   in these parts ; but in the warr the English had with the Indians 14 or 16 yeares sence the Mohauke shewed a reall Respecte and have not sence donn any knowne hostele actes against them

5   The English engage not in any warr before they have full and satisfiing euedence that in all Respects and consideracons it is Just and before peace vpon Just tearmes hath ben offered and Refused

6   The Mohaukes are neither in Subiection nor in league with the English soe that wee can neither Require any accoumpt of theire warrs or other proceedings nor haue wee meanes to enforme our selves what they can say for themselves if all other considerations were cleared

7   To make warr with the Mohaukes may endanger our Naighbor Indians of which diuers professe christianitie and the Rest doe rather expect Just protection from vs then that wee should expose them by our voulentary Inroadeing the Mohaukes

8 .   Though the English in these Jurisdictions are free to pforme all Naighbourly offices of Righteusnes and peace towards the French Collonie, yet they foresee they can neither pmitt volenteers or Avxiliarye forces to bee taken vp against the Mohaukes nor that the French or Easteren Indians to pase through the English Jurisdictons to envade them ; but they shall expose both the Christian and other Indians and some of the smaler English plantations to danger.

9   The English are much vnsatisfied with that mischeuivs trade the French and Duch haue had and still continew selling guns powder and shott to all

the Indians of which wee have daily complaints and by which the Indians are animated and apte to grow ensolent not onely against Indian Converts and Chatechumini but against the Christians of Europe

If the English Collonies were assured of the Justice of this warre and engaged with the French to prosecute against the Mohaukes yett wee haue noe such short and convenient passage either by water or land to approach them as may bee had by hudsons Riuer to and beyand Ourania fort which is in the Duch Jurisdiction

*They hope the Ancient peace and amity betwixt England and France wilbee continued and confeirmed which they both desire and as fare as lyes in them shall by all due meanes Reddilye promote

They conceiue that the honered Deputies haue power and authoritie at p^{r}sent to agree and settle a free Comerce betwixt the English and French Collonie in these parts, But if the said Deputies vpon Reasons knowne to themselves see cause to limitt the English Collonies to such Restrictions or Rather prohibitions as the vnpriuilidged French are vnder that they may not trad till they haue first procured a pticulare lycence from the Govr and Counsell of New France at least till they haue Issued the p^{r}sent diferences and settled peace with the Mohaukes ; A fitter Season for these Treaties must bee attended which the Comissioners shall Reddyly Improue when it is p^{r}sented

The English Collonies as in the 2^{cond} Article are Reddy vpon a fitt opportunitie to shew due Respect to all true Converted and Christian Indians and much more then to others ; but while they live at such a distance from the English Jurisdictions they neither may promise nor can afford them any protection to Secure them from Danger ;

10

11
*236

12

A Petition and Letter from Mr Eliot dated September 3^d i65i was Read and the contents considered and the ensueing answare Returned

Reverent Sir,

latter

Wee haue Read and considered both youer petition and ˏ letter dated the 3^d p^{r}sent by which wee Conceiue youer hope continueth that the Indians doe Really Imbrace the Gospell a work (if true) worthy of due encourragement but the honer of Christ and of the Collonies in the 2^{cond} place Requireth that all Christian prudence bee vsed to Judge aright of the Indians Scope and aime in theire profession least they should onely follow Christ for loaues and outward aduantage Remaining enimies to the yoak and gouerment and sensuring our *our slightnes and aptnes to bee deceiued nor is this caution altogether

*237

needles; wee feare that som of those very Indians who haue drunk in (through youer continued labour) somthing of the knowlidg of Christ coming into these ptes shew little of the sauor of it in theire carriage sorting themselues with the Indians and as it is feared complying to mnch to their way of Sabboth breaking ℓc yet by what wee haue heard from youer selfe ℓ others wee haue better hopes of som of them for whom wee blesse god and shall not neglect theire due encourragment as wee haue oppertunitie Wee wrote to the corporaɔ͂n the last yeare (of which posibly you haue not heard) that M͏ʳ Winslow might for his encourragment Receiue out of what was giuen an 100ᵗ supposing they might haue Concorded with vs; that hee or other Iustruments Imployed in that work might eate of yᵉ fruit of it, but adding that if they thought otherwise; It might bee charged and should bee paied by the Collonies which latter they more Incline vnto; and as wee conceiue will furnish him as mony comes in and charge it vpon vs; but money yet comes in slowly by those collections soe that yet wee haue onely Receiued a pcell of Tooles which wee desire may bee Improued to the sole end propounded in the Collection; that such as either haue approued themselues in a Christian Course or vpon due consideraɔ͂n hold a disposition to learne may by a free gift of howes and axes or such like Instruments bee duely encourraged but if any after Receipt fall of; A marke would bee sett vpon all such that they deceiue not soe eazily the 2ᶜᵒⁿᵈ time but betwixt giueing and lending howes ℓc as lending may bee ordered there wilbee little diference and Indian Trades are or may bee driuen by others wee doe not yet conceiue it any part of our worke Wee haue entreated our Worthy frinds M͏ʳ Bradstreet and Captaine Hathorne to Confer with youer selfe and youer brother to Consider his Imployment in Reference to the worke and to allow such encourragment as they Judge meet; who will also consider with a speciall Respect such Indians as soe Improue theire oppertunities to learne as that they may bee fit to teach others; you ar pleased to mention 20ᵗ p annum you haue Receiued for 4 yeares near past; and of 10ᵗ *10ᵗ from M͏ʳ Andrews ordered for som yeares though you know not how many; Wee heare of som other Gifts and pticularly of an 100ᵗᵗ or more sent from exeter or som of those Westeren pts pt for youer selfe and pt for M͏ʳ Maihew and pt for yᵉ Indians but in what proportion wee vnderstand not; Wee take notice from you that M͏ʳ Leueridg and M͏ʳ Blinman are fitting themselues for the worke It wilbee great mercy if the Lord please to p͏ʳsent more Instruments and fitt mater for them to worke vpon M͏ʳ Higgenson hath spent som time formerly about the Indian language and M͏ʳ Peirson hath done the like and continueth with much seriusnes therin Wee shall thinke them all worthy of due (though diferent) encourragement; wee desired the corporaɔ͂n

the last yeare to pay there for the bookes and other nessesaries ; and pticularly
encluded the i0ᵗ wee conceiue you now againe mention To brother Parke of
Roxberry it seemes it was not payed ; and money, may still com in more
slowly then is expected ; wherfore wee haue desired Mʳ Bradstreet and Captaine Hathorne to see him Justly satisfyed out of the goods sent ; Wee shall
add noe more but Rest

youer Loueing Frinds

September i2 i65i

1651.

September.

The following Letter was directed to Mʳ Maihew

Sʳ

Wee haue heard of the blessing God hath bestowed on youer laboure
in the Gospell amongst the poore Indians and desire with thankfulnes to take
notice of the same and from the appeerance of these first fruits to bee stired
vp to seeke vnto and waite vpon the great lord of the haruest that hee would
send forth more labourers into his vinyard and soe bedew theire labours with
the former and latter showers of his spiret that good corn may aboundantly
Spring vp and this barran Wildernes become a fruitfull feild yee the garden of
God ; and that wee might not bee wanting in the trust comitted to vs for the
furtherance and encorragement of this work wee thought good to let you
vnderstand there is paid by the corporacion in london 30ᴴ for part of Mʳ
Gennors librarye and as they enforme vs a Catalogue of the bookes sent ouer ·
(which is for youer encoragement) Wee hope you haue Receiued or els desire
you would looke after *after them from Mʳ Eliott or any other that may haue
them or if ther bee any error wee desire to heare it ; there are som howes and
hatchetts sent ouer for the Indians encorragement of which youer Indians may
haue pt if you think meet and bee pleased to giue them a note to Mʳ Rawson
of Boston of what shalbee needfull for theire vse especially those that bee
most willing to labour Wee are allsoe enformed there is an 100ᴴ giuen by some
of exeter toward this work of which som pt to youer selfe but know not
the quantitie Wee would bee glad to heare how the work of God goes on
amongst them with you that soe wee might enforme the corporation in England and haue our harts the more enlarged to God for them soe with our best
Respects wee Rest

youer very Frinds

Newhauen Sept: i2 i65i

*239

For the better ordering and Carrying on the affayres of the Iudians in
Respect of the gifts procured for them by the corporačõn in England the Comissioners have made choise of Mʳ Edward Rawson as a Steward to Receive
and dispose of the same ; and haue entreated the Comissioners of the Massa-

1651. chusets to treat with him about his Imployment ꝑ sallary and if hee accept
therof to deliuer him the ensueing Comission if hee Refuse the said Co-
September. missioners are desired to appoint and agree with som fitt ꝑson for that work
for this yeare next ensueing

Wheras you Edward Rawson gent: are Chosen and appointed by the
Comissioners of the vnited Collonies as a Steward or agent for the Receiueing
and disposing of such goods and comodities as shalbee sent heither by the
corporaçõn in England for the propagating the Gospell amongst the Indians in
New England which you are Carfully to observe and ꝑforme according to the
trust comitted to you in the ensueing directcions.

first you are to take notice of all such goods or Comodities as shalbee
sent from the corporaçõn aforsaid them safely keep and make entry therof in
*240   a book for *for that purpose
2 condly   you shall deliuer and dispose of ˄ according to the directions of the
Comissioners or some two of them by a note vnder theire hands and not
otherwise

3 ly   you shall yearly give or send a true accoumpt of what you haue Receiued and desposed of, to the aforsaid Comissioners at theire ordinary
meeting and at any other time being therunto by them Required

Thomas Stenton being ordered by the Comissioners the last yeare to
gett an accoumpt of the number and names of the seuerall Pequots liveing amongst the Narragansetts Neantick or Mohiggen Indians ꝑd. Wherby
an agreement made after the Pequot warr are Justly Tributaries to the
English Collonies and to Receiue the Tribute due for this last yeare ; did
according to appointment attend the Comissioners this meeting as Interpreter
in the Indians occations. With him came Vncas the Moheggen Sagamore
with seuerall of his men Wequash Cooke came allsoe and som of Ninnacrafts
men Robert a Pequot Indian somtimes a servant to Mr Winthorp and some
with him and some Pequots liueing on long Iland Tho: Stenton Presented
som Papers with the names of som Pequots as they are at pᵣsent settled
vnder seucral other Sagamores but these papers being short and defectiue the
accompt could not now bee ꝑfected but Tho: Stenton and the Indians Respectiuely brought in these following summes of Wampam toward the forementioned Tribute viz

Ninnecrafts Men brought in ————————— 9i ffaddome
Wequash Cooke ————————————— 54 ffadd

in pt of ye rest being about 30 Fadd (as hee said) hee promised to pay
to Tho: Stenton within a month

Robert and his Companie ————————————	56 ff
for long Iland Pequots ————————————	32 ff
Vncas in pt the rest hee is to pay to Tho Stenton	
within three monthes ————————————	79 ff
In the whole but all vntold ————————————	312 ff

This Wampam being layed downe Vncas and others for the Pequots
demaunded why this Tribute was Required; how long it should continew and
whether the Children to bee born heerafter were to pay it; All which being
considered the Comissioners by Tho: Stenton answared that the Tribute by
*by agreement hath been due yearly from the Pequots sence anno i638 for
sundry murthers without provoca$\tilde{co}$n commited by them vpon seuerall of the
English at seuerall times as they found oppertunity Refusing either to deliuer
vp the Murtherers or to doe Justice vpon them and soe drawing on a warr
vpon themselues to the great charg and Inconvenience of the English; which
warr through the good hand of ^{Or}God issued first in a conquest ouer that
Treacherus and bloody people; and after by agreement (to spare as much as
might bee) euen such guilty blood; in a smale Tribute to bee paied in different
proportions by and for theire males according to theire different ages yearly but
hath not hitherto been satisfyed though demaunded Wherfore the Comissioners
might haue Required both an account and paiment (as of a Just debt) for the
time past but are contented (if it bee thankfully accepted to Remitt what
is past accounting onely from i650 when Tho: Stentons Imployment and
Sallary begun

*241

2^{condly} though 12 years Tribute were due before this last yeare and
thoug the agreement was for a yearly Tribute to bee paid by them and theirs
soe longe as they continrue in this pt of ye Cuntry yet the Commissioners
somthing to ease theire sperits in Reference to this Just burthen and to engage
them to an inoffenciue and peacable Carriage not onely towards the English
Collonies but to the Indians amongst whom they liue thought fitt and
declared that the paiment of this Tribute shalbee limmited to ten yeares of
which this last yeare to bee Reconed the first; after which time vnlesse they
draw trouble vpon themselves they shalbee free

Thirdly though by agreement the said Tribute extended to men growne
to youthes and to all male children yet the Comissioners are further Content
and doe heerby declare and conclude that the Rest Submitting and duly paying the said Tribute all male Pequot Children which shalbee borne heerafter
this time are and shalbee free and noe tribute to bee Required for them

1651.

September.

*242

Eltweed Pomery of Windsor in Conecticot Jurisdicton haveing often petitioned the Comissioners about a mare of his wilfully killed by a Pequot Indian called Poquoiam soone after the foremencioned warre when all sorts of horses were att an high prise ; conserning which *which Mr Israell Stoughton Generall for the Massachusetts made an agreement with Myantinomo one of the prinsipalle Narraganssett Sachems with or vnder whom the said Poquoiam lived on behalfe of the offender ; as by the Testimonyes of Tho: Stenton and Ser,eant Jefferies hath been proued by which the said Myantonimo engaged to pay or satisfy for the said mare the summe of fourty pounds of which there hath been yet noe pt satisfied though often demaunded And Myantonimo haveing been dead now about eight yeares the said Eltweed Pomery hath by himselfe and his agents often made his addresse to the Comissioners att theire meetings for aduise and assistance therin ; And the last yeare vpon the Request of the Comissioners the souldiers sent from the Massachusetts to Ninecraft to Require satisfaction for other Just debts had alsoe order in pticulare to demaund this for the mare of Ninnecrafts and of the Narragansett Sagamore the mare being killed by his brother in law and hee Inheriting a considerable pte of Myantonimoes estate namly his pte of the Pequots of wh Poquoiam is one and hath liued with Ninnecraft which was donn but without fruite ; Vpon consideracõn of the prmises the Comissioners thought fitt that the said money bee againe demaunded of Ninnecraft or that the said Poquoiam bee deliuered in their hands but vpon Refusale or delay that some fitt man bee sent duely accompanied by order and direction from the Gouerment of Conecticott to Require it with allowance of the prsent charges and if it bee not forthwith paied to make seizeure of the vallue of fourty pounds with the charges and to bring it away with them And heerof the Narraganssett Indians now present were willed to enforme Ninnecraft onely if after such payment or sezure Vncas or Wequash cooke shall by entertaining counselling or protecting Poquoiam hinder Ninnecraft from Recovering the same of him in such case the said fourty pound shalbee accounted due and bee Required from them or either of them

A letter from Mr Williams directed to the much honered Gouernor of the Massachusetts and dated July 25. i65i conteining sundry complaints made by the Narraganssett Sachems against vncas being Receiued the Comissioners Read the pticulars to Vncas who was Reddy to make answare in his owne defence ; The Comissioners enquired who were sent on behalfe of the Narragansett Sachems to cleare and proue the said charge and to consider *and enforme conserning Vncas his answares Tho: Stenton acquainted the Comissioners that Ninecrafts had once Resolued to send som men to prosecute the

*243

said complaints but after pretended feare and danger from Vncas Tho: Stenton endevored to Remoue his feare and offered to acompanie or secure himselfe or messengers but all would not serue ; none were sent soe that there could bee noe prosseedings therin

Vncas Complained that Saquasson som yeares sence as is well knowne began hostile actes vpon him to the desturbance of the publicke peace wherupon hee was ocationed to fight him and in the Issue ouercame him and Conquared his Countrey which though hee gaue to the English and did not oppose the favore they were pleassed to shew him in sparing his life yet hee cannot but looke vpon himselfe as wronged in that Saquasson, as hee is enformed is set vp and endeavored to bee made a great Sachem notwithstanding hee hath Refused to pay an acknowledgment of Wampam to him according to engagments

The Comissioners disclaimed any endeavors of theires to make Saquassen great and are Ignorant of what hee affeirmes conserning the other yet Recomended it to the Gouerment of Conecticot to examine the case and to provide that vpon due proofe Vncas may bee owned in what may be Just and equall and Mr Ludlow was entreated to promote the same

Captaine Tapping and Jonas Wood in theire owne name and in the behalfe of Mr Fardom and John Ogden and others of South hamton by petition &c enformed the Comissioners that theire peace is much endangered by that large Trade the Indians haue with the Duch in guns powder and shot by which meanes they are at least as plentifully furnished as themselues as apte to giue valleyes of shot in theire entertainements and complements and by exersise are become good markes men ; but withall growne ensolent and Iniurius against the English som of them as the petitioners haue ben enformed haue *haue lately driuen som of the English Cattle into the Water and soe drowned them to the great damage of the owners ; They further complaine of Iniuries susteined from the Duch sence they remoued from theire Jurisdiction to one of the English Collonies thogh They first gaue notice to the Duch Gour therof and vnderstood not that it was any way offensiue yet since som considerable ptˢ of theire estates are attached ; or by authoritie as they heare stayed and kept from them ; and that Imprisonment is threatoned if they com in pson to Improue or Remoue their estates ; All which being duely considered the Comissioners expresse the deep sence they haue of the mischevivs Trad of selling &c and soe Armeing and animateing the Indians both against themselues and vs and that they would gladly vse all due meanes to suppresse it ; They further told them that if they could proue the Indians wilfully drowned theire Cattle They would consider som Just course for theire Satisfaction but themselues acknowlidg they want due proofe ; lastly

*244

in Reference to such estates as they haue within the Duch Jurisdiction The Comissioners wrot to the Duch Gouerner as followeth

To the Duch Govern^r

Much Honrd Sir

Severall of Southhamton haue p^rsented their Greiuances to vs sence Wee mett at New haven which wee are slow to Receiue vpon the onely complaint of the pties Interest M^r ffardom Captaine Tapping John Ogden and Jonas Wood haue (as wee heare) som considerable pts of theire estates yet within the limits of youer Jurisdiction whether they may freely Remoue them to the plantation where they dwell or whether all or any pte bee sequestered attached or vpon any offence or other Respect deteined ; is to vs (whatever Reports are brought)

*245 yet doubtfull ; they *they haue been exersiseed whom they might Imploy to Receiue speedy and satisfying enformȧồn but wee conceiue much time wilbee spent and lost in treating by attornies or deputies And beleiveing the Justice of New England and New Netherland is Squared by one Rule wee pswade them to mannage theire owne ocations in youer Jurisdictions desireing for them and hopeing wee may promise that for this single Journey Captaine Tapping and Jonas Wood who are most enclined to waite vpon you at ye Monhatoes shall haue the fruite of a safe conduct that theire psons may com and goe at libertie what euer debts or offences may bee alledged or proued against them as any of youers in a like case and vpon a like motion of youers shall haue with vs and that in all prosses and proceedings for or against them whether vpon private or publike questians the issue may hold forth Justice with moderacon ; and that if there shalbee occation a satisfiing Reason may bee giuen in an a naighborly way as was donn in Govert Locormans and shalbee in any like case which may well bee done without p^riuduce to any Jurisdiction whether youers or ours ; wee Rest

youers in all due
Newhaven   Respects
September 11: i65i

To the Honord Comissioners for the vnited Collonies now assembled at Newhauen

The humble petition of Jasper Graine William Tuttill and many other the Inhabitants of Newhauen and Totokett

Humbly Sheweth That wheras divers yeares sence seuerall Marchants and others of Newhauen with much hazard, charge and lose did purchase of the Indian Sagamores and theire companies the true propriators seuerall large

Tracts and ꝑcels of land on both sides of Delaware Bay and Riuer and did p'sently begine to build and *and to set vp factories for Trad and prepared to set vp plantations within theire owne limmits wherby the Gospell alsoe might haue been carried ⸿ Spred amongst the Indians in that Most Southerley ꝑt of New Englaud And the vnited Enlish Collonies might before this time been enlarged with conueniency both for themselues and posteritie had not the whole work by hostile and Iniurivs opposition made both by the Duch and Sweeds been then hindered

And wheras youer petitioners streitened in the Respectiue plantations; and finding this pte of the Countrey full or affoarding little encorragement to beginne any considerable new plantations for theire owne Comfort and conueniencye of posteritie; did vpon a serius consideraꝯn of the premises and vpon encorragement of the Treatye betweene the honered Comissioners and the Duch Gouerner the last yeare at Conecticott by agreement and with Consent of the said Marchants and others Resolue vpon a more difficult Remoue to Delaware; hopeing that our aimes and eudeauors would be acceptable both to God and to his people in these Collonies being assured our title to the place was Just; and Resolueing (through the healp of God) in all our carriages and proceedings to hold and mainteine a Naighborly corespondence both with the Duch and Sweeds; as was assured them both by the tennor of the Comissions and by letters from the honered Gou^r of this Jurisdiction; To those ends and with these purposes p^rparations were made in the winter a vessell was hired and at least fifty of vs sett forward in the Springe and expecting the fruite of that wholsom aduise giuen at Hartford the last yeare in the case by the arbetrators Joyntly, Those chosen by the Duch Gou^r concuring in it; wee went to the Monhatoes which wee might haue avoyded; and from our Honered Gou^r p^rsented a letter to the Duch Gou^r vpon pusall wherof (without further provocation) hee arrested the two Messengers and Comitted them to a private house close prisoners vnder a guard; that donn he sent for the M^ster of the vessell to com on shore as to speak with him and comitted him alsoe after which two more of the companie coming on shore and desireing to speak with theire naighbours vnder Restreint *Restreint hee comitted them as the rest then desireing to see our Comissions and Coppie them out promiseing to Returne them the next day though the Coppes were taken and the Comissions demaunded hee Refused to deliuer them and kept them and the men Imprisoned tell they were forced to engage vnder theire hands not then to proceed on theire voyage towards Delaware but with lose of time and charg to Returne to Newhauen; Threatening that if hee should after find any of them in Delaware hee would seize theire goods and send their ꝑsons prisoners into Holland and accordingly they Returned though theire damage therby as they conseiue doth amount to aboue 300ᵗ All which youer petitioners Refere to youer wise and serius consideraĉõn and being assured you will haue due Respect to the honer of the English nation which now suffers by this Iniurius affront taken notice of by all the Naighboring Indians ; They humbly desire that som Course may bee agreed and ordered for the due Repaire of theire loses satisfaction for theire vnjust Imprisonment with libertie and encorragement to Improue theire Just Rightes in Delaware for the future to which purpose they further humbly offer to Consideraĉõn

first That Delaware in the Judgment of those that haue often and seriusly viewed the land and considered the Climate is a place fitt for the enlargment of the English Collonies at present and hopfull for posteritie that wee and they may enjoy the ordinances of Christ both in Sperittuall and Ciuell Respects

2ᶜᵒⁿᵈˡʸ they feare that if the English Right bee not seasonably vindicated and a way oppened for the speedy planting of Delaware ; the Duch who haue layed alreddy an Iniurius hand both vpon our psons and Rightes they haueing (as is Reported) lately begun a new fortification and plantation vpon our duly purchased lands ; will dayly strengthen themselues and by large offers draw many of the English to settle and plant vnder them ; in soe hopfull a Place which will not onely bee dishonerable to the English Nation but enconvenient to the Collenies and of mischeuius Consequences to the psons who shall soe settle in Reference to that lycencius libertie theire suffered and practised

*248

*Thirdly as the Petitioners haue not in theire Eye any other considerable place within the limitts of New England either for the enlargment of the Collonies at present or for the comfort and conveniency of posteritie soe if the Duch may thus oppenly opose vs in our psons and Rights if they may plant and fortifye vpon the land which themselues the English Sweeds and Indians know to be ours; It may encorrage them to encroach and make further hostile attempts vpon som or other of the smaler English plantations to bring them vnder theire Gouerment and may annimate the Indians (with whom the Dutch engratiate themselues by a larg Constant mischevius Trad in guns powder and shott to despise and make assaults vpon vs ; Wherfore they againe humbly entreat youer advise with seasonable and sutable assistance ; according to the weight and Import of the Case ; That all youer Consultations and laboures may tend and Issue in the honer of Christ and welfare of the Collonies

The forgoeing Petition being p^rsented and Read The Comissioners tooke into Serius consideraçõn the contents therof and what was to bee donn therin

They considered the English Right to Delaware by pattent The Right of the Marchants and other Inhabitants of Newhauen to sertaine tracts and pcells of land there by purchase The Iniury donn them by the Duch both formerly and this last Summer in theire hostile and forceable proceeding against them as the petitioners Relate and the great affronts therby giuen to the English Nation the ensolency of the Duch and the Contempt it is like to bring the English into among the Indians if som speedy course bee not taken to prevent it by Righting the oppressed

As alsoe the Comodiusnes of the place for plantations and how preiudiciall it may bee to the English in these ptes if it should bee planted by enimies or people of another nation not being vnmindfull of the stright accomodacions of many in seuerall places and the benifite of Trade with the Indians in Delaware if prudently managed

They likwise considered what had pased betwixt the Duch Gou^r and the Comissioners the last yeare at hartford and that advise giuen by the Delegates of them both for the quitet and peacable Improuement of theire seuerall Rightes in Delaware tell the aforsaid diference shalbee determined in Europe

*The Comissioners Vpon these and seuerall other consideracions thought meet to Write to the Duch Gou^r to protest against his jniurius proceedinges to assert the English Right and to Require satisfaction for the Damage donn to our frinds and confeaderats of Newhauen ; And to declare vnto the petitioners in way of answare to theire petition that howeuer wee think it not meete to enter into a present Ingagement against the Duch Chusing Rather to suffer Iniuries and affronts (at least for a time) then in any Respects to seem to bee to quicke ; yet if they shall see cause againe to endeavore the planting of theire formencioned purchased lands in Delaware at any time within these i2 monthes and for that end shall at theire owne charge Transport together i50 or at least an i00 able men well armed with a meet vessell or vessels and Amunition fitt for such an Enterprise all to bee allowed and approued by the Maiestrates of Newhauen Jurisdiction or the greatest pte of them that then in case they meet with any hostile opposition from the Duch or Sweeds whiles they carry themselues peacable and Inoffenciuely that may call for further Aide and assistance The Comissioners doe agree and conclude that they shalbee supplyed by the seuerall Jurisdictions with such a number of souldiers as the afforsaid Comissioners shall Judge meet they the said plaintifes bearing the charges therof ; for the true paiment wherof the vnpur-

*249

chased lands and Trade there with the Natiues shalbee engaged tell it bee satisfyed provided alsoe and it is agreed that such psons as shall Transport themselues to the aforsaid lands in Delaware either out of Newhauen Collonies or any of the other three shalbee and Remayne vnder the Gouerment and Jurisdiction of Newhauen tell the Comissioners of the vnited Collonies shall otherwise order the same

To the Duch Gouerner

Much Hono^red Sir

Before wee parted last yeare at Hartford you gaue vs hopes of a comfortable meeting at Newhauen this yeare what derections you had from Europe to maynteine peace and Neighborly Respects with the English in america you then shewed and best know what other Comissions you haue sence Receiued; But all the Collonies take notice that now you walke in contrarye pathes you told vs of a protest you must make against such as should plant or Improue (though but theire just Rightes in Delaware; Wee saw noe cause for that but know that both youer predecessor and youer selfe had without cause formerly protested against som of the Collonies; But in youers dated aprell the 11th i65i Stil: nouo sent to the Gou^r of Newhauen wee obserue you threaten

*250   force of armes and *and Martiall opposition euen to bloodsheed against such as shall goe about to Improue what they haue proued to bee Justly theires in Delaware; and yet shew noe more of any Just title you haue therevnto then you did at Hartford which left all the Delegates both for the English and the Duch therin vnsatisfyed; in the said protest you alsoe affeirme that the planting ℈ce of Delaware by the English enterest is contrary to the provisionall agreement made betwixt youerselue and the Comissioners for the English Collonies which wee marvell at; those Records clearly expressing the contrary Wee hoped alsoe that according to youer promise (at Hartford Wherin Mr Willet and Mr Baxter engaged Greenwidge before this should haue been settled as a Member of Newhauen Jurisdiction but instead of that wherof wee yet heare nothing) the complaints of diuers of our Confeaderates of Newhauen Collonie are Renewed wee can not but expresse our like sence of y^t eniurius carriage of youers towards them who neither attempted nor entended any thing against the Duch or Duch Right in any portion or privilidge they may Justly claime there; as the generall court of the Massachusets did in their letters May 14th i65i But wee are further enformed that you haue sence begun som fortification or plantation vpon som pt or pts of the English land which giues vs cause to feare that you more Respect private advantages then publicke Righteusnes and peace wee must therfore as formerly soe againe assert the English Right especially to theire purchased lands and protest against youer eniurius hostile carriage in Imprisoning some of theire psons deteining theire Comissions and engaging them to theire great damage to returne before they could inioy theire Just libertie without shewing either Right to the land in question or any Just cause of such proceeding, vnlesse a pretence of a title should satisfy which the English vpon as good grounds can make to the Monhatoes, And wee heerby further professe and protest that by these vnneighborly and vniust courses you are the sole auther and cause of all such inconveniencies and mischeifes as may follow therupon the Comissioner and Collonies haueing Just cause and ground to vindecate and Improue the English Rightes and to Repaire theire confederats who haue been soe wronged and damaged ; Wee heare alsoe that you haue againe Imposed that offensiue Custome of Recognicõn at the Monhatoes which vpon our former complaint was for a time taken of; which fayrely tends to desturbe if not to cutt of all Trade betwixt vs in these pts ; These things wee Rather thought nessesarie to write and leaue to youer consideracõn because wee yet heare of noe Returne you haue made to the generall Court of the Massachusets ; if to that or this you please to send answare to the Gouerner of Newhauen wee shall from him receiue Informacõn and the better vnderstand our way soe wee rest

youer loueing ffrinds

Newhauen
Septem: i5
i65i

*The coppy of a letter sent from the Comissioners　　　*251
To Mr Cottington

Sir,

Wee are enformed that it hath pleassed the Parliament or Counsell of State to Comitt the publick Trust of Goverment in the Iland vnto youer hands wherin wee can not but desire that truth and Righteusnes may soe flurish and that the Gospell professed by the English in this wildernes may not bee brought vnder any Just Reproch It is p'sented to vs that som notorius Delinkquents who are lyable to hiest sensures making escape out of seuerall of the Collonies; Repaire to youer Iland as to a Cittey of Refuge hoping therby to avoid the stroake of Justice and wee may well expect offenders in like and other kind wilbee easily apprehensiue of theire advantages and Improve them for the future if such a dore bee open which occationeth vs to direct these few linnes to youer selfe ; and desire to Receive enformacion from you and from youer Counsell what wee may expect in the formencioned cases

or when any fugetiues out of any of the English vnited Collonies shall heerafter seeke shelter there; Whether vpon Surtifficate from som of y⁰ Maiestrates of the seuerall Jurisdictions where the offences comitted may bee best
vnderstood and Receiue its due sensure you will deliuer vp ₵ returne such
delinkquents and fugetiues to bee proceeded with in theire pper place according to theire demeritts as the collonies vpon due consideracõn for the pro-
moteing of Justice and Righteusnes find cause to doe amongst themselues Or
.whether you entend to Receive and keep such vnder youer protection vntell
they bee pursued and Impleaded in youer courts and the Respectiue cases
there Issued as wee heare hath been somtimes pretended which wee Judge
very obstructiue to the waies of Justice We shall add noe more but oʳ due
Respects to youerselfe and soe Rest

youer very loveing
ffrinds

Newhaven the i3th of
September i65i

*Vpon a letter Received from Mʳ Dunster President And the ffellows of
Harvard Colledge the following answare was Returned

Much Respected ffrinds

By youers of august 27ᵗʰ wee vnderstand that the former colledge buildings are in a .decaying condition and will Require a considerable charge ere
long for a due Repaire and that through the encrease of Scollers many of
them are forced to lodge in the Towne: which proves many waies enconvenient and will nessesarily Require an enlargment of youer buildings; for which
you ppound and wee haue seriusly considered whether any healp may bee
had from the collections for the ppagateing the Gospell amongst the Indians
but can not find by the Acte of Parliament (now pused) that any such libertie is graunted and by a letter lately Receiued from that corporacõn wee
pceive that an hundred pounds appointed by the Comissioners to pay Mʳ
Winslow as a gratificacõn of his paines in the said Collections is like to be
charged backe and borne by the Collonies without any allowance thervnto
from the collections; yet wee now desire Mʳ Winslow to. enquire the mind
of the corporacõn therin our selues conseiveing that the advancement of learning heere may alsoe advance the worke of christ amongst the Indians and
accordingly out of that Stock (as it coms in) should gladly contribute might ·
wee doe it without offence; but if an other enterpretacion by made in England The Comissioners will propound to and Improue theire seuerall enterests in the Collonies that by pecks half bushels and bushels of Wheat according as men are free and able the Colledge may have some Considerable yearly

healp towards theire occations; and heerin if the Massachusetts please to
give a leading example the Rest may probably the more Reddyly follow ;

This following letter was prsented from the Inhabitants of Warwicke

May It please this honored Comittee to take knowlidg that wee the
Inhabitants of Sowamett *allias Warwicke haueing vndergone diuers oppres-   *253
sions and wronges amounting to great damage sence wee first possessed this
place being forced therby to seeke to that honerable State of old England for
Releife which did eneuitably draw great charge vpon vs to the further
Impairing of our estates and finding favor for Redresse wee were willing
to wave for that time (in regard of the great troubles and Imployment that
then lay on that State) all other losses ⎨ wrongs wee then vnderwent soe
that wee might bee Replanted in and vpon that our Purchased Possession and
enioy it peacably for time to come without desturbance or molestation by those
from whom wee had formerly suffered; but sence our gratius graunt from the
honorable Parliament in Replanting of vs in this place wee haue ben and
dayly are pressed with Intollerable greivivances to the eating vp of our
labours and wasting of our estates makeing our lives together with our wiues
and Children bitter and vncomfortable; Insomuch that groneing vnder our
burthens wee are Constreined to make our addresses to that honorable Parliament and state once againe to make our Just complaint against our causlesse
molestors who by themselves and theire agents are the onely cause of this our
Reuttering of our destressed condicōn ; May it please therfore this honored
Assembly to take notice of this our solleme entelligence (given vnto you (as
the most Publicke authorized society appertaining vnto and Instituted in the
vnited Collonies whom our complaints doe conserne that wee are now prparing
ourselves with all convenient speed for old England to make our greivances
knowne againe to that State which fale vpon vs by Reason that the order of
Parliament of England conserning vs hath not ben obserued, nor the Injoy-
ment of our graunted priuilidges pmitted to vs ; That wee are as it were
bought and sold from one pattent and Jurisdiction to another

In that wee have ben prohibited and charged to acquite this place since the
order of Parliament given out and knowne to the contrary

In that wee have had Warrants sent vs to Summon vs to the Massachusets court ; And officers imployed amongst vs to that purpose *purpose;   *254

In that these Barbarius Indians about vs with euill minded English
Mixed amonst vs vnder pretence of some former psonall Subiecttion to yᵉ
Gouerment of the Massachusetts Countenanceing of them Cease not to kill
our Cattle offer violence to our families, villifye Authoritie of Parliament

vochsafed to vs Justifying theire practises with many Menaces and threatenings as being vnder the protection of the Massachusetts

In that Wee are Restrained and haue been this 7 or 8 yeares past of
common comerce in the Countrey and that onely for matters of Consience

In that our States formerly taken from vs Remayne yet vnrestored with .
these additions therunto

These and the like are the grounds of our complaints with our serius
desires that you bee pleassed to take notice of them as our sollonne Intelligence given heerof that as youer selues shall thinke meet you may giue
further sesonable Intelligence to youer severall Collonies whom it may Conserne soe that theire agent or agents may haue seasonable Instructions to make
answare and wee heerby shall aquite our selues that wee offer not to proceed
in these our complaints without giveing due and seasonable notice therof

By mee JOHN GREEN juni

Warwicke the first   Clark in the behalfe of

of September i65i   the Towne of Warwicke

Vppon occation of the foregoeing letter and som descourse about this
busines the Comissioners for the Massachusetts pᵣsented this ensueing
Declaraĉŏn

That in Anno i643 seuerall complaints were made to the Comissioners of
the vnited Collonies then mett at Boston against Samuell Gorton and his
companie and som of them of weightye and great Conisernment to all the
Jurisdictions; Informaĉŏn was alsoe given that the said Gorton and his companie had been sent to once ₵ againe by the generall Court of the Massachusetts *with a safe conduct both for theire coming and Returne that they might
give answare and satisfaction wherin they had donn wronge; It then came
into consideraĉŏn vnder what Gouerment or Jurisdiction the said Gorton and
his companie lived; the Comissioners take notice that the Indian Sachems
proprietors of the place had volĩentarily Submitted theire psons and lands
somtimes before to the Goverment of the Massachusetts; The Comissioners
of Plym: claimed enterest therin by pattent but vpon such consideracions as
was then pᵣsented Resigned the same to the Massachusetts with the consent
and approbacon of the Rest of the Comissioners

The Gouerment of the Massachusets haveing now both English and
Indian Right and title to the aforsaid place where Gorton and his companie
lived derived to them; the Comissioners did Joyntly thinke It fit and
accordingly advised the Maiestrates of the Massachusets to proceed against
them according to what they should find Just engaging the Rest of the Juris-

*255

dictions to approue of and concure in the same as if theire Comissioners had
been present; Att the aforsaid conclusion vpon the aforsaid grounds the generall court of the Massachusets brought the said Gorton and severall of his
companie to theire tryall and Just sensure according to the Jointe advise
giuen them by the Comissioners which hath neuer sence been disowned by
any of the Jurisdictions but allowed of by theire silent approbacõn; though
pte of theire sensure vpon other grounds hath hetherto been suspended and
the said Gorton and his companie pmitted peacably to Reside on the aforesaid lands notwithstanding the manifould complaints both of the English and
Indians vnder the gouerment of the Massachusetts of great and Insufferable
Iniuries donn by the said Gorton and his companie *donn* to them both to
theire psons and estates which occasioned seuerall addresses from the Massachusets both by Message and Writting to Gorton and his companie for
Reparacõn but in vaine; To the Comissioners for counsell and advise being
vnwilling to engage further (as at first) without a Joynt concurrance and
approbacõn *of the other Jurisdictions but in the meane time were continew-   *256
ally burthened with complaints from the English and Indians there vnder our
Gouerment and charged with breach of promise in not Righting their wronges
and doeing them Justice according to Couenant

The Inhabytants of Warwicke neuer exhibited any complaints to the
Jurisdiction of the Massachusets of any wrongs or Iniuries donn them by
English and Indians there which had they donn they should haue Receiued
equall Justice with any other

And when there arose a diference betwixt the Massachusets and
Plymouth conserning the Jurisdiction of the aforsaid place; The Gouerment of Plymouth not allowing of what theire Comissioners had done
therin; though for a long time they had been sillent The Comissioners of
the Massachusets Refered the Determinacõn of that difference to the rest
of the Comissiones at Boston in Anno 1649 who aduised to issue the same
by hearing a Naighbourly Treaty betwixt the two Jurisdictions of the Massachusets and Plymouth Wheruupon the generall court of the Massachusets sent
two Deputies to the generall court of Plym: with Comissiones and Instructions to Resigne and Submit the aforsaid lands and psons Residing therin to
the Gouerment of Plym: they onely promiseing to doe eqvall Justice both
to English and Indians there according to our engagements but the Gouerment of Plym: Chose Rather to Ratifye and confeirme the aforsaid Resig-
nacõn of theire Comissioners which accordingly was donn by an authentique
Writting signed by the Gouʳ ℓc

The court of Massachusets againe demaund satisfaction of Gorton his

*257

companie but are slighted and neglected by theire Comissioners they desire aduise of the Rest of the Comissioners at Hartford in anno i650 and are sollemly aduised againe to Resigne the aforsaid place and psons to Plym: *and that Gouerment to Receiue them Judging that way in seuerall Respects most expedient for all the Jurisdictions the Gouerment of the Massachusets obserue the aduise given and make a 2^{cond} Tender as aforsaid but were Refused by the Gonerment of Plym: by all that hath been said it may appeer to the honered Comissioners of the seuerall Jurisdictions and any other that may take Notice therof that the Goverment of the Massachusets haue from first to last been alwaies Reddy to herken to the aduise and counsell of the rest of the Comissioners and to acte accordingly in the case aforsaid ; And haue out of theire owne Treasury allowed a large quantitie of corn to the Indians vnder theire Gouerment there to keep them aliue The Cattell of Gortons Companiy haveing destroyed Most of theires Rather then by force to comple them till all other meanes and waies of prudence for Issueing these and the like differences were vsed which wee haue done to the vtmost of our power with much Patience and forbearance but complaints are dayly Renewed and subiects oppressed our Gouerment and Jurisdiction ouer them slighted and contemned and our promise and covenant both to English and Indians there for theire Just protection charged by them to bee Infringed and broken to the great dishoner of god our Religion and of our profession amongst the hethen Wee therfore desire and entreate to know of the Rest of the Comissioners that in case wee meete with opposition from the aforsaid people of Warwicke in following the aduise of the Comissioners giuen at theire last meeting at hartford what aide and assistance each Jurisdiction will afford vs for the Righting of our Iniuried and oppressed people And bringing Delinkquents to Condigne Punishment.

To which Declaracion the Comissioners for Conecticott and Newhauen ptly by way of Concession and ptly by way of exposition answared that at a meeting of the Comissioners in i643 diuers complaints of weighty consideraçon were psented from the Massachusetts collonie against Samuell Gorton and his companye conserning which noe Satisfaction by any fayre meanes could bee obteained, wherupon the Comissioners Joyntly thought fitt that the maiestrates of the Massachusetts If the said companie persist in theire Stubburnes should proceed against them according to what they shall find Just pmising the concurrance *of the collonies in what should warrantably bee donn; but the Comissioners haue neither Receiued enformacion from the Massachusets nor complaint from Samuell Gorton and his companie Conserning these proceedings ; soe that they haue hade neither call nor meanes

*258

to owne nor disowne them; Att the aforsaid meeting Anno i643 a question alsoe grew betwixt the Comissioners for the Massachusetts and Plym: to which of theire Pattents that Tract of land on which Samuell Gorton and his companie were settled did apperteine; each Collonie claimed it as pte of theire Jurisdiction but in the Issue the Comissioners for Plym: consented that it should belong to the Massachusets from which the other Comissioners (being neither conserned nor vnderstanding where the Right lay) saw noe cause to desent but sence sundery complaints at seuerall meetings haue been brought from the Massachusetts of Iniuries donn by Samuell Gorton and his companie Inhabitants of Warwicke to som English and Indians subiect to the Massachusets Jurisdiction and the question was againe Reviueed betwixt the Massachusets and Plym: to which Jurisdiction that Tract of land belongeth the Comissioners from time to time gaue counsels of peace according to theire best prsent light Anno i649 they advised that the Right of place with other things in difference might bee Issued in a Naighbourly Treaty betwixt those two Collonies and that all offensiue carriages might bee suppressed; in Anno i650 vpon like complaints they aduised that the Massachusets aqvite and Relinquish theire claime to the foremencioned Tract of land and that Plym: Reassume it That Warwicke might bee placed vnder theire Jurisdiction to which it belonges that a comfortable Isue might bee put to ye former Difference and Justice haue a free Passage, But if then the Inhabytants of Warwicke should Refuse to Submitte to that Gouerment they aduised that the wholsome directions giuen by the honorable Committee of Parliament in that case be forthwith duely attended; That the Inhabitants of Warwicke might bee convenced and accordingly Submitt; and the Comissioners for Conecticott and Newhauen then wrote to the Gouer of Plym: advising therunto wee were sence Informed that the Gouerment of the Massachusets herkened therunto and offered to settle Warwicke and the land in question vnder Plym: but that Plymouth hath and still Refuseth to except them soe that offences are like to continew and encrease; The Comissioners therfore fearing inconvenience would provide Remedie but know not what to add to the aduise given in Anno i650 conserning Trespasses but that which is proved bee Recouered if noe other meanes will serue by legale force; but with as much moderacion as may bee; least *from a course of continued offences further qvarrells and actes of hostillitie should Springe and grow betwixt the Inhabitants of Warwick and theire formentioned naighbors

*259

The Comissioners for Plym: taking knowlidge of the long Declaration of the Massachusetts Comissioners Collected out of peeces of passages of many yeares and being vnsatisfied therwith thought meet to declare them-

1651.

September.

selues that what was done by Mr Winslow and Mr Collyare then Comissioners of Plym: in Anno 1643 Conserning the Resignačõn vp of any lands which Plym: had enterest in was not at all in theire power to Resigne vp any pte of Plymouths Jurisdiction to the Massachusets Neither could the Massachusets Receiue any such Resignačõu without being Iniurius to the third and sixt articles of Confeaderačõn (if any had been made) And Mr Winslow and Mr Collyare haue seuerall times publickely denied that they either did or entended to Resigne any pte of the Jurisdiction of Plym: to the Massachusets And by what Right of authority the generall court of the Massachusets had to send for Samuell Gorton or any companie inhabiting soe fare out of theire Jurisdiction wee vnderstand not, and how Just theire sensure was wee know not ; or what pte of sensure they haue Suspended and vpon what grounds wee apprehend not ; and conserning any Reference put to the determinačõu of the Rest of the Comissioners att Boston in Anno 1649 the Comissioners for Plymouth Refered none and what authentickᵉ Writting the Gou^r of Plym: signed the Massachusets Comissioners doe not shew but if they meane a writting signed by the Gouerner of Plym: and som pticulare psons Joyning with him bearing date the 7th of June 1650 Wee the Comissioners of Plym: for our pticulare psons can not owne it haueing protested against it in the Court of Plym: as being directly contrary to the order of the

*260

honorable committiee of the parliament of England *England* and Contrary to the articles of confederačõn With the Rest of the Collonies

And wheras wee are enformed that the court of the Massachusetts haue lately sent out seuerall Summons or Warrants to seuerall psons Inhabiting Warwick allias Showamett and Patuxet and haue made seizure vpon som of theire estates Wee doe heerby protest against such proceedings if any such bee ;

The foregoing Conclusions were signed by the Comissioners at Newhauen the 16th of September 1651.

THEOPH: EATON Pres^{dt}

EDWARD HOPKINES	SIMON BRADSTREETE
ROGER LUDLOE	WILĿAM HATHORNE
STEUEN GOODYEERE	TIMOTHY HATHERLEY

John Browne in the busines Conserning Delaware doth dessent from the other Comissioners

Inspexi — Anno — 1716 —

[The following petition of Humphrey Johnson, and answer of the Court thereto, more properly belong with the Records of the General Court.]

*The humble petition of Humphrey Johnson of Hingham to ye Hono^rd Court assembled in plymouth this third of June 1684 sheweth that whereas ye hono^rd Court in answere to my adress 1683 doe declare it is not proper to this Court to determine title of land, ye Hono^rd Court may please to remember my adress was to request ye Hono^rd Court to answere their ingagement to my adress 1676. when they could come to a full vnderstanding ye ca_ to aford me releife according to law ₵ equitie ₵ you^r petitioner doth humbly conceaue ye Court in 83 had a full vnderstanding ^ ye case ₵ ye relieffe, I request for is that those deuiti_ of lands in Sittuate granted by order of Court 1671: ₵ signed by three of ye Hono^rd maiestrates may be laid out which grants will appear if ye Hono^rd Court please to giue your petitioner opertunity, I shall produce a Copy of ye Committies Determination signed by gouerno^r Winslow ₵ your law saith all grants of lands remaine for euer to ye grantee he his heires ₵ asigns also ye Hono^rd Gou^r, Hinckley may please to remember that in ye yeer 1677 himselfe declared those perticuler grants made by ye Comittie in Sittuate 1671 were yet binding

And you^r petitioner doth humbly conceiue that it is proper to this Court to make good such grants of proprietie granted either by themselues or theire predecessors: further you^r petitioner doth humbly request ye Hono^rd Court to order I may have my execution serued forthwith that was countermanded July 1683 for now y° then plaintiffe if here namely Jerimiah Hatch of Sittuate, you^r petitioner doth humbly request this Hono^rd Court to condescend to giue me their answere ₵ I shall acknowledg it to be a vndeserued fauou^r ₵ if ye Hono^rd Court shall giue such an Answere that may put an end to ye long Controuersie betwixt sittuate men ₵ my selfe that so ye Court may haue no more trouble concerning that matter ₵ you^r petitioners family may be setled in their iust rights: ₵ you^r petitioner shall euer pray

HUMPHRY JOHNSON

Hingham third June 1684.

*The Generall Courts answere to the said petition of Humphry Johnson ffolloweth viz: said Court doe not find any act or order of Court that doth hinder or preuent ye petitioxx or any other person from ye recouery of his iust right in due course of law, And that if ye petitioner hath a good title to any land within ye Township of Sittuate that is by that Towne or any

person therein detained from s^d pet‿ioner that if he see cause to bring his action against ye party detaining to any of ye Courts of triall that may haue proper Cognissance thereof, ₵ proue his title to ye land demanded he may recouer it with his damages.

And concerning ye execution mentioned in the petition ye Court are fully informed by ye petitioner himselfe that since ye date of his petition he hath receiued full satisfaction concerning that matter.

The Courts answere to y^e before written petition:

p^r NATHANIELL MORTON

Secretary

GENERAL INDEX.

GENERAL INDEX.

www.ingramcontent.com/pod-product-compliance
Lightning Source LLC
Chambersburg PA
CBHW061723270326
41928CB00011B/2092